Other Insight Guides available:

Alaska
Amazon Wildlife
American Southwest
Amsterdam
Argentina
Arizona & Grand Canyon
Asia, East
Asia, Southeast
Asia's Best Hotels
  and Resorts
Australia
Austria
Bahamas
Bali & Lombok
Baltic States
Bangkok
Barbados
Belgium
Belize
Berlin
Bermuda
Brazil
Brittany
Buenos Aires
Burgundy
Burma (Myanmar)
Cairo
California
California, Southern
Canada
Caribbean
Caribbean Cruises
Channel Islands
Chicago
Chile
China
Colorado
Continental Europe
Corsica
Costa Rica
Crete
Cuba
Cyprus
Czech & Slovak Republic
Delhi, Jaipur & Agra
Denmark
Dominican Rep. & Haiti
Dublin
East African Wildlife
Eastern Europe
Ecuador
Edinburgh
Egypt
England
Finland
Florida
France
France, Southwest
French Riviera
Gambia & Senegal
Germany
Glasgow
Gran Canaria
Great Britain

Great Railway Journeys
  of Europe
Great River Cruises
  of Europe
Greece
Greek Islands
Guatemala, Belize
  & Yucatán
Hawaii
Hungary
Iceland
India
India, South
Indonesia
Ireland
Israel
Istanbul
Italy
Italy, Northern
Italy, Southern
Jamaica
Japan
Jerusalem
Jordan
Kenya
Korea
Laos & Cambodia
Lisbon
Madeira
Malaysia
Mallorca & Ibiza
Malta
Mauritius Réunion
  & Seychelles
Melbourne
Mexico
Miami
Montreal
Morocco
Namibia
Nepal
Netherlands
New England
New Mexico
New Orleans
New York State
New Zealand
Nile
Normandy
North American and
  Alaskan Cruises
Norway
Oman & The UAE
Oxford
Pacific Northwest
Pakistan
Peru
Philadelphia
Philippines
Poland
Portugal
Provence
Puerto Rico
Rajasthan

Rio de Janeiro
Russia
Sardinia
Scandinavia
Scotland
Seattle
Sicily
South Africa
South America
Spain
Spain, Northern
Spain, Southern
Sri Lanka
Sweden
Switzerland
Syria & Lebanon
Taiwan
Tenerife
Texas
Thailand
Trinidad & Tobago
Tunisia
Turkey
Tuscany
Umbria
USA: On The Road
USA: Western States
US National Parks: West
Venezuela
Vienna
Vietnam
Wales

INSIGHT CITY GUIDES
(with free restaurant map)

Barcelona
Beijing
Boston
Bruges, Ghent & Antwerp
Brussels
Cape Town
Florence
Hong Kong
Las Vegas
London
Los Angeles
Madrid
Moscow
New York
Paris
Prague
Rome
St Petersburg
San Francisco
Singapore
Sydney
Taipei
Tokyo
Toronto
Utah
Venice
Walt Disney World/Orlando
Washington, DC

INSIGHT **CITY GUIDE**

FLORENCE

APA PUBLICATIONS

Part of the Langenscheidt Publishing Group

L

✳ INSIGHT GUIDE
Florence

Editor
Maria Lord
Art Director
Klaus Geisler
Picture Editor
Hilary Genin
Cartography Editor
Zoë Goodwin
Production
Kenneth Chan
Editorial Director
Brian Bell

Distribution

UK & Ireland
GeoCenter International Ltd
The Viables Centre, Harrow Way
Basingstoke, Hants RG22 4BJ
Fax: (44) 1256-817988

United States
Langenscheidt Publishers, Inc.
36–36 33rd Street 4th Floor
Long Island City, NY 11106
Fax: (1) 718 784-0640

Australia
Universal Publishers
1 Waterloo Road
Macquarie Park, NSW 2113
Fax: (61) 2 9888 9074

New Zealand
Hema Maps New Zealand Ltd (HNZ)
Unit D, 24 Ra ORA Drive
East Tamaki, Auckland
Fax: (64) 9 273 6479

Worldwide
Apa Publications GmbH & Co.
Verlag KG (Singapore branch)
38 Joo Koon Road, Singapore 628990
Tel: (65) 6865-1600. Fax: (65) 6861-6438

Printing

Insight Print Services (Pte) Ltd
38 Joo Koon Road, Singapore 628990
Tel: (65) 6865-1600. Fax: (65) 6861-6438

©2006 Apa Publications GmbH & Co.
Verlag KG (Singapore branch)
All Rights Reserved

First Edition 1989
Fourth Edition 2006

ABOUT THIS BOOK

The first Insight Guide pioneered the use of creative full-colour photography in guidebooks in 1970. Since then, we have expanded our range to cater for our readers' need not only for reliable information about their chosen destination but also for a real understanding of that destination. Now, when the internet can supply inexhaustible (but not always reliable) facts, our books marry text and pictures to provide that much more elusive quality: knowledge. To achieve this, they rely heavily on the authority of locally based writers and photographers.

How to use this book

The book is carefully structured both to convey an understanding of the city and its culture and to guide readers through its sights and activities:

◆ To understand Florence today, you need to know something of its past. The first section covers the city's history and culture in lively, authoritative essays written by specialists.

◆ The main Places section provides a full run-down of all the attractions worth seeing, as well as places to eat. The main places of interest are coordinated by number with full-colour maps.

◆ The Travel Tips listings section provides a point of reference for information on travel, hotels, shops and festivals. Information may be located quickly by using the index printed on the back cover flap – and the flaps are designed to serve as bookmarks.

◆ Photographs are chosen not only to illustrate geography and buildings but also to convey the moods of the city and the life of its people.

book, most notably **Christopher Catling**, as both updater and writer, who first fell in love with Florence when he was a student archaeologist excavating Roman villas in the Tuscan countryside. Other writers included: former Florence resident and TV presenter **Lisa Gerard-Sharp**; American lawyer and journalist **Tim Harper**; art historian **Paul Holberton**, who specialises in Renaissance art and architecture; **Forrest Spears**, a fashion designer resident in the city; actor, writer and film producer **David Clement-Davies**; and **Susie Boulton**, who was so hooked on the city in her student days that she once sold ice cream to pay for her accommodation there. Previous updaters of the book include **Nicky Swallow**, who has lived in Florence since 1981 when she got a job as a violist in the opera orchestra. She wrote a large part of the existing Travel Tips.

Many of the pictures are by the team of **Anna Mockford** and **Nick Bonetti**, regular Insight photographers. They ably captured the beauty of both the city and surrounding region. **Jerry Dennis** is another Insight regular whose photographs feature strongly.

Thanks also go to **Neil Titman**, who proofread the book, and to **Elizabeth Cook**, who compiled the index.

The contributors

This new edition of *Florence* was edited by **Maria Lord** and builds on the success of earlier editions. The Places section and Travel Tips have been restructured and thoroughly updated by **Sarah Birke**. She knows this part of Italy very well after studying law at the European University Institute in Fiesole.

The history chapters were completely revised by the journalist **Bruce Johnston**, who also wrote the lively new chapter on Contemporary Florence. The wide-ranging new chapters on that essential element of the city, art and architecture, were written by sculptor and art historian **Dr John Lord**.

The current edition builds on the excellent foundations created by writers of previous editions of the

CONTACTING THE EDITORS

We would appreciate it if readers would alert us to errors or outdated information by writing to:

Insight Guides, P.O. Box 7910, London SE1 1WE, England. Fax: (44) 20 7403-0290. insight@apaguide.co.uk

www.insightguides.com
In North America:
www.insighttravelguides.com

Maps

Travel Tips

THE BEST OF FLORENCE

Art, culture, food and shopping...
Here, at a glance, are our top
recommendations for a visit

CHURCHES

Much of Florence's artistic glory lies in its churches, in
their architecture, paintings and sculpture.

- **Ognissanti**
This church is home
to wonderful frescos
by Ghirlandaio, Botti-
celli and Gaddi. *See
page 163.*
- **Orsanmichele**
This converted me-
dieval grain market is
a showcase for
Renaissance sculp-
ture. *See page 132.*
- **San Lorenzo**
The complex of San

Lorenzo contains
many treasures, in-
cluding the ornate
Cappelle Medicee.
See pages 142–5.
- **San Marco**
As much an art
gallery as a church,
San Marco has some
of the finest works by
Fra Angelico. *See
pages 147–9.*
- **San Miniato al Monte**
In a beautiful position

ABOVE: the copy of Michelangelo's *David* outside
the Palazzo Vecchio.
LEFT: the ornate facade of the Duomo.

overloooking Flo-
rence from the hills,
this Romanesque
basilica has wonder-
ful decoration. *See
pages 183–5.*
- **Santa Croce**
A beautifully deco-
rated and spacious
church, Santa Croce
was the burial place
of many famous
Florentines. *See
page 117.*
- **Santa Maria del
Carmine**
One of the city's
great treasures is
here, the frescoed

Cappella Brancacci.
See page 173.
- **Santa Maria del
Fiore (the Duomo)**
Florence's great
cathedral, with a
campanile by Giotto
and crowned by
Brunelleschi's superb
cupola. *See pages
89–94.*
- **Santa Maria
Novella**
Behind the splendid
facade is another
treasure house of art,
including Giotto's
splendid crucifix. *See
pages 159–61.*

FLORENCE FOR FAMILIES

● Although Florence may not seem the most family-friendly of cities, dominated as it is by renaissance *palazzi* and works of art, there are numerous attractions that children might find enjoyable. The newly expanded Egyptian collection at the **Archaeological Museum** *(see pages 152–4)* is full of mummies. The **Science Museum** *(see page 107)* contains working experiments of Galileo. The **Anthropological Museum** *(see page 116)* is crammed with curiosities including Peruvian mummies, Indian shadow puppets and Eskimo anoraks made from whaleskins. For children with a gruesome fascination for the human body, **La Specola** (in the Museo di Zoologia; *see page 171)* exhibits realistic anatomical waxworks of body parts. The **Boboli gardens** and the **Cascine** are Florence's two main parks where kids can run around and let off steam, whilst one of the few children's playgrounds is to be found in **Piazza dell'Azeglio**. Children may also enjoy taking a ride on one of the horse-drawn carriages found in **Piazza della Signoria**.

ABOVE: a horse gets a well-earned break from carting tourists.
LEFT: the Palazzo Vecchio seen from Piazzale Michelangelo.
BELOW: wonderful silks from Antico Setificio.

VIEWPOINTS

Florence is surrounded by hills from where there are stunning views over the city.

● **Bellosguardo**
Meaning literally "beautiful view", this spot above Oltrarno is in a wonderful location. *See page 174.*

● **Fiesole**
The view from this hilltop suburb – site of the original Etruscan settlement – gives a panorama over the whole city. *See page 190.*

● **Piazzale Michelangelo**
From this open square, the view over the city rooftops and the Arno is simply breathtaking. *See page 185.*

SHOPPING

● **Via Tornabuoni**
This is Florence's most prestigious shopping street and home to its most famous designer brands, including Ferragamo, Gucci and Pucci. *See pages 164–5 and 226.*

● **The Markets**
Florence has a number of markets, selling everything from leather goods to fruit and vegetables. Two of the best are the Mercato Nuovo and Mercato Centrale. *See pages 133 and 139.*

● **Giulio Giannini e Figlio**
Florence is famous for marbled paper and this is one of the finest shops. *See page 226.*

● **Antico Setificio**
The place to buy very high quality and locally made fabrics, especially silks. *See page 226.*

MUSEUMS AND GALLERIES

● **Accademia**
A wonderful collection, home to Michelangelo's *David*. *See pages 156–7.*

● **The Bargello**
The city's greatest collection of sculpture. *See pages 126–7.*

● **Museo Archeologico**
The city's archaeological museum has the finest collection of Etruscan artefacts to be found anywhere. *See pages 152–4.*

● **Museo Horne**
A charming villa with part of the collection of an English art historian. *See page 108.*

● **Museo dell'Opera del Duomo**
Sculptural treasures from the cathedral. *See page 94.*

● **Museo di Storia della Scienza**
Florence has made great contributions to the advance of science, all documented in this museum. *See page 107.*

● **Museo di Zoologia "La Specola"**
An unusual display of wax anatomical models – all very realistic and not a little gory. *See page 171.*

● **Natural History Museum**
Spread over several sites, one of the best sections of this university-run institution is the Anthropolical Museum with its many fascinating exhibits. *See pages 116 and 150–1.*

● **Palazzo Pitti**
A huge Medici *palazzo* containing a number of museums and some extraordinary paintings. *See pages 176–9.*

● **Palazzo Vecchio**
Florence's town hall is superbly decorated and has many treasures. *See page 102–5.*

● **Uffizi**
The world's greatest collection of Renaissance art. *See pages 110–13.*

ABOVE: Giambologna's *Rape of the Sabine*.
LEFT: the Appennino sculpture at Villa Demidoff.

VILLAS, PARKS AND GARDENS

● **Giardino di Boboli**
Exquisite formal gardens behind the Palazzo Pitti. *See pages 176–7.*

● **Giardino dei Semplici**
Peaceful botanical gardens. *See page 151.*

● **Villa di Castello**
Beautiful Renaissance gardens. *See page 193.*

● **Villa Demidoff and Parco di Pratolino**
The gardens here contain extraordinary Mannerist sculpture and grottoes. *See page 193.*

● **Villa Medicea Poggio a Caiano**
Thought by many to be the perfect Medici villa, with frescoed halls and beautiful gardens. *See page 193.*

● **Villa Medici (Fiesole)**
Delightful, with superb views of the city. *See page 192.*

● **Villa Medicea della Petraia**
An elegant villa set on a sloping hill and decorated with wonderful frescos. *See page 192.*

EATING OUT

- **Acqua al Due**
  Book ahead for this very popular restaurant. *See page 124.*
- **Baldovino**
  Run by a Scottish couple but with no deep-fried pizza in sight. *see page 124.*
- **Buca Lapi**
  Wopnderful *bistecca* served in the basement of the Palazzo Antinori. *See page 167.*
- **Caffè Italiano**
  Excellent Tuscan food

- in a 14th-century *palazzo. See page 124.*
- **Cavolo Nero**
  Elegant Mediterranean dishes. *See page 175.*
- **Cibrèo**
  Very popular modern Tuscan food. *See page 124.*
- **Coco Lezzone**
  Beautifully prepared traditional food. *See page 167.*
- **Enoteca Pinchiorri**
  Thought by some to

ABOVE: pizza topped with tomato and rocket.
LEFT: Andrea del Sarto's *St John the Baptist,* in the Palazzo Pitti.

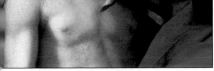

be the best restaurant in Europe. *See page 124.*
- **Frescobaldi**
  Classic Tuscan food and an exceptional wine-list. *See page 109.*
- **Godò**
  A little way out of town but with excellent food. *See page 125.*
- **La Giostra**
  Acclaimed food, particularly the *crostini. See page 125.*
- **Gustavino**
  Creative dishes but no fuss. *See page 109.*

- **Oliviero**
  Everything is fresh, from the pasta to desserts. *See page 109.*
- **Pane e Vino**
  Chiefly famous for its excellent wine list but it also serves very decent food. *See page 185.*
- **Pugi**
  Possibly the best pizza in town. *See page 155.*
- **Sostanza**
  A real Tuscan dining experience, famous for its steaks. *See page 167.*

TOP WORKS OF ART

Botticelli: Adoration of the Magi, Annunciation, Primavera, Birth of Venus, Uffizi.
Cimabue: Madonna, Uffizi; Crucifixion, Museo dell'Opera di Santa Croce.
del Sarto: Madonna of the Harpies, Uffizi; Last Supper, San Salvi; Coming of the Magi, Santi Annunziata; St John the Baptist as a Boy, Palazzo Pitti.
Donatello: Judith and Holofernes, Palazzo Vecchio; St George, David, Bargello;

Crucifixion, Santa Croce.
Fra Angelico: Last Judgement, Crucifixion, San Marco.
Ghirlandaio: Adoration, Spedale degli Innocenti; St Jerome, Last Supper, Ognissanti; Life of St Francis, Santa Trinita.
Giotto: Madonna, Uffizi; St Stephen, Museo Horne; Crucifixion, Santa Maria Novella.
Lippi: Madonna with Angels, Uffizi; Tondo of the Madonna and Child, Palazzo Pitti; Madonna and Saints, Santo Spirito.
Masaccio: Trinity, Santa Maria Novella; Life of St Peter,

Expulsion from Paradise, Cappella Brancacci.
Michelangelo: Doni Tondo, Uffizi; Bacchus, Bargello; Madonna and Child, Cappelle Medicee; David, Galleria dell' Accademia.
Raphael: Madonna of the Goldfinch, Uffizi; Madonna della Seggiola, La Valeta, Palazzo Pitti.
Titian: Venus of Urbino, Uffizi; Portrait of a Grey-eyed Gentleman, Maddalena, Portrait of a Lady, Palazzo Pitti.
Uccello: Battle of San Romano, Uffizi; Universal Deluge, Santa Maria Novella cloister.

THE INEXHAUSTIBLE CITY

Doctors in Florence have found that Stendhal was right: trying to experience all of the city's art, culture and history too quickly can make you ill

Getting acquainted with Florence is a little like taking up chess; the more you know about it, the more you realise there is to learn. Consequently, to many visitors Florence can be intimidating. Trying to see all the highlights only reveals more highlights to be seen, and the impossible task is especially frustrating because of the physical compactness of the city. Visitors frequently drive themselves to distraction or exhaustion or both in their desire to see everything the city has to offer.

Florentine hospitals actually document about a dozen cases a year of "Stendhal Syndrome". First described by the French writer, who suffered from it in 1817, the syndrome is a reaction to the overwhelming beauty of Florence. Symptoms range from dizzy spells to complete collapse requiring bed rest. "Sensory overload" is how modern travellers describe their feelings of too much art, too much culture, too much history, and just too much Florence. A glass of wine and an hour or two of reading a trashy novel or watching the students play out their coquetry in the city's squares and cafés are usually adequate therapy to renew the spirits and revive one's interest in seeing some more of Florence's almost numberless treasures.

All this is to say that visitors to Florence shouldn't try to do too much too fast. The people who seem to enjoy and appreciate the city most are those who leave parts of it unseen, reserving something for their next visit – for Florence is a city to which nearly every visitor vows to return.

Florentines describe themselves as an inhospitable, wary of foreigners. However, reticence is reserved for those who view Florence as a museum and its people as servants to the tourist industry. For them, the pleasures of carrying out life's routines amid such splendour are matched by the frustrations: narrow streets pose daily problems of how to get to work or where to park, while momentous issues, such as the proposal to build a new satellite city, provoke passionate debate. These complex undertones highlight the real marvel of Florence: the fact that it has survived at all, despite floods, warfare and the threat from development; the fact that it is very much part of the modern world as well as a monument to past achievements, with one foot in the 21st century and the other in the Renaissance. ❑

PRECEDING PAGES: the shadow of the baptistery on the facade of the Duomo; the Ponte Vecchio reflected in the Arno. **LEFT:** Florentine rooftops from Brunelleschi's cupola.

ETRUSCANS TO MEDICIS

Ancient traders sowed the seeds of Florence's artistic
flowering, but it was a wealthy banking dynasty
that propelled the city to the international
cultural renown it enjoys today

Florence was originally a Roman settlement, and the classical flowering of the Renaissance owes much to Rome's civilisation. However, the vitality of 15th-century Florentine art is indebted at least as much to a culture that pre-dated Rome by centuries, that of Etruria. Rising above Florence to Fiesole, where the sunset steeps the city in colour, you come upon the remains of an ancient Etruscan town. The massive stone walls were laid in the late 7th century BC, long before Latins ever settled the Arno's banks. Today, Fiesole is just a satellite of the city, and for the traveller the Renaissance obscures an earlier dawn. But throughout Tuscany, hilltop villages founded by the Etruscans, as well as their harbours, tombs and statuary, testify to a remarkable and often overlooked civilisation.

Craftsmen and traders

The Etruscans (Tusci to the Romans, Rasenna as they called themselves) first flourished around 800 BC in the coastal regions of Tuscany and Lazio. Building their cities on high plateaux for defence, but with access to the sea, they soon rivalled the Greeks and Phoenicians as traders. Their wealth was founded on the rich metal deposits of the mainland and the island of Elba. With a genius for craftsmanship, they worked metals and exchanged them for luxury goods, and trading links soon extended as far as Mesopotamia, Syria, Cyprus and Egypt.

LEFT: Lorenzo de' Medici from a fresco by Gozzoli.
RIGHT: an Etruscan tomb painting in Tarquinia.

The Etruscans thrived as powerful traders for around 300 years. At their peak. their cities covered Italy from Campania to the Po valley. By forging links with the Greeks in the 8th century BC, they set up an outpost in Latium (Lazio). This small encampment was to become the city of Rome, and Rome would one day eclipse Etruria.

Unlike the Romans, the Etruscans never established a centralised empire. Their settlements remained largely independent from one another, and although the 12 main cities of Etruria were grouped in a loose confederation, this was primarily for religious purposes. That religion was complex and magical. Vases and

RICH LEGACY

Etruscan remains in Tuscany tell the story of a peaceful people, of a magical religion and of a delightful culture that attained a high degree of civilisation.

tombs are haunted by their gods and demons, such as the Lasa or winged women, symbolic of death, and Tulchulcha, a demon of the underworld. Temples and votive statues abound, while the Etruscans' special preserve was augury, interpreting the will of the gods in the entrails of wild animals, forks of lightning and the flight of birds. The Romans later

sible to modern scholars; a recent theory even roots their language in Indian Sanskrit.

Similarly, their origins elude us. Herodotus believed they came from Lydia in Asia Minor, led by Tyrrhenos, son of Athis, to settle on the shores of the sea that still bears his name. Yet Dionysius of Halicarnassus says the Etruscans themselves claimed to be indigenous to Italy, and the lack of any evidence of warfare at the early archaeological sites might support this. These lingering mysteries have captured the imaginations of writers from the Emperor Claudius, who wrote a 20-volume history of the Etruscans, to Virgil, Livy and D.H. Lawrence. All were fascinated by the art that these people

absorbed these beliefs and, as late as the reign of the Emperor Julian (AD 361–3), every legion of the army had an Etruscan soothsayer. But who knows if Etruscan soothsayers ever predicted the fate of their own people, for the Etruscans, powerful in the 5th century BC, had, by the 4th, completely succumbed to Roman rule.

The great enigma

Why this civilisation should have proved so fragile is just one of the enigmas that surround the Etruscans. Though their alphabet has been deciphered as being similar to Greek Chaldean, much of their language remains incomprehen-

produced: marble statues, colourful frescos, powerful bronzes, pottery of great delicacy – potent, erotic and, above all, humane.

Tarquinia

The search for the spirit of Etruscan art, which many have seen as akin to that of the Florentine Renaissance, begins on the parched hillsides of Lazio, in the underground necropolises or citadels of the dead that cluster round the hilltop city of Tarquinia. Most remnants of Etruscan civilisation come from tombs such as these: their myriad funerary urns, painted sarcophagi, and many household objects which accompanied the wealthy into the afterlife.

Though empty now, the tombs of Tarquinia, buried safe from the dust that blows hard across the region's wild landscape, are covered in remarkable frescos. The scenes of hunting, fishing, wrestling and feasting evoke a lively and luxurious people, fond of music and dancing, while erotic figures capture a sensuality and naturalism rare in any art.

A central element in these paintings is the wildlife. Dolphins, bulls and sea horses leap to life from the walls. In Tarquinia's terracotta horses and the famous bronze she-wolf – later to become the symbol of ancient Rome – the Etruscans displayed an extraordinary empathy with their natural environment and a supreme ability to record life in movement.

Tarquinia's frescos are the most complete. Elsewhere we have only tantalising scraps, "fragments of people at banquets, limbs that dance without dancers, birds that fly into nowhere", as D.H. Lawrence described them.

Illicit trade

How many tombs are yet to be discovered, even in the vicinity of Florence, no one knows. Tomb-robbers are more active than the archaeologists, and neither, with good reason, are prepared to disclose their discoveries to the public.

Yet it is not unusual, among trusted friends at intimate aristocratic dinner parties in the villas of the Florentine countryside, for some pristine Etruscan bronze figurine, mirror or brooch to be offered for admiration or sale. By law, all objects discovered underground become the property of the Italian state, but an ordinance of 1934 permits Italians to keep the antiquities they owned before that date. The difficulty of proving exactly when an object was acquired clearly works in favour of the tomb-robbers, and so the regrettable business continues.

Florentines justify their illicit trade by pointing to the inactivity of archaeologists, by asserting that art should be enjoyed, not left forgotten underground, and, above all, by claiming that "it is our heritage; we are Etruscans".

There is some truth in this statement, even if there is not in the arguments it is used to support. Cosimo I justified his conquests of Pisa and Siena as an attempt to reunify the ancient kingdom of Etruria, and the citizens of Florence warmed to this appeal. Renaissance artists saw themselves as inheritors of the Etruscan talent for sculpture and bronze casting, and many of the objects in the Archaeological Museum in Florence were once owned by the likes of Michelangelo and his contemporaries.

Bronze masterpieces

This compact museum, tucked away in the Via della Colonna, is untouched by the hectic traffic of visitors to the city. In the Room of Urns you often find yourself alone among sculptures of the dead and intricate marble friezes that rival the best Greece and Rome produced.

The Archaeological Museum's prize exhibits, however, are two exquisite bronzes, the Arringatore and the Chimera. The Arringatore (or Orator) dates from the 1st century BC, by which time Etruria had already been conquered by Rome. It portrays a member of the Metelli family, once powerful Etruscan aristocrats who had adopted a new name and achieved new status by winning Roman citizenship. At once dignified and disturbing, it captures the tension between new energies and a sense of melancholy for a culture destined to lose its own identity. It is a wonderful example of Etruscan realism and their mastery of bronze.

LEFT: dancing youths in a Tarquinia tomb painting.
RIGHT: the Chimera, an Etruscan masterpiece.

The wounded Chimera is one of the most celebrated masterpieces of high Etruscan art. The straining beast, part goat, lion and snake, bursts with a desperate energy as it struggles in mortal combat. Discovered near Arezzo in 1553, the Chimera was entrusted to the care of Cellini, who restored the two left legs, marvelling at the skill of the original makers.

The Etruscan demise

All over Tuscany one finds remains which bring the Etruscans vividly back to life. But Etruscan glories were fleeting. By the 5th century BC they were threatened by Gauls in the north and by local Italic tribes. The Romans,

The date of the founding of Florence is generally agreed to be 59 BC, when it was established as a *colonia* for retired Roman soldiers, distinguished veterans of Caesar's campaigns.

City of flowers

The source of the Roman name, Florentia, remains open to question. Perhaps the new city was named after the many wild flowers that grow in the Arno plain and on the surrounding hillsides, perhaps as an inspired piece of prophecy, since the word *florentia* could mean either "floriferous" or "flourishing".

The retired Roman soldiers built the first city walls almost in a perfect square, with sides of

exploiting their vulnerability, rapidly overcame Etruria. The Etruscans survived for two centuries as Roman subjects, but their culture became diluted and eventually they were absorbed into the fabric of a new society.

The Etruscans first settled the area in the 5th or 6th century BC, but their city was Fiesole, which now lies in the hills above modern Florence. The Etruscans, however, had a regular market at the ford across the Arno, near the Ponte Vecchio. A dispute in the Etruscan community apparently led some of Fiesole's residents to set up a separate community near the ford, but in around 300 BC the Romans engulfed it when they established a camp on the site.

about 400 metres (1,300 ft) in length. The southwestern corner, not far from Ponte Santa Trinità, was the closest point the walls came to the Arno. The fact that the river embankment was not itself defended suggests that the Arno played little part in the economy of the Roman city, initially at least.

Instead, the Roman settlers lived chiefly by farming the perimeter of the city. Out of this developed what was to become one of the principal industries, both in Roman times and in the centuries that were to follow – wool-dyeing.

ABOVE: the Roman theatre in Fiesole.
RIGHT: the 13th-century Bargello.

Even in those early days, the city was setting itself apart in style and attitude. The Romans who settled Florence were dedicated to the Horatian and Virgilian ideal of *rus in urbe* – the countryside in the town. It is an ideal that has characterised Florence through the ages, for even now, while many Italians aspire to a chic city apartment, Florentines desire a country villa with a vineyard and olive grove.

Bandits tamed

The wealth and splendour of Florence from the 13th century onwards owed much to this same marriage of town and country, of nature and necessity. As the city prospered, she grew to resent the parasitical habits of landowners who descended from their hilltop fortresses to rob any mule trains that passed through their domain. Armies were formed to counter the threat, while defeated landowners were forced to live in Florence to learn to read and write.

Forced to be civilised, they nevertheless built in the style of the countryside. Travellers over the centuries have commented on how much the 12th- and 13th-century Romanesque churches of Florence, with their wide arcades and shallow aisles, their decorative motifs of leaves, flowers, seashells and sun rays, have a chapel-in-the-woods atmosphere.

Palaces – *palazzi,* the grandiose term that Florentines give to any townhouse of pretension, were built with massive fortress-like walls and towers, gaunt reminders of their rural prototypes. Yet, in both public and private construction, the emphasis was on sunlight and warmth, bringing the glorious golden outdoors

of Tuscany inside, past the columns and through the spacious arches and open windows. Courtyards were filled with greenery, potted plants and flowers, in part because of the *rus in urbe* heritage but also to deflect the intense summer heat – another example of Florence's traditional mix of the pragmatic and the ideal.

Early suburbs

Through the 14th century there was little building outside the city walls, but as the robbers and murderers, highwaymen and renegade soldiers were tamed, the hills around Florence once again became dotted with villas built by the Medici and other wealthy families. These

ENLIGHTENED CITY PLANNING

Unlike many cities in Europe, Florence was planned from the start. Much of its appeal stems from the grid system of its streets, that one moment creates a grand vista, the next opens into an intimate piazza, and often provides glimpses of the cathedral or one of the city's domed churches.

Public buildings too (the cathedral, the Palazzo Vecchio and town walls) were planned and built thanks to a property tax and the patronage of the guilds, striving to outdo each other in the splendour of their buildings. The first fruit of this communal endeavour was the new set of walls, built by the Comune in 1173–5 to protect the city that had grown beyond the limits of the Roman and later fortifica-

tions. In 1250 there were more than 100 towers some 65 metres (215 ft) high that wealthy families had built as status symbols to crown and protect their urban palaces. The Comune imposed a height limit of 29 metres (95 ft), and the families had to scale them down to conform with the building style that has characterised Florence ever since.

By the late 13th century Florence had grown to 100,000 inhabitants. New walls, begun in 1284 and completed in 1333, encompassed 100 sq. km (40 sq. miles) but proved unnecessary. Plague in the following decades killed over half the inhabitants, and areas of the new city were still greenfield sites when expansion began again in the 1800s.

villas were the start of the modern suburbs, although the people who built them as a refuge from the summer heat of the city also saw them as a vital ingredient of the humanistic philosophy that regarded a person as incomplete if they did not study the natural world and find time for relaxing, reading, thinking and pursuing hobbies or sports.

During the 15th century, Florence was virtually unrivalled as a cultural and commercial centre. Unique in its artistic contribution, it also enjoyed a singular political position, clinging doggedly to republicanism long after rival towns had succumbed to despotic rule, tolerating Cosimo de' Medici's leadership so long as it remained unofficial and benign. In this the city had some justification in styling itself the "new Rome".

How Florence reached this state of commercial superiority and political independence is a story of self-awareness and creativity, emerging from centuries of continuous and frequently violent conflict.

The wool trade

As early as the 11th century, Florentine merchants began importing wool from northern Europe and rare dye-stuffs from the Mediterranean and the East. They quickly developed specialised weaving and dyeing techniques that made the wool trade the city's biggest source of income, an industry that employed approximately one-third of her inhabitants by 1250.

Soaring profits fuelled that other Florentine mainstay, banking. Financiers exploited the established trade routes, creating a network of lending houses. In 1252 a tiny gold coin was minted in the city that became the recognised unit of international currency, the florin.

Guelf versus Ghibelline

Emergent capitalism and the rapid expansion of the city served to fuel the long-standing conflict between two factions, the Guelfs and the Ghibellines. The whole Italian peninsula was embroiled in the struggle, but the prize – and therefore the vehemence of the feud – was all the greater in Florence.

In broad terms, the Guelfs supported the Pope and the Ghibellines the Holy Roman Emperor in a battle for territory and temporal power. In Florence, the parties fought in the streets, attacking their enemies and retreating to their defended palaces.

In the ups and downs of the conflict there were no decisive victories, and new alliances were created every time an old one was defeated or its supporters sent into exile. In general, though, the new men were in the ascendant. The Florentine banking system reached its zenith in the late 13th century when the Parte Guelfa secured a monopoly over papal tax collection, and in 1293 the Ordinances of Justice barred the nobility from state office, concentrating power in the hands of the trade guilds.

THE FLORIN

In 1252 Florence minted modern Europe's first gold coin, the florin, which soon became a standard currency throughout the continent. (Indeed, until the introduction of the euro, the Dutch florin still carried the name of the old Florentine coin.) The minting of the florin coincided with a spectacular growth in the city's wealth and population throughout the 1200s. By the end of the century the city walls were scarcely able to contain its 100,000 inhabitants. Florence was one of the five most populous cities in Europe, and one of the richest. Both banking and the wool trade were booming, and the new opulence created new possibilities for art and culture.

Black versus white

But just as the *magnati,* aristocrats, survived as a powerful element in the city, so the Guelfs themselves began to split, as powerful families jostled for prominence, and the family vendettas grew apace. The origins of the new conflict – between the Blacks, the Neri, and the Whites, the Bianchi – lay outside Florence, in a feud between two branches of the Concellieri family in Pistoia. It was just the excuse that the rival Florentine Cerchi and Donati families needed. They took up opposite sides in a quarrel that gained momentum and in 1302 led to the exile of Dante, among others, who were all expelled from the city in a mass purge of the Whites.

The enigma of Florence

During the 14th century, Florence was the richest city in Europe; the cathedral, the Palazzo Vecchio and the church of Santa Croce were all begun, industry boomed and Florentine artisans were renowned for their skills in metal-casting and terracotta, as well as the weaving and dyeing of cloth. Pope Boniface summed up the enigma of the city when he described the world as composed of five elements; earth, air, fire and water... and the Florentines.

Moreover, whereas factionalism in other Italian city states favoured the rise of *signori,* despots who exploited instability to impose

Dante's revenge

Dante exacted revenge by populating the Hell and Purgatory of his *Divine Comedy* with his enemies, inventing suitable punishments so that out of the conflict was born a great work of art, one that helped establish the Florentine dialect as the progenitor of the modern Italian language. Equally remarkable is the fact that Florence still prospered even though it was, in the poet's own words, like a fevered woman tossing and turning in bed in search of rest and relief.

LEFT: Gustave Doré's view of Dante's *Inferno.*
ABOVE: Florence conquering Tuscany, by Vasari.

their own personal authority and establish hereditary dynasties, Florence for a long time (and despite the infighting) did not succumb. Instead, it evolved its own style of broadly based government.

The city was never democratic in any modern sense of the word, for the huge artisan community had little real power. However, the government did encompass a variety of interest groups, with a council whose members were elected from the city's 21 guilds and executive officers chosen from the seven major guilds, appointed to posts for a finite period to ensure that no individual could dominate.

Capitalism in crisis

New-found stability was continually put to the test and yet survived. In 1339, Edward III of England reneged on Florentine debts, precipitating a banking crisis, and, three years later, the first terrifying symptoms of the Black Death appeared in the city. It re-emerged seven times during the century, carrying off more than half the population.

Internal revolts, such as the 1378 rebellion of the *ciompi,* the lowest paid of the city's wool workers, who demanded the right to form a guild and be represented on the council, often resulted in the powerful merchant families closing ranks against "popular" ele-

ments. But each time this happened the leaders were sent into exile: first the Alberti, then the Strozzi and finally the Medici.

Wars with foreign powers and neighbouring states also tended to unite factional leaders in a common cause: that of the defence and then the expansion of the Florentine republic. Between 1384 and 1406, Florence won victories over Arezzo, Lucca, Montepulciano and Pisa – the prize that gave the city direct access to the sea.

Style wars

Success helped to confirm that aggressive independence and sense of Florentine identity that played a shaping role in the cultural awakening of the Quattrocento. By the beginning of the 1400s, the guilds, as well as individual patrons, had begun to find new ways of expressing the rivalry that was previously the cause of so much bloodshed, but was now to benefit, rather than threaten, the city. Patronage of the arts became the new source of prestige, a means of demonstrating wealth and power. The oldest of the guilds, the wool-importers, the Arte di Calimala, set the precedent with its lavish expenditure on the baptistery and its competition to choose the best artist to design the great bronze doors.

As well as private patrons, Florence's many religious foundations also began to compete in the sponsorship of artists. All could justify their patronage on grounds of piety – initially Renaissance art was religious, and only later secular and classical – or as an expression of community responsibility and civic pride. At root, though, it was the same old desire to excel, dressed in a new guise.

Nouveau riche artists

Patronage made many a Florentine artisan wealthy. Ghiberti, who trained as a goldsmith and was only 25 years old when he was awarded the commission for the baptistery doors, founded a workshop and foundry that employed countless craftsmen, many of whom became famous and courted in their own right. Fra Filippo Lippi's sexual peccadilloes were tolerated – he was even allowed to relinquish his monastic vows and marry the nun he seduced, so long as he continued to produce brilliant art.

Florentine humanism

In this changing environment, it was also possible for intellectuals and artists to play a role in political life. Humanist scholars emerged from their absorption in classical texts to make new claims for Florence as the true inheritor of Roman virtues.

In 1375, Colluccio Salutati, the great classical scholar, became Florentine Chancellor, bringing to everyday politics all his immense learning, and swaying opinion by the power of his Ciceronian rhetoric. Other scholars followed him: Leonardo Bruni, Carlo Marsuppini, Poggio Bracciolini and Cosimo de' Medici.

Dawn of the Medici dynasty

Cosimo proved too persuasive, too popular for his political opponents. Heir to the banking network established by his father, Giovanni, he supported the guilds against government attempts to expropriate their funds to finance its military operations. He suffered the fate of all who threatened to wrest or win power in Florence and was banished from the city in 1433. Exile lasted only a year, for, with the backing of Pope Eugenius IV, he returned in 1434 and acted as unofficial leader for the next 30 years. Thus began a period of unparalleled peace and stability, and the founding of what was to become the Medici dynasty.

The Medici family ruled Florence almost continuously from 1434 to 1737. There is scarcely a corner of the city which does not have some connection with the family.

The Medici coat of arms is ubiquitous: a cluster of red balls on a field of gold. Some say it represents the dented shield of Averardo, a legendary knight from whom the family claimed descent. Others think the balls are medicinal pills – the family name suggests descent from apothecaries. Another theory explains the balls as symbols of money, like the traditional pawnbroker's sign, reminding us of the banking foundations of the family fortune.

The bank was established by Giovanni di Bicci de' Medici (1360–1429), one of nearly 100 financial institutions in the city at the start of the 15th century. Its rapid expansion to become the most profitable bank in Europe had much to do with the family's special relationship with the Pope. When the bank secured a monopoly over the collection of papal revenues, the family fortune was made.

Giovanni's son, Cosimo de' Medici (1389–1464), spent his early years travelling around Europe in pursuit of new business. Father and son preferred to stay out of Florentine public life, aware that the price of popularity with one faction was the enmity of another; too many public figures had been exiled when their party fell from power and, to a businessman, exile was clearly incompatible with running a successful enterprise.

Cosimo's arrest and exile

Nevertheless, when Cosimo was arrested and charged with treason in 1433, he was no longer able to stand in the wings. For the previous five years Florence had been involved in inconclusive wars with neighbours. The cost was bringing the city to the verge of economic crisis.

Cosimo had agreed to serve on the war committee, but resigned in 1430, having failed to win support for an end to the costly campaign. He left for Verona where, according to rumours spread by the rival Albizzi family, he was plotting to invade Florence and seize power. He was summoned to return to the city, on the pre-

text that his advice was required, and then arrested and sentenced to 10 years' exile.

Triumphant return

In the event, Cosimo's absence from Florence was brief. After a disastrous defeat by the Milanese in 1434, Florence was in no position to pursue its wars. Support for the Albizzi crumbled, the sentence of exile was revoked and Cosimo returned to a tumultuous welcome in September 1434. Though the people of Florence welcomed Cosimo as if he were a conquering king, he himself was characteristically ambivalent about taking up the reins of power. He stayed very much in the back-

LEFT: Cosimo de' Medici receiving the model of San Lorenzo from Brunelleschi and Ghiberti.
RIGHT: Cosimo I romanticised by Vasari.

Florentine Firsts

From something as down-to-earth as street paving and eyeglasses to grand concepts such as capitalism and the theory of the universe, it is sometimes difficult to grasp the breadth of Florence's contributions to the modern world.

Old records show that street paving began in Florence in the year 1235, and by 1339 the city had paved all its streets – the first in Europe to do so. And while Florentines had little to do with the discovery of the New World, Amerigo Vespucci pro-

vided the word "America", and Leonardo da Vinci created the first world maps showing America. A tablet in Santa Maria Maggiore church documents another first: "Here Lies Salvino d'Amato degli Armata of Florence, the Inventor of Eyeglasses, May God Forgive His Sins, Year 1317."

Two developments in music are among the most solidly documented Florentine firsts. The pianoforte was invented in Florence in 1711 by Cristofori, and the origins of opera are traced to the performance, in 1600, of *Euridice*, a new form of musical drama written by Iacopo Peri in honour of the marriage in Florence of Maria de'

Medici to Henri IV of France. An earlier marriage was the impetus for modern table manners. When Catherine de' Medici wed the future Henri II and moved to France, she was apparently appalled at the French court's table manners; unlike in Florence, no one used a fork. Before long, all of Paris society was imitating her. It is also possible that Catherine, equally appalled at French food, sent for her own chefs, and was responsible for the birth of French haute cuisine.

Many other firsts, of course, are related to the arts. Donatello's *David* (1430) is regarded as the first free-standing nude statue of the Renaissance. Donatello is also credited with the first free-standing equestrian statue of the Renaissance.

The grandiose claim that Brunelleschi is the father of modern architecture is one of the least contested. He was the first Renaissance architect to evolve the rules of linear perspective, and he developed a new approach, detailing specifications in advance and separating design from construction.

Machiavelli, through *The Prince* and other works, is credited with inventing both modern political science and modern journalism. Another literary great was Dante. Though much of his work was written in exile, Dante's highbrow Florentine language was so admired that it became the basis for modern Italian. Also in literature, Guicciardini is credited with laying the groundwork for modern historical prose, Petrarch for modern poetry and Boccaccio for the modern prose narrative.

In the financial world, it is arguable that 13th-century Florentine banks were responsible for modern capitalism, and that the city's medieval merchants were the first of a new, and eventually dominant, social class. But there is less doubt that those early Florentine financiers originated credit banking and double-entry book-keeping, both of which contributed mightily to the success of capitalism. Finally, it is well documented that in 1252 Florence became the first city to mint its own gold coin, the florin, which was widely used throughout Europe.   ❑

LEFT: Dante sketched by A. Bronzino.

ground, manipulating rather than governing, maintaining the appearance, at least, of private citizenship and respecting the city's republican aspirations. Hence the story that Cosimo turned down a first design by Brunelleschi for the family palace because it was too ostentatious. Hence, too, the contemporary accounts of Cosimo's cryptic character, the complaint that you could never tell what he was thinking. Both as a politician and as a businessman running an international bank, he was a master of guile, persuasion and discretion.

Enthusiastic humanist

Cosimo was also a keen supporter of the movement we now call humanism – a name which, though Renaissance in origin, was not used in this sense until the 16th century. In the 15th century the nearest equivalent was "orator".

In its early stages, in Cosimo's time, the movement emphasised the instruction to be gained from studying the classical past. It was nourished by a great belief in the overriding power of the word: persuasion, knowledge and good sense, leavened by the grace of God, were enough to make the world the way it should be.

The orators were pre-eminently diplomats or statesmen: men such as Leonardo Bruni, Chancellor of Florence, Aeneas Sylvius Piccolomini, later Pope Pius II, and Cosimo himself. The origin of the movement can be traced to 1397–1400, when a Byzantine, Manuel Chrysoloras, was invited to Florence to teach ancient Greek, a language all but forgotten.

From the start, the humanists were motivated by the excitement of discovery, and throughout the 15th century they scoured the world for antique manuscripts. Cosimo himself funded the travels of Poggio Bracciolini, who became famous for his discovery of the lost works of Cicero in a remote monastery. Cosimo founded the public library at San Marco to house a portion of his massive collection of manuscripts – the rest form the core of the Laurentian Library. He also paid for the education of Marsilio Ficino so that he could translate the then-unknown dialogues of Plato.

Cosimo died in 1464, leaving Florence prosperous, peaceful and with just claim to the title of the "new Rome" – having given birth

contemporaneously to humanism and the Renaissance. Upon him the *signoria* conferred the title once bestowed upon Cicero of Pater Patriae, Father of His Country. Cosimo's son, the sickly Piero, inherited his father's gout and did not long survive. In 1469, Lorenzo was called upon to fill his grandfather's shoes.

Lorenzo, poet and statesman

Lorenzo was no great patron of the pictorial arts. He owned few paintings and preferred the more princely pleasures of collecting antique gemstones, coins and vases (now in the Argenti Museum). Yet his portrait is familiar to the world through Botticelli's *Primavera* where, as

Mercury, he chases away the clouds that may spoil the idyllic scene. The picture was painted not for him but for his cousin and namesake.

The youthful and athletic figure in Botticelli's picture is hugely flattering. In reality Lorenzo had a beak nose and a projecting lower jaw that almost engulfed his upper lip. But to portray him as Mercury, god of eloquence, conciliation and reason was entirely just.

Lorenzo was an outstanding poet, writing satirical, often bawdy, sometimes romantic verse in his native tongue. Whereas in Cosimo's time it would have been unthinkable to read or write seriously except in Latin, Lorenzo promoted the study of Dante's work in the univer-

RIGHT: Lorenzo as glamorised by Botticelli.

sities and encouraged respect for Boccaccio and Petrarch, also writers in the *volgare* (vernacular). The language of these writers would soon become the standard for all Italian literature.

Moreover, Lorenzo was, like Cosimo, a humanist, much taken with the new philosophy of neo-Platonism that his grandfather's protégé, Ficino, had begun to develop; the ethereal quality of Botticelli's painting may also owe something to Ficino's quasi-mystical, half-magical theories as well as Lorenzo's love poetry.

As for reason and conciliation, although Lorenzo preferred literary pursuits to affairs of state, he won respect throughout Italy for his attempts to heal old rifts and pacify warring city

states. His aim was an alliance of states strong enough to defeat external threats, including the ambitions of the Holy Roman Emperor.

Papal dealings

Ironically, it was the Pope who proved to be Lorenzo's greatest enemy, for his own territorial ambitions depended on a divided Italy. It was Sixtus IV who took the papal bank account from the Medici bank, contributing to its near bankruptcy. Sixtus, too, was behind the Pazzi conspiracy of 1478 which aimed to murder Lorenzo and destroy the Medici. Sixtus even sent his allies, the Neapolitan army, to attack Florence, but Lorenzo so charmed the King of Naples that peace terms were rapidly agreed.

The news probably hastened Sixtus's death. Lorenzo took care to cultivate his successor, Innocent VIII, and succeeded in having his son, Giovanni de' Medici, created a cardinal, aged 13, thus planting a Medici in the heart of the papal domain. Three weeks after Giovanni's consecration, in 1492, Lorenzo was dead. "The peace of Italy is at an end," declared Pope Innocent, who himself died two months later, and his prophecy proved correct. In 1494, the French King Charles VIII invaded Italy and marched with a huge army to the walls of Florence. Piero de' Medici, Lorenzo's son, hoping to win the king's friendship, surrendered the city. Florentines slammed the doors of the Palazzo Vecchio in his face and that night the family fled.

Savonarola

Into the vacuum stepped Girolamo Savonarola, Prior of San Marco (1491–8), who was convinced that Charles VIII was an agent of God, sent to punish Florentines for their obsession with pagan philosophies, secular books and profane art. He presided over the city for four terrible years, when to wear unbecoming dress was punishable by torture and when children were rewarded for reporting their parents' misdemeanours. Savonarola had fanatical supporters and equally determined opponents: opinion turned against him when he was excommunicated and the threat of papal interdict fell over the city. His lasting achievement was the new republican constitution adopted in 1494 and, even after he was executed in 1498, the republic continued to flourish under the leadership of Piero Soderini, assisted by Niccolò Machiavelli.

THE MEDICI LEGACY

We have generations of Medici to thank for the fabulous collections of art amassed by the family – and Cosimo's court painter Vasari to thank for the Uffizi building which houses so many of them. Florence itself is indebted to the last of the Medici, Anna Maria Lodovica, for the fact that the great Medici art treasures are still to be seen in the city. On her death in 1743 her will stated that the family's vast wealth and hoards of art were to become the property of the future rulers of Tuscany – on condition that none of it should ever be moved outside Florence. Had it not been for her, the treasures of the Uffizi and the Bargello could well have been dispersed long ago.

Return of the Medici

In 1512 the nascent republic suffered a heavy defeat at the hands of the Spanish, and the Medici forced their way back into the city, led by Cardinal Giovanni. The following year he was crowned Pope Leo X, and Florence celebrated for four days. Machiavelli, regarded as a threat by the Medici, was imprisoned and tortured, then allowed to retire from public life. He began working on *The Prince*, a justification of his own actions in office and a reflection on the qualities that make an effective leader.

Much misunderstood, his work is regarded as a defence of ruthless autocracy. Until now, this had not been the Medici style, but the family became determined to hold on to power with all the force at its disposal. Two Medici popes, Leo X and his cousin Clement VII, ruled Florence from Rome for the next 15 years through the agency of Alessandro de' Medici, widely believed to be the bastard son of Pope Clement.

A brave attempt to re-establish the republic in 1527, when Rome was sacked by imperial troops, was put down by combined imperial and papal forces in 1530. Alessandro was crowned Duke of Florence and proved to be the first of generations of Medici dukes who, secure in their power, were corrupt, debauched and tyrannical. When he was murdered by his cousin and occasional bedfellow, Lorenzaccio, Florence was relieved of a great burden.

When the council met to elect a successor, they chose another Cosimo; this time son of the respected Giovanni delle Bande Nere and Maria Salviati, granddaughter of Lorenzo the Magnificent. Those who voted for him perhaps believed that he would accept constitutional limitations to his power and act only after consulting appointed counsellors. They were wrong – it soon became evident that under his rule, they would enjoy less, not greater freedom.

Cosimo I set about destroying all opposition. First he defeated an army of republicans in exile and had the leaders publicly executed, four a day, in the Piazza della Signoria. Then he brought the cities of Tuscany to heel, attacking them with such force and brutality that Siena, for example, lost half its population. (To this day many Sienese refuse to set foot in Florence for this very reason.) Unlike former Medici, he was no enlightened patron of the arts. Such work as he did commission – the frescos of the Palazzo Vecchio – were for his own self-glorification or for practical purposes: the Uffizi was built to bring all the administrative functions, the guilds and the judiciary, under one roof and under his control.

Cosimo's achievements

He thus created an effective administration, forced Tuscany into political unity and brought security to the region. Whereas Cosimo de' Medici, in the 1400s, had been just one of several powerful heads of Florentine families,

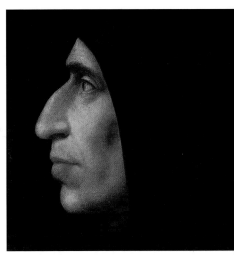

Cosimo I was truly a monarch, the government his council and his followers courtiers.

Ironically, after his death, Florence achieved something approaching the self-governing status that had so long eluded the city previously. Cosimo's descendants, who nominally ruled Florence for another six generations, proved so indolent, degenerate, drunken and debauched that they had little taste for affairs of state, which was left to the government machine created by Cosimo. Yet no one again challenged their right to rule, and when the last Medici, Anna Maria, died in 1743, there was genuine grief at the passing of a dynasty and the end of a chapter in the city's colourful history. ❏

LEFT: the Medici coat of arms.
RIGHT: Girolamo Savonarola, an unbending ruler.

FOREIGNERS AND FLOODS

Florence's best ambassadors have long been international celebrities with a taste for good living and a thirst for culture. But recent times have been darkened by political corruption and the threat of flooding

The twilight of the Medici era ushered in a relatively sedate period under the bureaucratic rule of the House of Lorraine. But it also saw the flourishing of a rich relationship between Florence and its foreign visitors, which had begun the century before.

When asked what made life worth living, Sir Harold Acton, the grand old Anglo-Florentine man of letters, aesthete, and voluptuary, recalled Cyril Connolly's words with pleasure: "Writing a book, dinner for six, travelling in Italy with someone you love." Years later, as an old man before his death in 1994, Acton confirmed that judgement: "I believe Florence has given me all this."

Before the 17th century, foreign visitors were likely to be mercenaries or spies, posing as diplomats. Gradually, a few adventurous eccentrics such as Fynes Moryson published their encounters with witty, if outlandish, Florentines and their barbarous architecture.

A century later, the attraction of an alien psyche, a perfect climate, the architecture, a low cost of living and undervalued works of art made Florence an essential stop on any European tour. The cynical Tobias Smollett decried this new cultural traffic as "an exchange of snobbery, vices and fashions," since travel was an option open only to the aristocracy. As the product of a narrow if leisured background himself, he saw even upper-class Florentines as noble savages at best and horse thieves at worst. Smollett's

jaundiced views were perhaps influenced by his unfortunate nocturnal arrival in Florence: he and his wife had to trudge four miles round the old city walls before finding an open gate.

Court consuls

By 1737, Horace Mann, the English consul to the Grand Ducal court, protested against the numbers of English in Florence: "If I had to invite them all to dinner, I'd be ruined." He welcomed the cultivated company of the politician Horace Walpole and the poet Thomas Gray as a change from the usual "cheesecake" English. Mann himself was of a noble line of consuls to Florence, an institu-

---

LEFT: debris from the 1966 flood outside Santa Croce.
RIGHT: the English poet Percy Bysshe Shelley.

tion dating back to 1456. He tolerated his onerous contacts with the rapidly expanding expatriate colony, but was considerably more at ease with Florentine aristocrats.

Unfortunately for him, his budget did not allow him to compete with the splendour of masked balls held by the Corsini and Niccolini in the Pergola theatre. Mann was, in fact, witnessing the last days of the Medici era.

Parties aside, Mann was an industrious consul, a rarity in a British community devoted to merriment and culture alone. The Anglophile Mario Praz put it more bluntly: "For centuries the Italians have gone abroad to work and the English to enjoy themselves."

receive their titles. Hadfield, clutching a punchbowl, is also in the picture. Among the decorations on the walls are the Medici coat of arms, a copy of the *Dancing Faun* in the Uffizi, and, echoing it on another wall, a bust in which the artist has depicted himself with faun-like ears.

During the Napoleonic Wars, travel to Florence was suspended, but the unfortunate case of Joseph Forsyth highlights the dangers of idle tourism. After a happy exploration of the region, Forsyth was imprisoned by the French for 12 years and died soon after his release in 1814, the first known martyr to tourism.

The antics of the *jeunesse dorée* were further enriched by a British-owned Florentine inn, Carlo's, which flourished from the mid-1700s to the death in 1776 of its owner, Charles Hadfield. A painting in the National Trust stately home of Dunham Massey, Cheshire, by the caricaturist Thomas Patch – a friend of Reynolds who had escaped to Florence from Rome in 1755 amid a homosexual scandal which had dashed plans to start a British academy there – offers an intriguing insight into the British community. It shows a punch party for 13 gentlemen of fashion held at Hadfield's restaurant in 1760. Many of those present had yet to

Generals and governesses

Following the British victory at Waterloo, the middle classes joined the throngs of aristocratic dilettanti and literati heading for Florence. Renaissance scholars, persecuted rebels, demure governesses and eloping couples incongruously filled the ranks. As Samuel Rogers observed: "If rich, one travels for pleasure; if poor, for economy; if sick, to be cured; if gifted, to create."

Shelley and Byron

In his famous phrase, Shelley called Florence a "paradise of exiles", an escape from persecution and poverty to art and sunshine. He

FOREIGNERS AND FLOODS ♦ 33

marvelled at the city, "the white sails of the boats relieved by the deep green of the forest which comes to the water's edge, and the sloping hills covered with bright villas".

Byron was more interested in the people than the landscape. "What do the English know of the Italians, except for a few museums, drawing rooms and a little reading?" With his glamorous Italian mistress and his active involvement in the movement for Italian independence, Byron challenged English insularity. The majority of his contemporaries simply ignored the natives in favour of Florentine art and architecture.

The lure of art

Now that art was on the agenda, foreign visitors flocked to see the Uffizi sculptures and Botticelli's *Medici Venus*; however, the "Primitives" such as Giotto and Cimabue were not admired until John Ruskin made an impassioned plea in 1860; and Masaccio and Piero della Francesca were not fully appreciated by visitors until the 20th century. But from the 18th century, Florence had become an important market for art and antiques, providing grand tourists with souvenirs to take home to their country piles.

From the 1820s, a clutch of discerning English clergy arrived and promptly carried away some of Florence's greatest Renaissance treasures, including Masaccio's *Madonna and Child*, now in London's National Gallery.

The poet and essayist Walter Savage Landor (1775–1864) was the only collector ever to own a Cimabue. Landor boasted often: "Nature I loved, but next to nature, art." After an unsuccessful lawsuit in 1858, he fled to Florence permanently and decorated his Villa Gherardesca with paintings by Raphael and Fra Filippo Lippi. Forgetting his own litigious and unsavoury past, Landor designated Florentines "beyond all others, a treacherous, mercenary race".

Along with many of his peers, Landor was struck by the contrast between the city's glorious past and mundane present. He called Florence "the filthiest capital in Europe", and described villas overrun with "tame pigs, rotten grapes, smelly goats' cheese, children covered with vermin".

Florence Nightingale (1820–1910), the founder of modern nursing, who was born in the city after which she was named, would have had little sympathy for the querulous Landor. In 1837 she returned, intending to study language and art in an early Florentine

finishing school. But instead, so the legend goes, she sealed her fate by nursing a sick Englishwoman back to health.

Victorians abroad

According to her contemporary, the American poet William Cullen Bryant (1794–1878), Nightingale did well to escape the conventional Grand Tour. In his diaries, he perfectly captures the spirit of Victorian Britain abroad. "As the day advances, the English in white hats and white pantaloons come out of their lodgings, accompanied by their hale and square-built spouses, and saunter stiffly down the Arno."

LEFT: *Villa di Belvedere* by Adolfo Tommasi.
RIGHT: an early photograph of Santa Maria Novella.

By the 1850s, escapees from mid-Victorian England made Florence *une ville anglaise* according to the Goncourt brothers. In the morning, the English would go for a "constitutional" in the Cascine Park; residents and visitors alike met at Vieusseux library for a chat; then it was time for *i muffins* at *i tirummi* (tearooms). Italian language and society were forced into retreat as the English acquired shops, paintings and villas.

As Henry James said, from the splendour of Villa Palmieri: "If you're an aching alien, half the talk is about villas." He ruefully pondered on the fate of Florentine villas, not built "with such a solidity of structure and super-

fluity of stone, simply to afford an economical winter residence to English and American families." Against local custom, the English chose their villa for its view rather than for its architecture, function or size.

The Casa Guidi view

The Brownings, Florence's most celebrated literary couple, were no exception: the view from the "Casa Guidi Windows" slipped neatly from reality into Elizabeth Barrett Browning's most famous poem. Since the invalid Elizabeth was largely confined to home, her veranda, "not quite a terrace but no ordinary balcony", was central to her happi-

ness. There among the lemon trees, Elizabeth, the ardent republican, saw the Austrians invade the cowed city. The Florentines had "constrained faces, they, so prodigal of cry and gesture when the world goes right".

Elizabeth never tired of praising Italy at the expense of England. "Our poor English want educating into gladness. They want refining not in the fire but in the sunshine." Or, as Virginia Woolf put it: "So Mrs Browning, every day, as she tossed off her Chianti and broke another orange off the branch, praised Italy and lamented poor, dull, damp, sullen, joyless, expensive, conventional England." The improvement in Elizabeth's health and happiness was said to have been partly due to the chianti cure Robert used to wean her off her addiction to laudanum.

Robert Browning loved Florence because, in his own words, "I felt at home with my own soul there." He channelled his erudition into theology, psychology and botany while organising literary salons, writing prodigiously and looking after his "Lyric Love". However, neither of the poets had time for Florentines, although both felt a very genuine passion for the city.

When Elizabeth died, her last words were for Italy. Today, the Browning Institute has refurnished Casa Guidi in cluttered and eclectic Victorian style decorated in green and pink, Elizabeth's two favourite colours. The inscription on the wall is a tribute from *Firenze grata*, a grateful Florence: "In her woman's heart blended learning and the spirit of poetry and made of her work a ring of gold joining Italy and England."

So many talents

Florentine literary critics such as Oreste del Buono believe that the Browning circle's preciousness has obscured the rest of Florence's foreign community. Precious or not, its members were aware of living in a mythical time.

The American community was enriched by Henry James's thoughtful analysis. In the German community, Adolf von Hildebrand surrounded himself with painters and composers. One evening Liszt played Chopin at dinner.

Strauss, Wagner and Clara Schumann all stayed at Hildebrand's villa on the slopes of Bellosguardo. A stone's throw from the Brownings, Dostoyevsky was finishing off

The Idiot. The Florentine Slavic community flourished under Count Demidoff's patronage of the arts. Tchaikovsky lived and worked fruitfully in Via di San Leonardo; even Maxim Gorky and Alexander Blok made an entrance on the scene. Yet not all Florence's visitors were great authors and artists. The obscure epitaph on Arthur Clough's tombstone reads: "Died at Florence November 13 1861, aged 42 – came to Florence in search of good health and died of a fever."

Italy's capital for a day

In 1865 Florence briefly became the capital of the newly united Italy. Although its exalted role would last only five years before Rome was then made the permanent capital in turn, Florence underwent profound and rapid change during this time. An ambitious plan of expansion and modernisation sadly led to the demolition among other things of the old city walls, and their replacement with a wide ring of avenues punctuated with large piazzas in keeping with the French urban taste of the times. Quarters for the middle classes and Piazzale Michelangelo were built.

Later, old areas of the centre including the Ghetto were declared to be in dangerous condition and unwholesome, and were razed, and the soulless Piazza della Repubblica was created partly in their place.

Great collectors

At the beginning of the 20th century, the Anglo-Florentine community was as much a part of the fabric of the city as the Medici villas it inhabited and the art collections it had founded. The collections assembled by people such as Harold Acton's parents, Arthur Acton and his American banking heiress wife Hortense Mitchell, the American art critic and connoisseur Bernard Berenson, and the British architect Herbert Horne, remain a tribute to the enduring effect of the "Grand Tourists" on Florence.

Bernard Berenson (1865–1959) was the archetypal collector. Alan Moorhead describes how the penniless young Berenson "had gone over the frescos in these Tuscan churches inch

by inch, riding out every morning on his bicycle with his pockets full of candles." Fittingly, his Villa i Tatti is now Harvard's Center for Renaissance Studies.

On his death, Harold Acton instead left his superb Villa La Pietra, together with his art collection and 40,000 rare volumes, to New York University, and another property near the

Arno to the British Institute. However, in an unexpected twist, his will has been challenged by the children of a late Florence innkeeper, Liana Beacci, claiming that she was Sir Harold's illegitimate sister due to an affair which Arthur Acton had with his secretary, and so entitled to part of the estate. DNA testing has come out in her favour, but NYU is fighting the claims tooth and nail, and the case continues.

Mixed impressions

World War I chased away most of the foreign visitors and residents. D.H. Lawrence had a tourist's experience of the political aftermath

Famous visitors to the city: the composer Tchaikovsky **(LEFT)** and the novelist D.H. Lawrence **(RIGHT)**.

of the war. He saw the shift from socialism to Fascism as different forms of "bullying". Under socialism "servants were rude, cabmen insulted one and demanded treble fare". Under Fascism, he reported that taxis had a lower price, but so did life; the socialist mayor of Fiesole was murdered in front of his family. In the 1920s and 1930s, the Grand Tour resumed, but for society figures and intellectuals rather than aristocrats. Aldous Huxley dubbed Florence "a second-rate provincial town with its repulsive Gothic architecture and its acres of Christmas card primitives". But E.M. Forster was besotted with the city's alien vivacity.

river and the Allies on the other, the retreating Germans abandoned Florence, blocking the Ponte Vecchio with rubble from demolished medieval buildings at either end and blowing up all the other bridges across the Arno. A few hours after the last German left, reconstruction of the bridges began. Legend has it that all of the bridges would have been blown sky high had it not been for Hitler's fond memories of the Ponte Vecchio.

The great flood of 1966

Despite post-war construction and the economic boom years that followed, Florence would awake to an even worse shock 22 years

In 1947, Dylan Thomas came to create or vegetate in the "rasher-frying sun". After initial excitement, he became steadily drunk and shamelessly collapsed in front of Florence's literary elite in the Giubbe Rosse café. Undaunted, Thomas damned them all as "editors who live with their mothers, on private incomes, and translate Apollinaire".

World War II

The Second World War severely affected the city, especially in 1944 as the Germans, pursued by the advancing British forces, retreated. After a two-week pitched artillery battle between the Nazis on one side of the

later. Shortly before dawn on 4 November 1966, after 48 centimetres (19 inches) of rain had fallen in 48 hours, the River Arno burst its banks. Thirty-five people were killed, 16,000 vehicles destroyed and hundreds of homes left uninhabitable as the muddy floodwaters rose to more than 6 metres (20 ft) above street level. Heating oil was swept out of broken basement tanks. Bella Firenze, Beautiful Florence, the world's cultural capital, the city of art and dreams, was a stinking black morass.

The water crashed through the museums, galleries, churches and crafts shops. Thousands of works of art were damaged, some dating back to the 12th century – paintings, statues, frescos, tapestries and manuscripts, scientific instruments and ancient Etruscan pottery. The city had suffered from floods in the past – about one really serious inundation each century – but the only other event that caused as much devastation as the 1966 flood came during World War II.

Florence's unique place in cultural history carries with it the heavy burden of preserving its treasures for the rest of the world. Consequently, it has become a leading centre for art restoration – and a focal point for arguments over how, when, whether and what should be preserved of humankind's past achievements.

Memories of the flood

There was no such doubt over what to do in 1966. Florentines did what they have always done when disaster strikes their city. Even as the flood-waters subsided, the task of reversing the damage began.

Francis Kelly, an American artist who later wrote a book about the restoration, was one of hundreds of art students who had gathered that year, as every year, to study in Florence. "It was the students who jumped into the mud and pulled out paintings, statues and manuscripts, who were the real saviours of Florence," he says. Forming a human chain down into the fetid bowels of the National Library's basement, they passed out old manuscripts that could easily have been lost.

Student volunteers flocked to Florence from around the world to help the army, which had sent in thousands of conscripts. They helped to wrap Japanese mulberry paper over paintings to keep the paint from buckling, and they helped scrape the slime off the base of Michelangelo's *David*. Living in makeshift dormitories and wearing blue overalls supplied by the government, many students gave up months to help with the restoration, to clean up the streets and pump out basements.

Kelly himself remembers walking into a huge hall lined with famous paintings, all damaged. "It was terribly dismaying," he recalls. "Hanging beside each painting was a bag of paint flakes that had broken off."

LEFT: Adolf Hitler and Benito Mussolini salute at Florence's Tomb of the Fascist Martyrs.
RIGHT: a flood marker, reminder of a constant threat.

Money and expertise

When word of the flood spread, millions of dollars in public and private money poured in from around the world. Art-restoration experts arriving from America and Europe agreed that it could take 20 years for all the damaged art objects – those not totally ruined – to be restored and for Florence to recover. They were half right. Florence has definitely recovered, but almost half a century on, the task of restoration is still not yet complete, although most major works that were damaged are back on display. The banks of the Arno have been re-dug and reinforced, and valuable art objects have been moved to higher, safer places.

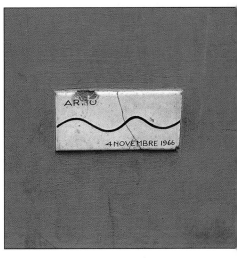

Experts admit, however, that another major flood could occur, while administrators fail to agree on steps to prevent this.

The damage to the Archaeological Museum, so inundated that curators resorted to digging techniques they had used to recover artefacts from long-buried civilisations, has now all but been repaired, but the reconstruction of ancient Etruscan tombs, once a popular feature of the museum gardens has only recently been completed, and they are still not yet open.

At the National Library, the institution hardest hit, students looking for rare reference books may still expect to be told, "That book has not yet been restored from the flood." In all, 1½ million volumes were damaged, two-thirds beyond repair. But more than 500,000 modern books were saved, along with 40,000 rare or historic volumes.

Rapid advances

After being dried and treated with chemicals to prevent further deterioration, those volumes were stored – not in the basement this time – to await restoration. The library's full-time staff, once 80-strong, are now greatly reduced, but they are through much of the restoration task. Many believe that this sort of restoration effort would have been necessary even without the flood. Moreover, sci-

entific advances in restoration now allow all manner of ageing, deteriorating or damaged works – not only those rescued from the flood – to be saved.

Benefits of the flood

In the oldest part of medieval Florence, among the tiny jewellery and woodworking shops, Paola Lucchesi and Beatrice Cuniberti have a thriving studio restoring antique maps, prints and manuscripts for private collectors. They regard themselves as students of the flood, benefiting from techniques that might never have been developed but for that disaster. Paola Lucchesi acknowledges that her

LIVING WITH THE THREAT OF FLOODING

The threat of flooding is something that sticks in the mind of every Florentine. November normally brings heavy rain, and one eye is always kept on the level of the Arno. After a particularly prolonged period of wet weather, groups of people can always be seen on the bridges observing with apprehension the turgid, swirling mass of water below.

Since November 1966, attempts have been made to ensure that the disaster will not be repeated; the river bed near the Ponte Vecchio has been deepened and the river banks around Ponte Amerigo Vespucci have been reinforced by massive walls. Changes in the river's level are scrupulously monitored by computers and video cameras.

But few Florentines believe that, should the water reach the 1966 levels, disaster could truly be averted. Throughout the city, both inside and on the facades of buildings, small plaques have been mounted on the walls showing the 1966 flood levels. This is particularly mind-boggling in the area around Santa Croce, one of the lowest parts of the city. The actual water marks are still visible on some buildings which have not been repainted since the disaster.

On 4 November 1996, the 30th anniversary of the flood, newspapers and TV news programmes were full of shocking black-and-white images of the devastation, a solemn reminder and warning that it must not happen again.

speciality, paper restoration, was an unknown field before the flood, but developed rapidly as experts gathered in Florence to swap information and work together to develop now-standard drying methods, chemical treatments and rebinding techniques.

In the same huge hall where Francis Kelly painstakingly pieced together paint flakes in 1966, Marco Ciatti presides over a laboratory belonging to an institute founded by the Medici and now run by the Italian Ministry of Culture, employing a large number of specialists in the restoration of paintings. A similar laboratory on the other side of Florence restores statues and stonework. Using gamma rays, spectropho-

metres (20 ft by 10 ft), most are back on display, with only a few still waiting to be restored. Techniques developed by the laboratory are being used on other important works that were not damaged in the flood but are in need of restoration.

Few, perhaps, foresaw that there would be a positive side to the tragedy of 1966, but there has been. Millions of people a year now visit the city – more than 10 times the pre-flood record. They can now see works of art in a condition that would make Ruskin, the Victorian writer who popularised the work of the so-called Florentine "primitive" artists, green with envy.

tometers, gas chromatographs and other sophisticated equipment, Ciatti's artists work alongside chemists and microbiologists who analyse the canvas and pigment "structure" of deteriorating paintings before deciding on the best way to conserve or reconstruct damaged areas. Larger paintings, which take up to three years to complete, are painstakingly retouched using brushes and paints re-invented in the style used by the original artist.

Of 3,000 rescued masterpieces, many of them huge canvases up to 6 metres by 3

LEFT: pictures for restoration laid out in the Uffizi.
ABOVE: a restorer at work in San Marco.

The damage of politics

Although there are pockets of conservatism across the region, notably in places such as Lucca, Tuscany displays an independent streak, and Tuscans, by and large, vote for the left. With the Communist Party evolving an progressive, pro-regionalist stance, after World War II a "red belt" developed across central Italy, run by left-wing coalitions.

At a national level, however, by the early 1990s, more than 50 post-war "swing-door" governments had come and gone. To many observers, the source of this crisis lay in Italy's administration and dubious morality. Senior party leaders tended to die in office, governments suffered from opportunism, not lack of opportunity. *Partitocrazia* (party influence) supplanted democracy, extending from government to public corporations, infiltrating banking, the judiciary and media, and the public tacitly condoned this "old boys' network".

Clean hands

The early 1990s saw a series of political scandals involving bribes, and the result was the *Mani Pulite* ("Clean Hands") campaign under the fiery leadership of Antonio di Pietro, a former magistrate who became Italy's most popular public figure when he spearheaded inquiries into public corruption.

self-imposed exile in Tunisia in January 2000, with international arrest warrants hanging over his head for a string of corruption charges and convictions. Andreotti, who was instead charged with Mafia ties, was eventually let off after a mammoth trial lasting years. His acquittal was later held up on appeal by state prosecutors. However, in a long report published afterwards to show how they had reached their decision, appeal judges said that Andreotti had been found to have enjoyed "friendly" and direct relations with the Mafia "up until 1980", but not later – meaning that due to statutory time limitations he could not now be prosecuted.

A seemingly vast network was uncovered in which public contracts were awarded by politicians to businesses in return for bribes. Italian public life was convulsed by the scandal, dubbed *Tangentopoli* – literally, "Bribesville". Dozens of MPs and businessmen came under investigation. A number were preventively held in jail, some even took their lives. The Christian Democrat Party, whch had dominated Italian politics since the war, collapsed. Two former prime ministers – the socialist leader Bettino Craxi and the Christian Democrat veteran and seven times former prime minister Giulio Andreotti – were investigated.

Craxi slipped through the net and died in

Mafia bombing

In the midst of the political upheaval, in May 1993 Florence suffered yet another devastating blow, when a bomb planted by the Mafia behind the Uffizi gallery rocked the city, both physically and psychologically. Five people were killed, and priceless paintings and sculptures damaged, while a handful were destroyed. The fabric of the Uffizi's buildings was damaged, and several medieval buildings around the corner were virtually destroyed, while the *pensione* used to film the Merchant-Ivory film *A Room With a View* was so devastated that it was forced to close for good.

The Mafia's widely perceived aim was to

use the attack, and others in Milan and Rome, to force the Italian state into submission, and agree to a deal of mutual convenience with the Mob, as had been enjoyed with the Christian Democrats. The jailed Sicilian Godfather, Salvatore "Toto" Riina, was sentenced to life for the Uffizi bombing, along with other crime bosses in 1998. However, the more refined minds thought to have been behind the attacks have never been brought to book.

The return of the corrupt

Meanwhile, while no area of Italy appeared to have been left untouched by corruption, including Florence which had its share of scandal, in the end few if any *Tangentopoli* politicians served any real time in jail. Many, initially ostracised, were later rehabilitated, while a number of those originally embroiled have since returned to politics, "running", as the writer Ennio Flaiano once said of Italians in general, "in aid of the winner".

In a frank interview in July 2005, the film director Bernardo Bertolucci told the *Corriere della Sera*: "Italy lost a great opportunity after *Tangentopoli*. It should have had a real examination of conscience, in order to understand how on earth it could be that there were so many corrupt figures populating our landscape, accomplices of a system which goes from small tips in return for small favours, to large *tangenti* [bribes] for big contracts. And instead we have wound up with an illegal prime minister, who was elected amid conditions of almost complete control of the media."

He was referring to Silvio Berlusconi, the media tycoon turned prime minister.

Silvio Berlusconi

Elected in March 1994 on an anti-corruption ticket and depicting himself as the new face of Italy, his centre-right coalition – including neo-Fascist elements – resoundingly collapsed in November the same year, after he came under investigation himself for graft. Following his extraordinary return to power in 2001 with the largest majority in post-war history – despite the by now many accusations of corruption

against him – he immediately set about pushing through a series of laws to spare himself and his cronies from prosecution. A number of politicians whose career had appeared to be finished in the wake of *Tangentopoli* had meanwhile joined his coalition, including from apparently opposed and incompatible parties at the other end of the spectrum.

Berlusconi headed a family empire that spanned telecommunications to insurance and building. It included top football club AC Milan, the Mediolanum bank, Italy's largest publishing house, Mondadori, leading daily paper *Il Giornale*, the popular news magazine *Panorama*, and three commercial TV channels

representing nearly half of Italy's viewing figures. Thanks to his indirect control also of state broadcasting, from where his satirical opponents had been banished, he was thought to control one way or another some 95 percent of Italian television.

Berlusconi's opponents pointed to a glaring conflict of interests between his roles as businessman and prime minister, and said he shamelessly used his TV channels to promote his cause. Berlusconi the populist shrugged this off: "the people decide", he said; and the people did, indeed, seem prepared to overlook everything in favour of political stability and strong, if idiosyncratic, leadership. ❑

LEFT: demonstrators at the European Social Forum, held in Florence in 2002.
RIGHT: Silvio Berlusconi, a controversial premier.

Decisive Dates

10th–8th centuries BC Settlements on the site of Florence.

4th century BC Fiesole is well established as a powerful Etruscan city with walls and temples.

351 BC Etruria conquered by the Romans.

59 BC Foundation of the Roman colony of Florentia, which grows rapidly at the expense of Fiesole.

3rd century AD Christianity is brought to Florence by eastern merchants.

5th–6th centuries The city is repeatedly sacked by Goths and Byzantines.

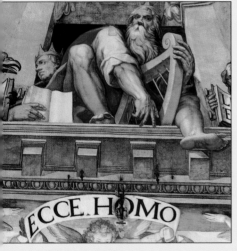

ECCE HOMO

570 Lombards occupy Tuscany, ruling Florence from Lucca. Two centuries of peace, during which the baptistery was built.

774 Charlemagne defeats the Lombards and appoints a marquis to rule Tuscany, still based in Lucca.

1001 Death of Marquese Ugo, who made Florence the new capital of Tuscany. Florence is now a prosperous trading town.

11th century Most of the city's churches are rebuilt.

1115 Countess Matilda, the last of the marquis, dies leaving her title to the Pope. Florence becomes self-governing Comune and conquers the surrounding countryside.

1125 Florence conquers Fiesole.

1216 Start of civil strife between rival supporters of the Pope and of the Holy Roman Emperor over issues of temporal power fuelled by class warfare and family vendettas. The papal party prevails in Florence.

1252 The minting of the first florin, which is to become the currency of European trade.

1260 Florentines suffer disastrous defeat by the Sienese at Montaperti. Florentine supporters of the Emperor dissuade the Sienese from razing the city.

1284 New town walls erected that define the limits of Florence until 1865. Florence is one of Europe's richest cities.

1293 Strife between Guelf (papal) and Ghibelline (imperial) parties is now an outright class war. The merchant Guelfs pass an ordinance excluding aristocratic Ghibellines from public office.

1294 Construction of the cathedral begins.

1299 Palazzo Vecchio is begun.

1302 Dante is exiled.

1315 Palazzo Vecchio is completed.

1338 Florence is at the height of its prosperity, despite continuing instability.

1339 Edward III of England defaults on massive debts incurred fighting the Hundred Years War. Two powerful banking families, the Bardi and Peruzzi, go bankrupt and the Florentine economy is in crisis.

1348 The Black Death sweeps through Tuscany. In 50 years it wipes out three out of five people in Florence.

1378 Revolt of the *ciompi*, the lowest-paid wool-industry workers, demanding guild representation and a say in government. Their demands are met but the merchant families reinforce their oligarchy.

1400–1 Competition to design new doors for the baptistery announced, marking the rise of Florence to intellectual and artistic pre-eminence.

1406 Florence defeats Pisa.

1433 Cosimo de' Medici exiled for 10 years, his growing popularity in Florence a threat to the merchant oligarchy.

1434 Cosimo de' Medici returns to Florence. He is to preside over 30 years of stability and artistic achievement.

1464 Death of Cosimo, hailed as Pater Patriae, Father of His Country. Start of brief reign of his sickly son, Piero the Gouty.

1469 Lorenzo, grandson of Cosimo, takes charge of the city at the age of 20 and proves himself to be an able leader.

1478 Pazzi conspiracy seeks to destroy the Medici dynasty but reinforces the popularity of Lorenzo.

1492 Piero, Lorenzo's son, takes over.

1494 Charles VIII of France invades Italy and Piero surrenders Florence to him. In disgust, citizens expel Piero and, under the influence of Savonarola, declare Florence a republic with Christ as its ruler.

1498 Pope Alexander VI orders the trial of Savonarola for heresy and fomenting civil strife. He is burnt at the stake.

1504 Michelangelo completes his statue of David, symbol of republican Florence, which is placed in Piazza della Signoria.

1512 Florence defeated by an invading Spanish army. The Medici take advantage of the city's weakness to re-establish control, led by Giovanni, son of Lorenzo the Magnificent and now Pope Leo X, and his cousin, Giulo (later Pope Clement VII).

1527 Clement VII tries to rule Florence from Rome but, when Rome is attacked by imperial troops, Florentines expel the Medici and return to a republican constitution.

1530 Pope Clement signs a peace treaty with Emperor Charles V and together they lay siege to Florence.

1531 Florence falls. Alessandro de' Medici is made Duke of Florence.

1537 Alessandro is assassinated by his cousin, Lorenzaccio. Cosimo I is made Duke, defeats an army of republicans and begins a 37-year reign. Many artists, including Michelangelo, leave Florence, which declines as a centre of artistic excellence.

1555 Cosimo I starts to reunite Tuscany.

1564 Cosimo I unexpectedly resigns and his son, Francesco, is appointed Regent.

1569 Cosimo I created Grand Duke of Tuscany by Pope Pius VI in belated recognition of his absolute control over the region.

1574 Cosimo I dies.

1610 Galileo made court mathematician to Cosimo II.

1631 Galileo is excommunicated.

1737 Gian Gastone dies without a male heir. The title passes, by treaty, to the Austrian imperial House of Lorraine.

1743 Anna Maria Lodovica, last of the Medici, dies, bequeathing her property to the people of Florence.

1799 The French defeat Austria. Florence is ruled by Louis of Bourbon.

1815 Florence is again ruled by the House of Lorraine, but clandestine organisations, set on securing independence from foreign control, gain popular support.

1848 In First Italian War of Independence, Tuscany is the vanguard of the uprising.

1860 Tuscany votes to become part of the emerging United Kingdom of Italy.

1865 Florence is declared the capital.

1871 Rome becomes the capital.

1887–1912 Tuscany remains economically buoyant, helped by textile production, and becomes a haven for foreign writers.

1919 Mussolini founds the Fascist Party.

1940 Italy enters World War II.

1944 Retreating Nazis destroy the bridges of Florence, leaving only the Ponte Vecchio.

1957–65 Florence transforms from an agricultural economy to a service and culture-based economy.

1966 Florence devastated by floods. Many works of art destroyed.

1988 Florentines vote to ban all but residents' cars from the historic city centre.

1993 Bomb kills five and damages the Uffizi, destroying and harming artworks.

1998 Salvatore "Toto" Riina and other members of the Mafia given life sentences for planting the Uffizi bomb.

2005 The left win regional elections.   ❑

LEFT: a fresco from the Duomo dome.

RIGHT: retreating Nazis blow up Ponte Santa Trinità.

CONTEMPORARY FLORENCE

Tourist Florence remains fabulous, but the city's inhabitants aren't immune from the familiar 21st-century problems: petty crime, urban decay, traffic chaos and high living costs

Mention the name Florence, and you are almost certain to conjure up images of the Renaissance, when the extraordinarily rich flowering of artistic and intellectual life under the enlightened rule of the Medici princes, coupled with the city's immense banking wealth, made it the most important centre in Europe.

Florence today is undoubtedly one of the finest open-air museums in the world, and the tourism which this fuels has itself become a major new source of wealth. Rarely, however, is it considered as a city in contemporary terms, except perhaps for its shopping. Yet even here, the fine handicrafts and stylish fashion accessories for which it is now almost equally famous are ultimately rooted in Florence's own, early mercantile and creative traditions.

Yet struggling to break free of its historical straitjacket is another, more hidden Florence, which, when the surface is scratched, reveals itself to be a sophisticated, tuned-in, complex and even slightly troubled modern city, and anything but one suffering from the passive nature of a resigned tourist capital.

The three faces of Florence

As it happens, there are probably three Florences. The first is that of the old historic centre. While this continues to stand proud as a repository for everything that is the Renaissance, shopkeepers often treat it as an open-face mine to be shamelessly worked in order to reap the

fruits of the mass tourism which flocks there.

However, many locals have by now discarded it as a viable place to live. Draconian traffic restrictions and rising prices have become a real deterrent, as well as the awareness that the centre is increasingly resembling a kind of Disneyland, although not everyone would agree with such a view. Yet refined and sensitive Florentines, for all their left-wing ideals, can be viciously ironic under their breath when witnessing Third World street vendors commandeering whole streets alongside the Palazzo Vecchio as they pedal repro football jerseys of players with names like that of the Ukraine-born striker

---

LEFT: texting on the steps of the Duomo.
RIGHT: culture and politics on Florentine posters.

Andriy Shevchenko for AC Milan, who have nothing to do with the city.

The second Florence is *la Firenze delle colline*, meaning the magical hills that ring, and in some cases help form the city. Despite the rampant urban development down below, these lofty upper reaches remain a loyal tribute to the Renaissance vision of *rus in urbe*, meaning the importing of a little bit of countryside into the city. Miraculously, delightful villages and hills such as Fiesole and Settignano, with their magnificent villas, lines of cypresses, and convents and castles, are still practically untouched, as are those of Arcetri – where Galileo's observatory is situated – and Bellosguardo.

The third Florence, in the periphery, is by contrast a newly developing urban sprawl featuring ambitious projects meant to renew areas of degradation and carrying internationally known architectural names. While they may seem exciting to some, auguring well for Florence as a city of the future, the projects also raise important questions about how they will affect what, in the past, has been one of the world's great aesthetic capitals.

Brave new buildings

Central to this brave new, but chilling, world is a new university city being built by the architect Adolfo Natalini to cater for tens of thou-

sands of students. Occupying 320,000 square metres of space around the old Fiat factory in Novoli, the site also embraces a sprawling justice complex designed by Leonardo Ricci.

This is meant to incorporate all of Florence's law courts into one towering new complex. However, little thought appears to have been given to basic needs such as public transport, parking facilities and refectories, or pavements around the buildings, which despite the vast open spaces available have all been squashed together.

The giant new palace of justice, which is to rise to half the height of the Duomo, will become one of the tallest structures around, making a huge visual impact on the city, especially from a distance and when it shimmers in the sun, thus altering the famous landscape and skyline of Florence in the most radical way imaginable in the past 800 years. Measuring 240 metres in length, 156 metres in width, and up to 64 metres in height (the tower of the appeal court), the complex – designed in the 1970s – was only begun in June 2000, with completion due by 2007.

Two other architectural titans are also intervening in the outskirts near by: Sir Norman Foster is designing Florence's new station – measuring half a kilometre long – for Italy's future generation of high-speed trains, (called TAV, or *treni di alta velocità*), whose choice of position in the Macelli area has been hotly contested by environmentalists. Jean Nouvel is meanwhile transforming another former Fiat plant, in Viale Belfiore, into a 300-room hotel complex, complete with a 700-seat auditorium and parking for 1,500 cars.

Official figures show that in demographic terms Florence is now also changing rapidly. At the turn of the 20th century, this was a residential city of prudent rentiers, merchants and minor craftsmen, and where as late as the postwar period there ruled a rigid class system made up of landed gentry, solid *borghesia* and poor *contadini*. Today, Florence is profoundly middle-class, despite its left-wing council. The city operates a craft-and-services economy with industry restricted to the outskirts.

Rampant commercialisation had been kept in check by a sophisticated if provincial culture, and an abiding belief in good education, the family and the good life, although it now seems to be gaining the upper hand. Figures, meanwhile, show that to maintain their old principles, denizens are now fast abandoning the metropolis for smaller centres. Taking their place in town now are the *extracommunitari*, or Third World immigrants.

People

The 2001 census put the population at 356,000, 12 percent fewer than the 403,000 inhabitants officially recorded in 1991. Some 9 percent of inhabitants now are foreigners, led by Chinese (who in neighbouring Prato now number 16,000, many of whom are said to work in crammed sweatshops), followed by Albanians,

about 17 now die. The over-65s, meanwhile, account for 26.5 percent of the population.

Experts have for long been puzzling over the possible causes of Italy's low birth rate, given the country's tradition veneration of *bambini*. Interestingly, a recent study at the University of Florence found that the more the father of an only child helped out in the marital home – statistically, something shown to be little practised by Italian men – the more likely his wife was to want to have another baby. Among the other key reasons used to explain the drop in population is the chronicled exodus of Florentines to the smaller centres in search of a better standard of living.

Filipinos and Romanians. Meanwhile, the population of immediately neighbouring towns meanwhile has also declined, showing that the exodus has been further afield.

During the 20th century and up until the 1960s, when tourism turned into a proper industry, the number of inhabitants steadily increased, before peaking in 1971 at 458,000. Part of the problem since has been Italy's famously negative birth rate, now the second-lowest in the developed world. In fact, for every 10 people born in a year in Florence,

LEFT: a bespoke handbag-design shop.
ABOVE: eating *gelato* in Piazza della Repubblica.

Where to live

According to a Monitor property study reported by Censis, Italy's Social Investment Studies Centre Foundation, rents shot up in the city by 118 percent in the period between 1999–2003, compared to 47 percent in Milan and 70 percent in Rome. Florence regularly also tops the league of Italian cities with the biggest increase in property purchase prices.

There is now a real problem of historic shops in Florence being forced to close because of crippling rents, a reality which is also driving many citizens to live elsewhere. Nor is the city's great crafts tradition immune. Florence's delightful small neighbourhoods such as Sant'

Ambrogio, with their vital cross-section of corner shops where gilders, book-binders, printers and wrought-iron makers work, are the true essence of local life. But gentrification, along with higher prices. is now setting in.

Some locals complain that as a result of all this, Florence is losing some of its distinctive feel. Others warn that it is now entering a vicious circle already experienced by Venice, whereby locals are being priced out of their own city, as it turns into a factory for mass tourism, before inevitably ending up an empty husk.

But the Florence of today, while owing its fame and its tourism to its cultural feats of the past, is also a publishing, engineering, phar-

maceutical and furniture-making centre, where the overall urban workforce numbers the highest proportion of commuters in Italy.

Its important leather trade is reliant on the hundreds of tanneries found along the valley of the River Arno all the way down to Pisa, where they have created other seams of wealth, much in the way that the textile industry has done around Florence and Prato. Among those tapping into this *benessere* are Eastern European women, who may pick up future husbands with flourishing businesses while working as *entreneuses* in the local nightclubs.

Winemaking is another key industry, as is that of fine Tuscan food in general, where the accent is now on excellence, as can be seen by the rows of bottles for sale in shops of expensive and even designer olive oil.

Urban crime

Among the city's other negative aspects is widespread petty and other crime, testimony to the fact that Florence is no longer just a pretty place, but at times now also a seething metropolis, with a darker side racked by inner-city problems of a kind that might have provided Dante with an ideal setting for the *Inferno* were it to be written today. Bag-snatchers fly by on scooters in smart areas of town as they prey on tourists, although not exclusively, much as they do in Naples or Rome.

The urban decay seems to know no bounds. In 2003, an American priest long resident in the city, Fr Timothy Verdon, caused a stir when he railed in public at the way he said the entrance-ways to local churches had been turned into "open latrines and drug-dealers' dens", as well as places to throw "trash, cans, and bottles".

Just as *calico storico* – colourful historic football – may be played in Piazza Santa Croce, in front of the church of the same name, where Michelangelo, Rossini and Galileo are all buried, so too is cocaine now flogged by pushers outside the church of Santo Spirito.

Of course, much of the old centre in Florence otherwise remains much as it did 100 years ago. But many landmarks of the type that made the grand tourist's palms moist with excitement are now struggling to survive with dignity in their changing contexts: the old Protestant or so-called "English" cemetery in Piazza Donatello, for example, where the poet Elizabeth Barrett Browning is buried, may still be claimed to be an "island of peace".

But today it is an island in a sea of car exhaust emanating from avenues alongside which are solid with commuter traffic. The superb bastions of the Fortezza di Basso, designed by Antonio Sangallo the Younger, and considered a model of Renaissance military architecture, have now virtually been joined to the concrete slabs of a monstrous new car park immediately behind.

New music and new grub

Considering its size (pop. 355,000, or about 15 percent that of Rome, and with 100,000 people fewer than Edinburgh), the new Florence, along with its ills, appears to have a disproportionately vibrant nightlife for a small city.

This ranges from a rich seam of underground music wafting out of basement windows of a flurry of tiny and often hidden clubs, to a variety of traditional and experimental theatre, and an array of venues offering a wide selection of classical music and productions of the performing arts. In comparison to other, much bigger cities, the cultural life seems far richer.

There is also a new, creative and stylish slant now often being leant to the serving of food in a growing generation of trendy restaurants springing up, along with a positively

the Florentines' character as well as their palate. Traditionally, for example, many commuters as well as working Florentines who are unable to return home for lunch have eaten for years in unadvertised and packed back rooms of delicatessens, paying economic prices in return for delicious, wholesome fare and as often as not the owner's own prized olive oil and wine.

Now, in what may be a new application of the same philosophy, many good restaurants are adopting a novel policy of dropping their prices – often dramatically – by day in order to encourage custom, when it is not unusual to eat lunch for as little as 6 euros per person.

booming bar culture. Aperitifs and cocktails, with some extraordinarily exotic food thrown in – some of it on the house – are fast becoming a Florentine byword. The list of sophisticated yet often informal bar establishments of a kind rarely encountered in Rome seems to be growing in leaps and bounds, and now includes even the rooftops of luxury hotels, where people can drink by the pool.

To some extent, a certain flexibility has long existed in local catering which perhaps mirrors the simple pragmatism common to

LEFT: phone, fashion and facade.
ABOVE: a Florentine news-stand.

The newspaper scene

According to the national research institute ISTAT, Florentines read newspapers more than most Italians, and are better informed about politics. Yet however much it moves forward to resemble a progressive, modern city, Florence still struggles to shake off a lingering provincial side, as evidenced for example by the parochial coverage of the local media, led by the dull and conservative *La Nazione* newspaper.

Informed left-of-centre Florentines tend to read *La Repubblica*, which has a proper daily local-news insert. The more left-wing *L'Unità* has similar local coverage, something which the conservative *Corriere Della Sera*, Italy's leading daily newspaper, is planning to introduce. The English-language community, meanwhile, is now served by *The Florentine*, a weekly magazine with information on what's on, together with small ads and lively, informed articles of local interest.

A prisoner of its past

Part of the city's difficulty in fitting into the sophisticated new shoes that it would sometimes like to wear may be due to the way it has remained a prisoner of its original concept – namely, of a medieval-Renaissance city, and now, a museum one. Often Florence seems to have lost its chance of becoming a national

mover and shaker after briefly serving as Italy's capital in the late 19th century.

Often, the sensation of being stuck in time is reinforced by the way foreign and Italian visitors, as well as Florentines, appear reluctant to accept considering the city in any other but the most traditional terms.

A (not very) provocative art show in 2005 in which Michelangelo's newly restored statue of David was surrounded by art works by important contemporary artists was received to acclaim by local intellectuals, while failing, however, to impress the bulk of the Italian and foreign public, many of whom left angry messages in the visitors' book.

"This is pure blasphemy," howled one outraged American tourist, while a recurring comment was that the show was a "disgrace".

Similarly, a design by the Japanese architect Arata Isozaki to build a towering, minimalist loggia in Perspex, steel and stone to serve as a new exit for the hallowed Uffizi art gallery, has bitterly divided the city, with critics dismissing it as a "bus shelter", and even branding it the "Monster of Florence" – the name of a serial killer who once struck terror into the city. As the government in Rome entered the fray and tried to get the project stopped, triggering what would become a simmering row for years, *La Nazione* said Florence had "never managed to swallow" the idea. Thousands of its readers, it added, felt the same. The stalemate over the project has left the city hall in an embarrassing quandary, since Isosaki's design won a competition that it had sponsored. The city's administration had also promised to foot half of the €7.5 million cost, including Isozaki's €675,000 fee.

Deep down, the problem appeared to smack of provincialism. On the one hand, the authorities seemed desperate in a parochial sort of way to see their main gallery given something similarly daring and modern for their main gallery as the Louvre already had with its glass pyramid in Paris.

On the other hand, they were exaggeratedly opposed by provincial traditionalists who refused to consider any modern addition to the Uffizi, even though the loggia was planned for an uninspiring back entrance that had previously been ignored.

Yet, to be fair, Italian cities often have something provincial about them. It seems to be almost part of their original sin, and something that frequently adds to their charm. Florence's provincialism, though, is perhaps a cut above the rest, having a certain decadent grandeur, with a whiff of old St Petersburg about it, and perfume and cigarettes.

Curbing cars

Often the politics of the city, as with those of the Tuscan region that surrounds Florence, seem to be out of step with the rest of the country, however, and ahead of their time.

In early 2005 Florence – which is particularly sensitive to traffic problems – began a revolutionary clampdown in Italy on many larger 4x4 vehicles, or *gipponi*, complaining that besides fouling the air, they were too big for the narrow streets. They took up too much parking space, councillors said, and had become an "invasive fashion which is growing worse". Now other cities are considering similar measures. At the same time Florence also decided to restrict access from 2006 to any cars over eight years old, while in 2005, camper vans were banned from the centre. Now, hardly any cars except those owned by residents can enter the congested city centre, not only by day, but also by night.

Gay couples

In December 2004, other new ground was broken when Italy's constitutional court ruled in favour of the Tuscan region around Florence, saying that gay and other de facto couples could be legally recognised locally, unlike in the rest of the staunchly Catholic country. It also ruled for the first time that gay discrimination in Tuscany is an offence, in contrast to the rest of Italy.

The two provisions formed part of a new regional constitution created by Tuscany under the terms of a national law ushering in devolution. In its landmark decision, the constitutional court ruled that the two provisions, and nine others, could form part of a regional constitution after all, even if they were not enshrined in the country's constitution itself.

The ruling also helped to strengthen the region's growing political awareness by giving it its first institutional underpinning since the days when Tuscany was a grand duchy of the Medicis. "We Tuscans want a modern society, one which is founded not on discrimination, but on tolerance", said Claudio Martini, the president of Tuscany's regional government, afterwards. "We have tried to use devolution to create something serious, which instead of dividing the country will help to make it cohesive, and based on new values."

While Florence and Tuscany have long welcomed foreigners amid its rolling hills, the innate left-wing political stance and tendency of its people not to mince their words meant that when Silvio Berlusconi, the billionaire right-

wing prime minister, tried to buy a castle near Siena, locals were less than accommodating.

His political allies were mortified after he was booed and heckled during a visit to inspect the property. "Tuscany is the black hole of Western democracy. I'm ashamed of being a Florentine," said Roberto Tortoli, head of the premier's Forza Italia party in Tuscany and an under-secretary at the Environment Ministry. "It is anti-government, anti-American, anti-system, anti-everything."

According to commonly held perceptions, however, political correctness in Florence may assume proportions that are sometimes absurd. Locals of all political persuasions

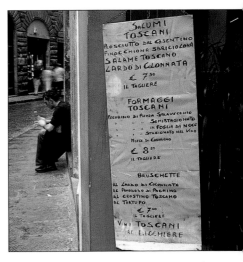

complain, for example, that despite the ring of steel thrown up around the city to keep traffic at bay, the old centre is suspiciously full of parked cars unable to be touched by the *vigili*, due to the sacred-cow status conferred upon them by handicapped stickers.

An antique bicycle race scheduled to begin and end on the Lungarno in the spring of 2004 had to be called off amid hilarity because, just ahead of the start, a car with a handicapped sticker suddenly managed to slip in, unnoticed by the organisers, and park smack on the starting and finishing line. "Florentines may be politically correct", said one native, "but like most Italians they are also *furbi* [cunning]." ❏

LEFT: the much-revered Uffizi.
RIGHT: the daily menu at I Paci.

ARISTOCRATS AND AGITATORS

**While the local nobility continue their tradition
of dominating social and economic life,
the city's lively intellectuals remain true to
another tradition: promoting radical causes**

After first making its fortune as a European wool capital in the Middle Ages, Florence, a merchant city, later turned to banking, another sector it would also dominate internationally. Thanks to the Medici princes who ruled the city almost uninterruptedly for three centuries, the city maintained its prosperity. But it could never match Rome's success, dominated as it was by the Pope's temporal influence. Soon, the artistic and cultural axis which had leant Florence added superiority shifted to the south.

Now, hundreds of years on, Florence seems a place locked in a remarkable time capsule. Many of the original landmarks and works of art are of course still there, with much of the aristocracy who commissioned them still ensconced in their same *palazzi*. To their credit, however, the Florentine aristocracy are no longer idle or absentee landlords, but are often dynamic entrepreneurs, yet who see themselves meanwhile as the rightful keepers of their city's collective memory and as arbiters of taste in modern society.

Old money, new commerce

The wine producer Bona Frescobaldi now pronounces on environmental issues, and also acts as the city's unofficial ambassador of style. Once, the entire contents of her dining room, including the furniture, glasses and silver, were flown to Japan to feature in an exhibition, to show how the Florence that counts really lives.

Sibilla della Gherardesca, whose family of counts stretches back 35 generations and was even mentioned at length in Dante's *Inferno*, is in charge of PR for Pitti Imagine, the Italian trade-and-apparel fair sponsor in Florence. Yet that has not stopped her from also writing a best-selling book about etiquette.

The local nobility continue to enjoy a key role in social and economic life, a detail that ensures that Florence, with its graceful manners extending across much of society, and its inherent Englishness – heightened by the way so many key families also married into English blood – continues to belong to another world. Ordinary Florentines happily live alongside the aristocracy, but are rarely deferential towards them.

Some of the great families have had to reinvent themselves to survive. Others like the Ferragamos – the fashion accessories dynasty descended from Salvatore Ferragamo, dubbed the "shoemaker of the stars" and who originated in Naples – are relative upstarts with humble origins, yet who already live as if to the manor born.

The Frescobaldi family, marquises and one-time merchant bankers who were already determining Florence's fate in the 13th century, excel in the production and distribution of fine wines, much as they did when they supplied the 16th-century court of Henry VIII. The difference is that now many of the 10 million bottles which they produce end up on the tables of middle-class homes around the world.

cult to grasp in Anglo-Saxon countries, where after only a few decades the different scions would probably be at each other's throats.

"It's incredible, but despite spending a lifetime living and working together, we've never experienced any bad feelings", explains Tiziana Frescobaldi, who handles the family company's PR, as well as dedicating her spare time to La Città Nascosta – specially guided tours, which she and two friends offer of parts of the hidden Florence which they love. Tiziana adds: "Part of the reason why we all get on may be that we have a great sense of belonging to a family, and to a city, which has strong merchant traditions."

Such a sense of continuity at home, let

What is surprising is the way in which 18 immediate members of the family manage to live full time under the same roof in the same *palazzo* which the Frescobaldi built near the Arno seven centuries ago. Other less permanently residing relatives instead come and go, occasionally helping to make up the numbers.

Almost all those living in the palace are also involved in running the company, which they do with remarkable harmony – a concept diffi-

alone in the workplace, would be impossible for many families to conceive. However, it is anything but unusual in Florence.

The Antinori, also marquises and historic winemakers, who are based in Florence's Palazzo Antinori, have a similar story. The noble Pucci family, a byword of 1960s chic whose fashion house has been relaunched with the help of outside investors, still live in Palazzo Pucci.

An intellectual elite

Florence has a lively intellectual life. Dominated by the contemporary historian Paul Ginsborg, a Londoner and Cambridge fellow

LEFT: a famous city brand.
ABOVE: the Florentine "Great and Good".

who teaches at the University of Florence, and Francesco "Pancho" Pardi, the city's academics provided much of the driving force for the *Girotondisti*, a spontaneous movement opposed to the prime minister Silvio Berlusconi, and his brand of politics, known as *Berlusconismo*.

Although the movement succeeded in the remarkable feat of gathering an estimated 1 million protesters in a square in Rome in September 2003, it later fizzled out.

Among the leaders of the Florentine intelligentsia is the political scientist and commentator Giovanni Sartori, known for his trademark Tuscan spirit and wit. Adrian Sofri,

the jailed but intellectually very active former leader of the defunct left-wing Lotta Continua movement, is an adopted Florentine who is originally from Pisa. Oriana Fallaci, the outspoken veteran journalist turned anti-Islamic pamphleteer in the aftermath of the attacks on the United States on 11 September 2001, and the opera and film director Franco Zeffirelli, who became a senator with Silvio Berlusconi's Forza Italia party, are both Florentines.

There are no industrialists in Florence even remotely on a par with the Agnelli dynasty of Turin who control Fiat. One of the most important, however, is Piero Targetti, the lighting fixtures tycoon. While Diego della Valle,

the owner of Tod's shoes who, now controls la Fiorentina, the city's football club, has become a permanent local fixture, even flying by helicopter to have lunch with Tony Blair when the British prime minister was holidaying nearby. Yet in fact he is from the Le Marche region.

The undisputed doyen of Florence's art world is Professor Antonio Paolucci, director general of fine arts for Tuscany, and a former cabinet minister. Another towering figure is Cristina Acidini, head of the Opificio delle Pietre Dure, the art-restoration institute created in the 16th century by the Medicis. Jonathan Nelson, a world-class Renaissance art historian, has settled in Florence, as has the acclaimed Indian conductor, Zubin Mehta.

A society figurehead

Of the nobles, Bona Frescobaldi, a friend of the Prince of Wales, stands out in sharp relief as a society figurehead. Princess Irina Guicciardini Strozzi, the Paris-born daughter of Russian émigrés, and whose eldest daughter Natalia is a ballet dancer and actress who was a protégée of Nureyev, is particularly active in the arts. Her husband, Girolamo, lectures in law, runs the family winemaking business and publishes the local Florence insert of the conservative *Il Giornale* newspaper, owned by the Berlusconi family.

The matron of the creative meritocrats remains Wanda Ferragamo, while her family's *aziendona*, or main enterprise in fashion accessories, is run by her son Fioruccio. Leonardo, her other son, makes luxury yachts in Sweden, and in Florence runs the family's growing chain of select, stylish hotels.

In the creative arts, Leonardo Pieraccioni, the film director, actor and producer, is a native, while the comedian and film director Roberto Benigni, while really from Prato, is considered an honorary Florentine. Staino, the *L'Unità* political cult cartoonist, is a Florentine born and bred whose characters embody the city's spirit and politics. Sandro Chia, the Transavanguardia School contemporary artist, is another native, who after years of living in New York has returned to Italy, where he spends much time in Tuscany and its capital.

Franco Pacini, the astrophysicist, is another Florentine, as is the popular singer Irene

Grandi, while in the world of international fashion there is the designer Roberto Cavalli. Paolo Galluzzi, director of Florence's Institute and Museum of the History of Science, is the only other Italian member of the Nobel Foundation apart from Umberto Eco.

Florence also has a wealth of creative and intellectual life at grass-roots level, where the so called Case del Popolo remain a vital institution. Bookshops also abound, as do places selling second-hand clothing, trendy hairdressers, and alternative food stores.

Young Florentines, often from working-class backgrounds, regularly gather in the Case del Popolo, literally Houses of the Peo-

place for recreation, offering library, sports and other facilities. Inevitably they often also became places central to the class struggle.

Across Tuscany and Florence, the typical Casa del Popolo is a single structure, which provides a manifold venue today for everything from theatrical performances and those by *cantastorie*, comedians, young bands, poets and artists, as well as a place to congregate and eat and drink together.

High-profile protests

The mood in such places ties in well with the leftist flavour that pervades the local administration of Florence, a city with a long anti-

ple, which provide the engine room, stage and escape valve for intellectual expression.

Present mainly across parts of the north and centre of Italy, but especially popular in Tuscany and Umbria, the Case del Popolo were created between the late 19th century and the post-war boom years. Left-wing by nature, they sprang from the Mutuo Soccorso, self-help cooperatives set up in the absence of state laws to alleviate poverty through the provision of low-cost food and other necessities, the organising of a rudimentary welfare system, and a

clerical history but whose post-war political nature also has a strong Catholic element, and which has known political autonomy since it began its rise to prominence in the 12th century.

It is partly in this vein that one should interpret modern Florence, which has been a focus for some high-profile protests, including an anti-war demonstration that drew half a million people from across Europe in November 2003.

In a controversial Italian referendum on assisted fertility that was declared null and void due to the failure to reach a 51 percent quorum, Tuscany came first in natiowide figures of voter turnout. ❑

LEFT: bicycles stacked up outside Louis Vuitton.
ABOVE: trade unionists voice their concerns in 2002.

FOOD AND DRINK

A traditional Florentine lunch is a seriously gastronomic event in which classic local dishes are accompanied by a vast proliferation of Tuscan wines

"I believe no more in black than in white, but I believe in boiled or roasted capon, and I also believe in butter and beer… but above all I have faith in good wine and deem that he who believes in it is saved." – Luigi Pulci

Whether Pulci is now being gently grilled on some infernal spit or playing his harp perched on an angelic soufflé, in life the 15th-century Florentine poet had a characteristically healthy appetite. In the city that sired the "mother of French cooking", Catherine de' Medici, the Renaissance heralded a new interest in food as an art.

Catherine was responsible for much of the renewed interest in the creation of original dishes during this period. Menus at Florentine banquets abounded with dishes such as pasta cooked in rose water and flavoured with sugar, incredible candied fruit and almond confectionery, the famous hare stew called *lepre in dolce e forte* – made with candied lemon, lime and orange peel, cocoa, rosemary, garlic, vegetables and red wine – and many more.

The claim that Gallic cuisine dates from the marriage of Catherine to Henri II of France in 1535 is based on the similarity between characteristic French and Tuscan dishes: *canard à l'orange* is not unlike the Florentine *papero alla melarancia;* vol-au-vents are found in Florence under the name *turbanate di sfoglia; lepre in dolce e forte* is still called *dolce forte* in French – although Italian and French

cooks are not in agreement about its origins.

Whatever the truth, the Medici were renowned for their multi-course banquets, and the Florentine's renowned preoccupation with his stomach increasingly got him into trouble with the Church. "You are great gourmands," railed one preacher. "When you eat ravioli it is not enough for you to boil them in the pan and eat them with broth, but you must put them in another pan together with cheese."

Simple fare

And yet sobriety rather than sensuality was, and remains, an important element in the Florentine character. Despite their love of food, Florentines

LEFT: *cantuccini*, a Tuscan speciality.
RIGHT: *bruschetta*.

never really warmed to the complex recipes of the sauce-loving Medici. Popular Renaissance dishes were simple and robust, with plenty of vegetables and plainly grilled meats, eaten for utility as much as enjoyment; nourishing the soul and spirit as well as the body. Busy people in a thriving commercial environment, they had little time for over-sophistication.

This solid element persists to this day. Florentines and Tuscans have been nicknamed the *mangiafagioli*, the great bean-eaters, because the pulse is used so much in local specialities. Thick soups and bean stews – served in terracotta pots, even in the most elegant of restaurants – and large steaks and heavy wines are

characteristic of a meal in Florence. Most Florentine food is healthy, hearty and draws on the raw wealth of the Tuscan countryside.

Eating Italian-style

Italians love their food, and Florentines are no exception. Usually, breakfast consists of just an espresso or cappuccino, drunk "on the hoof" in a local bar if not at home, perhaps with a *panino* (filled bread roll) if really hungry. The evening meal, too, is generally a fairly minor event, with perhaps a light soup or *frittata*.

But a traditional Florentine lunch – nowadays indulged in only at the weekend by many business people – is a different story. This is a truly gastronomic event, to be shared and savoured with friends and family at leisure – which explains the comparative hiatus in the city between 1pm and 3pm, when you'll often find churches locked, museums shut, shops closed and streets empty. A full-blown Italian meal will begin with an *antipasto* – a bit of salami, some roasted peppers. Then follows the first course, *il primo*, usually a pasta, risotto or soup. *Il secondo* is next, consisting of meat or fish and vegetables. Salad is always served *after* this, effectively cleansing the palate in preparation for *i formaggi* (cheese) and *i dolci* (dessert), the last often being fruit-based.

Markets and vegetables

The most colourful introduction to the city's food is a morning spent amid the vegetable stalls of the Mercato Centrale, hidden among the colourful stalls of the San Lorenzo market, on Via dell' Ariento. Here, the fruit of the hills – courgettes, tomatoes, mushrooms, peppers, potatoes and aubergines – form a bright tapestry of potential tastes. Florentines will happily eat any of these fried or brushed with Tuscany's purest *extra vergine* olive oil, and simply grilled until soft and melting.

But among these gaudy fruits, the undisputed aristocrat are the humble white beans or *fagioli*. Like the potato, the bean was introduced from the Americas by Florentine merchants, and it is now a staple of the city. In a soup or mixed with tuna fish, the little *fagioli* are a marvellously simple beginning to any Florentine meal.

Fresh Tuscan vegetables are rarely disappointing on their own, but together they make two of the city's great specialities, *ribollita*

OLIVE OIL

Tuscany's olive oil has long been famous for its quality and excellent flavour and texture. In recognition of this outstanding quality it is even accorded DOC status. Tuscans are passionate about olive oil; it is an important cooking ingredient, and its flavour and strength fundamentally affect the final dish. Quality is measured by acid content, the finest oil being Extra Vergine with less than one percent acid content. A few excellent oils from Florence and the surrounding area are Extra Vergine di Scansano, Extra Vergine di Seggiano cru Querciole, Extra Vergine del Chianti, Extra Vergine di San Gimignano cru Montenidoli, and Extra Vergine Badia a Coltibuono.

and *minestrone*. *Ribollita* means "reboiled" as in "recycled" – leftover vegetables are combined to create a dense and satisfying soup. The naturally thrifty Florentine might put any spare vegetable in the pan to make this filling potage – although traditionally it should include white *cannellini* beans and *cavolo nero*, a type of black cabbage indigenous to Tuscany – which is thickened with yesterday's stale bread. But Tuscan vegetables seem most at home in minestrone soup. Florentines are compulsive soup-eaters and, though they share a little of Italy's faith in pasta as the all-purpose dish, they really prefer their own rich and nutritious vegetable stews.

A feast of meat

Florence may seem a vegetarian's idea of Eden, but the Florentine is undeniably a red-blooded carnivore. For a start and a starter try *crostini di fegato,* chicken liver pâté on fried bread, delicious with a young white wine. A feast to follow is *fritto misto*, mixed meats fried in batter, or the peasant dish *stracotto*, beef stewed for several hours and especially satisfying in winter.

But, above all, Florentines specialise in plain roasted meats: *arista* (roast pork), beef, lamb at Easter and even wild boar in season. Tuscany's fertile pasture feeds some of the richest flavours in Italy, and Florentines refuse to clutter these tastes with over-adornment. Just as simple is their treatment of chicken and pheasant.

However, the master of meats – and as much a symbol of the city as the florin – is the famous *bistecca alla fiorentina* (steak Florentine). A huge, tender and succulent rib-steak from Tuscany's alabaster Chianina cattle, the *bistecca* is brushed with a drop of the purest virgin olive oil and charcoal-grilled over a scented wood fire of oak or olive branches, then seasoned with salt and pepper before being served, with the Florentine's characteristic lack of fuss. It is quite the most delicious meat in Italy.

In good restaurants, you will be able to see the meat raw before you order. If you can get a seat, the best *bistecca alla fiorentina* in the city is said to be served on the marble table tops of

Sostanza (Via Porcellana) or at Buca Lapi. But beware, the price on the menu is per 100 grams (3½ ounces) of raw meat, and you are thought mean if you order less than a kilo to share between two people.

Another famous Florentine meat dish is *arista alla fiorentina* – pork loin highly seasoned with chopped rosemary and ground pepper. The origin of this dish goes back to the 15th century. At the Ecumenical Council of 1430 in Florence, the Greek bishops were served the dish at a banquet and pronounced it *aristos*, which in Greek means "very good". The name stuck and became a feature of Florentine cuisine. It is a particularly useful dish

CHESTNUTS

In winter, the smell of roasted chestnuts *(castagne)* fills the air in Florence. *Castagne* are a Tuscan favourite, particularly in the mountain areas, where they are made into flour, pancakes, soups and sweet cakes. Keep an eye out at the Piazza Santo Spirito flea market for a small stand making fresh *necci*, delicious crêpes made with chestnut flour and served with ricotta cheese.

The chestnut season peaks around mid-October, when chestnut – and steam train – lovers can travel on a restored 1920s steam train from Florence's Santa Maria Novella station to Marradi's *Sagra delle Castagne*, or Chestnut Festival, to partake in the celebrations.

LEFT: hearty bean dishes.
RIGHT: preparing *bistecca alla fiorentina*.

because it keeps very well for several days and is even better cold than hot.

At the cheaper end of the culinary spectrum and in their rational desire not to waste, Florentines have even made a speciality out of tripe. *Trippa alla fiorentina*, cooked with tomatoes and sprinkled with parmesan, is a favourite and inexpensive dish, though the tripe's slippery texture and intense garlic flavour make it an equivocal choice for the uninitiated.

Sweeteners

If Florentine food tends to be filling, full of flavour but unsophisticated, Florentine *dolci* (desserts) make up for any lack of imagina-

thought by some to affectionately refer to the Duomo – or is perhaps a slightly irreverent allusion to the clergy. In the Tuscan dialect, a cardinal's skullcap is also called a *zuccotto*.

Gelato

No visit to the city would be complete without a taste of its ice cream. You can see why Florentines claim to have invented *gelato*, for the city is awash with a rainbow of flavours. Always look for the sign *Produzione Propria* (homemade), and before you try anywhere else, make for Vivoli on the Via Isola delle Stinche. It remains unrivalled for both flavour and variety. Here you'll find yet another "soup" – known

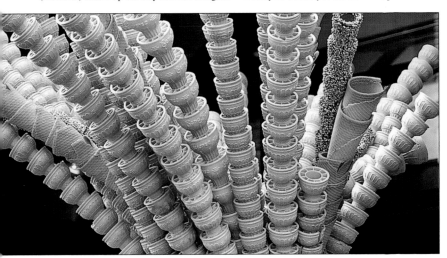

tion. In the city's bars, cake shops and *gelaterie* there is a constant carnival of colour. *Coppe varie*, bowls of mixed fruit and water ice, compete for attention with pastries and handmade sweets, huge slabs of nougat, chocolate "Florentines", *baci* – the angel's kiss – and, around carnival time, *schiacciata alla fiorentina*, a simple, light sponge cake.

One pride of the city is the incredible *zuccotto*, a sponge-cake mould with a filling of almonds, hazelnuts, chocolate and cream. Once eaten, it is never forgotten. There is no general agreement, however, as to the origins of its name. Literally translated as "small pumpkin", *zuccotto*, being a dome-shaped speciality, is

as *zuppa inglese,* which literally means "English soup" but is in fact trifle or trifle ice cream. Virtually a meal in itself, *gelato* is Florence's most delicious fine art.

Eating out

Whether for business or for pleasure, and invariably for both, dining is an important event for the Florentine. Once a languid affair, lunch during the working week is increasingly treated as a lighter snack as more businesses remain open through the lunch hour and the Florentines

ABOVE: *gelato* cones.
RIGHT: pasta with pine nuts and *grana*.

become more health-conscious. Caution is thrown to the winds, however, on a Sunday, when the midday meal is given great importance and may continue well into the afternoon. In the evening, Florentines usually eat at around 8.30pm. Lacking the Spaniards' nocturnal enthusiasm, the best restaurants close early. Visitors should also be warned that because so many Florentines take their holidays in high summer – to avoid the city's heat and its glut of tourists – many good restaurants are also closed throughout the month of August.

Many wines

In the region where soil and sunlight nurture Italy's most famous wine, Chianti, Pulci was not alone in extolling the virtues of the blushful Hippocrene. "I believe", wrote Leonardo da Vinci, " that where there is good wine, there is great happiness for men." Happiness may be harder to find, even in Tuscany, but good wine certainly isn't.

This is the kingdom of Sangiovese, the little grape that gives heart and strength to Tuscan classified reds, while innumerable other vines serve as royal subjects and even vie for the crown. This is the first lesson to be learnt about Tuscan wine – the subject is enormous. Quite apart from the diversity of growths and strains, Tuscany shares Italy's vast proliferation of vineyards and labels.

Chianti

Chianti is grown in seven regions surrounding Florence and Siena. Perhaps Italy's most potent symbol, Chianti is not just one wine, but many. In its seven zones, the variety of climates, producers and vineyards is staggering, ensuring a huge breadth of quality and complexity.

The heartland of Chianti lies either side of the Chiantigiana road (SS222) connecting the two cities of Florence and Siena, the "Via Sacra" (Sacred Road) of wine. This is the home of Chianti Classico, where the Chianti League was formed in the 13th century – a region that produces more consistently good wine than any other zone, except for the Rufina district. The latter, the most important wine-producing region near Florence, lies east of the city in the hills above the Sieve River.

THE FIRST FAMILIES OF WINE

Four names dominate wine production in Florence: those of the Antinori, Frescobaldi, Guicciardini-Strozzi and Ricasoli families. The first three have Renaissance palaces in the city; the Ricasolis are based near Siena, but are considered Florentine. These aristocratic families have been producing wine on their country estates for hundreds of years.

In the 1960s, a major depression in wine sales in Chianti forced many small farmers to sell their vineyards to large wine-producing families, who began to experiment with single-vineyard and propriety wines that are known as "super-Tuscans". As a result, the reputation of the Chianti region started to rise. Super-Tuscans such as Sassicaia, Tignanello (both Antinori wines) and Ornellaia are recognised as first-class wines. Despite being labelled *Vino da Tavola*, these "designer wines" are among the best in Italy, and they have come to represent the families that make them. In turn, the families are able to maintain their country properties and *palazzi* in Florence with the revenue that this new fame has brought.

Ricasoli now makes wine under two labels: Brolio and Ricasoli. The Frescobaldis have recently been experimenting with Californian grapes, and have formed a collaboration with Roberto Mondavi.

Although a tiny zone, it produces some of the giants of Italian wine: Selvapiana, Castello di Nipozzano, Fatoria di Vetrie and the new heavyweight, Montesodi.

The region surrounding Florence itself, the Chianti Coli Fiorentina, is the source of many of those characteristic straw-covered bottles – known as *fiaschi* – that once filled the city. (Now considered by many producers to be too "rustic", this emblem of the early days of Tuscan viniculture has largely been superseded by an elegant, square-shouldered bottle.) Chianti Coli Fiorentina wines tend to be heavy and coarse, but they can also be splendid with Florence's simple food.

White wines

Top brands to look for on Florence's wine-bar shelves include Vino Nobile di Montepulciano, Brunello di Montalcino and Brolio – all red wines. Although reds are by far the best-known and, for the most part, superior wines in the region, whites are also out there. They are light, simple and pleasant – but generally, despite continual improvements, could not be described as "great". Most are based on Trebbiano and Malvasia grapes and are named after the locality of their origin.

The main exception is the dry, elegant, but quite full-bodied Vernaccia di San Gimignano, from the famous town that lies west of Siena. White wines of note are also made from the French grape variety, Chardonnay. More and more producers have turned over one or more of their plots to this grape, and many have invested in *barriques* (oak barrels) from France in which to mature the wines. The end result is a great success.

The search for quality

The viticultural promiscuity of Tuscany makes standards hard to control, and quality does vary greatly. Concern for the quality of wine in the region began in the Chianti Classico area – just south of Florence – way back in the 1700s, when grapes and wines began to be classified and recommended methods of production were developed. The real mover in this area was Barone Bettino Ricasoli – a member of one of four of Florence's aristocratic wine-producing families *(see box on page 61)* – who, in the mid-19th century, conducted experiments that led to a specific formula for making the wine.

In 1924, the Consorzio Chianti Classico was founded to control production. To signify that a bottle was "Consorzio-approved" – contained the specified blend of grapes, had the minimum alcohol content and was properly matured – a neck label was introduced, printed with the *gallo nero* (black cockerel) symbol of the consortium.

Once in the European Union, Italy had to develop a country-wide wine law. In line with EU regulations, "quality" wines were designated Denominazione di Origine Controllata

LEFT: Chianti wines with the mark of the *gallo nero*.
RIGHT: vineyards in the beautiful Chianti hills.

(DOC), while DOCG guarantees the authenticity of certain favoured wines. After the 1986 methanol scandal, even stricter quality controls were enforced. These markings will help to identify Tuscany's best – but never take the region's ability to surprise for granted. Although considered by some to be the "lesser brethren" of the DOC wines, Tuscany has many remarkable *vini da tavola*, and one in particular, Sassicaia, has become a contemporary legend.

Individually named and often costly, these *vini da tavola* have become known as "super-Tuscans" and are often wines made solely with the Sangiovese grape – or Sangioveto, a superior clone. Sometimes they are a blend of San-

(single-vineyard wine) of Chianti Rufina from the Frescobaldi estate. So the one word is often all that is put on the list in a restaurant. In shops, where the label can be scrutinised before buying, life is easier.

The general, but not infallible, rule of thumb is that Classico is better than non-Classico. However, a good non-Classico producer can always outclass an average Classico estate. On the better, more matured, wines the label will state *Riserva*, which indicates the wine has been aged for at least three years, mainly in traditional oak barrels. For easy drinking, the lively Chianti non-*riserva*, informally called simply *normale*, comes into its own.

giovese and Cabernet Sauvignon, the French grape that produces excellent results in Tuscany. They are occasionally made solely with Cabernet. The only way to divine their constituents is to scan the label on the back of the bottle carefully (which still may not reveal all) or to ask.

To add even more confusion to the quest for good drinking, a single name on a wine list will not necesarily signify a "super-Tuscan". Many estates have a particular vineyard whose wine, when kept separate, is always better than the rest. Each is labelled with its vineyard name as well as its official designation: Chianti or Chianti Classico. Tuscans are expected to know that Montesodi, for example, is a particular *cru*

Vin Santo

After you have enjoyed the pleasantly enervating effects of a robust Chianti and a large Florentine steak, a delightful way to end the meal and ease the stomach is to follow the Florentine ritual of nibbling *biscotti di Prato*, hard almond biscuits, dipped in a glass of dark gold Vin Santo ("Holy Wine"). This dessert wine is made from white Trebbiano and Malvasia grapes picked late into the harvest – at "the time of the saints" (near to All Saints' Day, 1 November). Most Vin Santo is sweet, but some is dry. Nearly all of it is rare and expensive. Indeed, Vin Santo seems to liquefy the Tuscan sunlight and unleash the complex tastes of the land. ❏

ETRUSCANS TO EARLY RENAISSANCE

Nowhere else can rival Florence for its Early Renaissance masterpieces, in painting, frescos, sculpture and architecture

The earliest evidence of a substantial settlement at Florence comes from burial sites of the 10th to 8th centuries BC. This early Iron Age culture, known as Villanovan after a site in Emilia, produced burial urns typically comprising two conical vases joined together and often with a cap-like lid.

Elaborate examples have lids with small models of the deceased feasting. Cemeteries imply villages, and settlements may have been fortified. Alongside the burial urns were weapons, combs, bronze clasps and spindles, indicating a strong sense of an afterlife.

Etruscan style

The succeeding Etruscan civilisation was centred in Florence at the suburb of Fiesoli. They also believed in an afterlife and created elaborate underground houses for the dead, and occasional house-shaped burial urns (Museo Archaeologico). The Etruscan artistic style is a provincial variant of Greek, but with several distinct characteristics: a softness of figure-modelling (see the sarcophagus of Larthia Seianti, Museo Archaeologico), a greater attention to movement, and a somewhat unarticulated character to the figure, with a less strict sense of proportion. Figures were frequently attached to cinerary boxes either of stone, terracotta or bronze. Indeed, the Etruscans were skilled bronzeworkers, as the Mars and Arezzo Chimera show (Museo Archaeologico). A large altar excavated at Fiesole indicated a wealthy

LEFT: Raphael's *The Madonna of the Goldfinch.*
RIGHT: the Etruscan tomb of Larthia Seianti.

settlement with temple. After 264 the Etruscans were absorbed into the Roman world, though the Orator of *c.*100 BC (Museo Archaeologico) shows their culture persisted.

In 59 BC the Romans began to rebuild on the ancient Villanovan site, creating a grid-form town still discernible in the street layout around the Piazza della Repubblica. A temple of Isis, a semicircular theatre and a large amphitheatre were built, the latter near to Santa Croce. The Emperor Hadrian in the second century AD enlarged and marble-paved the forum, or central market/ceremonial square. Arches and marble buildings surrounded this, and an aqueduct was built to supply two bath houses (one on the Via delle Terme). The more prosperous structures had mosaic-tiled floors and marble wall facings, and by the third century wealthier citizens received burials in elaborately carved sarcophagi. Some pagan burials were sited along the Cassian Way.

Christianity arrives

Just before AD 250 Saint Miniato was martyred at Florence, indicating that Christians were established there. After 313, when the Emperor Constantine's Edict of Milan permitted freedom of worship, Christian burials, some in catacombs, became more common.

The next centuries were troubled. The

to other churches, San Remigio and Santissimi Apostoli. In form, many of these followed the established basilica plan of an aisled hall.

During the 11th century a new type of architecture took shape. In Italy it owes its character to northern Europe's adoption of a heavy, round-arched structure dominated by geometrical decoration, and which was known in Naples and Sicily on account of their Norman rulers. The style was modified by two other influences. One was Byzantine architecture, which preferred centralised plans with domes; the other was Roman, remains of which were still visible in Italy. The seeming

Ostrogoths laid siege to Florence in 405; in 541 another siege involved Byzantine occupation and in 570 the Lombards occupied Tuscany. Little remains of these times. A relief of King Agilulf between Angels (Bargello) gives some indication of contemporary accomplishment. The church of San Lorenzo is known to have been consecrated in 393, and Santa Reparata established on the site of the Duomo.

Under Lombard rule Sant' Apollinare, Orsanmichele and San Gaetano (originally San Michele Bertelde) were founded. The Emperor Lothair's establishment of Florence as the location of an ecclesiastical school led

continuance of Roman forms has led to this style being called Romanesque.

In Florence, polychrome marble panelling of geometric patterns was a feature of its two greatest Romanesque structures: the Duomo baptistery, reconstructed c. 1100, and San Miniato al Monte. The former, a domed octagonal building, perhaps following a Roman ground plan, exemplified a preoccupation with geometry, reflecting the concept of God the geometer/creator. San Miniato, a basilica church of nave and lower aisles, was completed by 1062, but had a decorative marble, five-bay facade added in the 12th century. Internally both are very rich: mosaics in the dome of the baptistery, a mix of abstract forms with occasional stylised birds and urns at San Miniato. The pulpits at San Miniato and San Leonardo in Arcetri give some idea of sculpture. The former has a stocky, column-like figure; the latter, reliefs of scenes from the life of Christ in a linear manner owing something to manuscript painting.

The Gothic

Europe in the years before 1200 saw a fundamental change of thought, in which the beauties of the world were now seen to reflect God's creation rather than being distractions from the contemplation of God as a meta-

ever, Italian Gothic varies from its northern counterpart, for there remained, especially in Florence, close links with Romanesque and Roman forms. The new emphasis was on spatial unity, light and harmony, with occasional pointed arches. Excellent examples are Santa Maria Novella (1279), Santa Croce, perhaps by Arnolfo di Cambio (1294/5), and the cathedral or Duomo (Santa Maria del Fiore), begun in 1300 by Arnolfo, continued by Andrea Pisano and subsequently Francesco Talenti.

The rebuilding of the Duomo reflects a growing prosperity related to the rise of the pro-Papacy merchant Guelf faction in Florence at the expense of the rival pro-Empire

physical being. The story of Saint Francis preaching to the birds demonstrates this, and it is no coincidence that his life begins to feature in so many works of art following his canonisation in 1228.

This change initiates the Gothic style, with its optimism expressed architecturally by a sense of verticality, weightlessness, unity and the use of ribs and pointed arches, and in painting and sculpture by a growing interest in the natural world and human values, often revealed through a cult of the Madonna. How-

Ghibellines. Thirteenth-century Florence was turbulent, and many aristocrats built defensive tower houses such as the Torre del Castagna and Torre del Alberti.

A variant of this type was the Palazzo Vecchio, begun in 1299, the seat of the priors of the guilds and of the Galfoniere of Justice, in effect the city's government. The ribbed vaulted Sala d'Armi is its best-preserved room. A contemporary domestic interior with simulated draperies and canopied cornices remains at the Palazzo Davanzati. The Duomo campanile or bell tower by Giotto, begun in 1334, continued the zest for decorative masonry with the addition of many sculptured

LEFT: an angelic mosaic from the baptistery.
ABOVE: a 13th-century mosaic, San Miniato.

reliefs. The guild church of Orsanmichele, 1337, at the time an open-halled corn market, was enclosed to form a splendidly decorated church, but corn was still stored upstairs.

External influences

Fourteenth-century Florentine sculpture derived from developments begun in the pulpits of Nicola and Giovanni Pisano at Pisa and Pistoia. The painters of the Sienese School had also moved towards a new, more accessible style. In Rome, Cavallini was exploiting a rudimentary perspective and simple modelling with light and shade. All these had some impact on Florentine art. Cavallini's methods

donna, (c. 1310–15, Uffizi), though still hieratic in arrangement, reveals saints and angels in total unity in adoration of Mary and Jesus, thus further humanising Cimabue's image.

In 1265, Nicola Pisano carved the Siena cathedral pulpit with the help of Arnolfo di Cambio. Pisano's style was a mix of Roman solidity coupled with Gothic liveliness and humanity of narrative (a trait amplified into the first convincing depiction of human feelings by his son Giovanni Pisano on the Pistoia pulpit). Arnolfo (d. 1302) designed the facade of the Duomo (the present facade dates from the 19th century), and for this several sculptures survive, including a Virgin of the Nativ-

were echoed in Cimabue, a Florentine who worked mainly at Assisi. In his Santa Trinità Madonna (Uffizi) he animated his figures to suggest humanity, thus breaking with traditional Byzantine formality. This may have influenced the Florentine, Giotto; his best work, at Padua, eliminates the usual Byzantine gold background – his frescos depict biblical figures with a clarity of design that makes meaningful and significant the well-observed actions in the narratives.

This low relief-like clarity of image is also seen in the damaged frescos in the Cappella Bardi (Santa Croce, c. 1315–20), depicting the life of Saint Francis. The Ognissanti Ma-

ity displaying his sense of simplified, monumental form. It was a manner adopted in Tino di Camaino's seated figure of Bishop Orso in the Duomo.

A comparable simplicity and fertility of invention was used on the panels of the south door of the Duomo baptistery (c. 1330–6), which depict – appropriately – scenes from the life of Saint John the Baptist. These were executed by Andrea Pisano (unrelated to the earlier Pisanos). Their rhythmic designs owe much to Giotto, for whom he contributed sculptures for the campanile, continuing to oversee its construction following Giotto's death in 1337.

International Gothic

Alongside Giotto, Arnolfo and others' massive, simple Gothic was a more gentle, sophisticated and elegant version, closely associated with courts and courtly chivalry, often termed international Gothic in that elements of its worldliness were found throughout Europe. A secular feel characterised Andrea Buonaiuti's frescos in the Capellone degli Spagnoli (Santa Maria Novella), which typically placed figures in rows one upon another.

More sophisticated was Gentile da Fabriano's *Adoration of the Magi* (Uffizi) for Santa Trinità, where the kings hold centre stage in courtly splendour; this elegant, decorative style resurfaced in Benozzo Gozzoli's Palazzo Medici-Riccardi frescos depicting Florentine notables and others within a procession of the Magi. But underlying all this Gothic work was still a hieratic scale and spatial incoherence.

Gozzoli's frescos were executed well into the 15th century and were commissioned by the Medici family. The Medici came to prominence in Florence with the rise of the merchant-orientated Guelph faction. They were bankers and came to be virtual rulers of the city, and also the most lavish patrons of the arts for more than a century. Few works of art, besides portraits, were without some religious connotation at this time, and for the Medici this was significant, for banking and the charging of interest – known as usury – was then deemed sinful, but the commissioning of religious works of art as gifts to the Church could help redress this sin.

The Renaissance

In 1401 a competition was held to determine which sculptor should execute a second pair of bronze doors to be erected on the north side of the Duomo baptistery. The trial pieces had to match the square-with-quatrefoil-shaped panels of Andrea Pisano's earlier doors, and the subject was to be the Sacrifice of Isaac (though for the finished doors the subject was changed to the Gospels). Lorenzo Ghiberti's competition piece shows Abraham energetically thrusting a knife towards Isaac kneeling on an altar. Behind Abraham is a sheep, and

an angel gestures from above, telling him to substitute the sheep for Isaac. The delicacy of modelling reflected the fashionable international Gothic style, and Ghiberti was therefore awarded the commission, which he fulfilled by 1424 in a spirited, and somewhat pictorial manner of – where appropriate – great charm.

The other main contender of the seven sculptors who submitted designs was Filippo Brunelleschi. His trial piece was far stronger, more logical in layout and less engaging. Here, Abraham raises the knife to Isaac's neck and – just in time – the angel grasps Abraham's wrist and points to the sheep now in Abraham's view *(see page 127)*. Already a

change of artistic direction had been taken, and the Renaissance initiated.

Renaissance is usually taken to mean the rebirth of Greek and Roman forms and values, either by imitation or by a striving for idealisation. More properly it is a rebirth of logic as a fundamental principle in the arts. Brunelleschi did little further sculpture, but turned his mind to architecture, where his first major building was the Spedale degli Innocenti (Foundling Hospital) of 1418, a Florentine orphanage. True, he revives Roman architectural forms – entablatures, pilasters, Corinthian-type columns, round-headed arches and pedimented windows – but it does not feel

LEFT: Gentile da Fabriano's *Adoration of the Magi.*
RIGHT: Gozzoli's *Journey of the Magi.*

Roman. It is too delicate. Gothic minimalist structure had been added to Roman forms.

The hospital's serenity lay, too, in an essentially simple mathematical geometry based on the height of a column: it is three columns high, the columns are apart by one column's height, the arcade is one column deep. These proportional principles Brunelleschi brought to his later churches, particularly San Lorenzo and Santo Spirito. His constructive genius was best displayed in the building of the dome of the Duomo, where he used an inner, corbelled, herring-bone brick swelling cone (that acted as its own scaffold) encased by a tiled dome supported on externally visible ribs.

A sense of perspective

The first artist known to have used this new perspective was Brunelleschi's friend, the sculptor Donatello. The plinth of his *Saint George* for Orsanmichele, 1418, showed an arcade in perspective. The *Saint George* itself showed Renaissance logic. He stands four-square; one senses flesh beneath the armour and bones within the flesh: his determined gaze suggests he is just the man to take on a dragon. Among Donatello's subsequent work, the bronze *David* (Bargello), one of the first large nude figures since antiquity and a stunning representation of an adolescent's body, is still static, but his children on the Singing Gal-

The whole was surmounted with a lantern reached by steps within the void between the two domes.

Brunelleschi's further claim to being the father of the Renaissance, and arguably Florence's greatest artistic genius, was his invention of measured perspective, a geometric means of creating a convincing illusion of space and solidity on two dimensions. Because its basis was measured geometry, artists were now able to get scale and proportion right, and because it was determined by the artist's viewpoint, a coherent arrangement of pictorial elements resulted: in effect, the subject was seen from the same position as the artist.

leries in the Duomo and his *Annunciation* (Santa Croce) reveal his mastery of movement. He created his great bronze equestrian statue of General Gattamelata in Padua between 1445 and 1450, but on his return to Florence his late work shows an emotionalism, best appreciated in the bronze Judith and Holofernes (originally a fountain centrepiece) in the Piazza della Signoria and his carved-wood *Mary Magdalene*.

A friend of Brunelleschi and Donatello was Masaccio, the first painter to use measured perspective. Of his few works, the Trinity Altarpiece in Santa Maria Novella shows the first true illusionist architecture. Set against a

Brunelleschi-type vault, Christ rises on the Cross, supported by God and the dove symbolic of the Holy Ghost. At the Cross's base are Saint Mary and Saint John above the two donors. Our eye level is that of the donors. Thus we look up at the other figures and into the architecture.

The Cappella Brancacci (Church of the Carmine) houses Masaccio's most extensive frescos, supplemented by others by Masolino and Filippino Lippi. Masaccio's show scenes from the life of Saint Peter and of Adam and Eve. His *Tribute Money* most clearly demonstrates the new perspective, and also a sense of solidity, logical scale and grouping of the

The body's geometric beauty

Others were quick to pick up perspective. Fra Angelico, a monk of San Marco, used it to create paintings of serene order, but, perhaps because perspective's rational scale tended to make figures seem small, he retained at times – as in the *Annunciation* (San Marco) – the older hieratic concept that size equated with importance, and also an international Gothic preciousness.

Andrea del Castagno, by contrast, emphasised sculptural solidity, with touches of *trompe l'œil* in his series of famous personages (Uffizi), whose feet overlap the sills on which they stand. To painters and mathematicians, like Piero della

figures. Though once fire damaged and restored the greying of colour towards the horizon shows aerial perspective.

But of greater significance than these technical matters is Masaccio's grasp of humanity: these are real people, some shivering with cold, some ill, others matronly, all relating to one another, and none more telling than the grief-stricken Adam and Eve expelled from Paradise. It was a remarkable achievement for a young man who died aged just 28.

Francesca of Urbino and Paolo Uccello of Florence, perspective's geometry evoked order and coherence. They may have seen a parallel in Plato's dictum that the nearer a body comes to pure geometry the more beautiful it is.

Uccello's three paintings of *The Rout of San Romano* (London, Paris, Uffizi) pick up this geometric solidity and the play of perspective, but more adventurous is his *Flood* (Santa Maria Novella), where a dynamic foreshortened perspective conjures an uneasy and dramatic scene of chaos. The discovery of a means to convey convincing images of the visible world led others, like Fra Filippo Lippi, to exploit their virtuosity in recording space, textures and forms

LEFT: a self-portrait by Filippino Lippi in the Cappella Brancacci.

ABOVE: Uccello's *The Rout of San Romano*.

as a means of making the biblical stories more immediate to their congregations.

Sculpture

Sculptors, too, became more concerned with capturing the immediate. Luca della Robbia, of a family of sculptors working in glazed terracotta, exploited this medium for decorative reliefs of largely religious sculptures, but began his career with marble-carving. In 1431 he carved his Cantoria or singing gallery for the Duomo, which features panels of music-making and dancing children of the utmost delicacy, their movements and gestures caught in mid-action. The "sweet style" is thus intro-

duced, and it echoes Ghiberti's further set of doors for the Florence baptistery begun 1425 – dubbed by Michelangelo "The Gates of Paradise". For these doors the panels were square, and Ghiberti exploited perspective architectural and landscape settings to show Old Testament subjects which appear as *tableaux vivants* akin to much painting.

Florence's historian Leonardo Bruni devised the scheme for these doors, and on his death in 1444 the sculptor Bernardo Rossellino created his tomb (Santa Croce) as a sort of tabernacle within Brunelleschi-type architecture. It was a pattern adopted by Rossellino's friend Desiderio da Settignano for the Mar-

suppini Tomb (Santa Croce). Both introduce sculptured portrait effigies. Indeed, the cult of portraiture, particularly as busts, truncated at chest level, gained in popularity after 1450, good exponents being Mino da Fiesoli, Antonio Rossellino and Benedetto da Maiano.

Thus, by 1460, the Renaissance had taken hold, and by then Leon Battista Alberti had completed his books on the arts – *De Pictura, De Statua* and *De Re Aedificatoria*, among the first modern treatises on the arts. That Alberti wrote all three indicates his wide knowledge: indeed, he exemplified the concept of the Renaissance "universal man".

As an architect Alberti brought an archaeological approach to his church, the so-called Tempio Malatestina (San Francesco) at Rimini, which revived a pilastered temple-like form. At San Andrea, Mantua, in addition to Roman references to architectural schemes of differing scales superimposed one upon the other, he also gave definitive form to the grotesque, a playful, decorative, antique-inspired motif of vine scrolls and devices of vases or candelabra mixed with animal and other motifs that became the standard emblem of Italian Renaissance design.

In Florence, Alberti's facade to Santa Maria Novella elaborated Brunelleschi's feel for geometry. His patron there, Giovanni Rucellai, also commissioned him to create a town house, or *palazzo* – the Palazzo Rucellai – whose elevation was enhanced by the use of the orders of architecture (pilasters based on antique Doric, Ionic and Corinthian columns).

Among the first of these new palaces built around a central courtyard, but outward-looking from the inhabited upper floors and cubic in conception, was the Palazzo Pitti, attributed to Brunelleschi. There followed Michelozzo's Palazzo Medici-Riccardi, 1444, and da Maiano's Palazzo Strozzi. This form persisted into the next century.

Classical mythology

The fall of Constantinople (Istanbul) to the Ottoman Turks in 1453 caused many refugees to flee to Italy, some bringing with them classical texts preserved in the libraries there. One result of this was to provoke renewed interest in pagan mythological subjects. The artist brothers Antonio and Piero Pollaiuolo picked this up along with a classical preoccupation with anatomy. Antonio's tempera painting of *The Martyrdom of Saint Sebastian* (London) shows the nude saint surrounded by four archers in vigorous poses seen from varied angles. A print and a sculpted relief of nude men fighting elaborated their anatomical studies; and their sculpture of Hercules and Antaeus (also known in a painted version) added specific mythological subject matter.

Piero di Cosimo, less interested in anatomical studies, adopted a more elegiac approach to mythology in his *Death of Procris* (London) and a narrative one in *The Liberation of Andromeda* (Uffizi). Di Cosimo also painted

tism, for, just as Venus was miraculously born out of water, so we are spiritually reborn through the water of baptism; this analogy was reinforced by the arrangement of the figures in Botticelli's beautiful painting which matched those of a traditional baptism, like that by Verrocchio (Uffizi).

Savonarola's influence

The problem came to a head in 1494–8 when Florence came under the spell of the militant Dominican, Savonarola of Ferrara. He condemned the propagation of antiquity, and many books and paintings, including some by Botticelli, were burnt. Botticelli's later work

portraits, as did many contemporaries including Baldovinetti, who favoured profiles, and Botticelli, who painted one of the first full-face portraits.

The secularising tendencies of portraiture and mythology worried many who had seen the arts as essentially supporting the Christian Church. In consequence, philosophers like Marsilio Ficino and Pico della Mirandola attempted to reconcile Christianity with paganism. In consequence, Botticelli's *Birth of Venus* (Uffizi) was seen as reflecting bap-

became emotionally spiritual, especially his *pietàs* at Milan and Munich.

Verrocchio's workshop was among the busiest at the end of the century. A goldsmith by training, he sculpted charming terracotta Madonnas, a robustly active equestrian statue of General Colleoni at Venice, portrait busts of the Medici wearing quasi-Roman armour, the delightful marble *Girl with Primroses* and also a youthful bronze *David* (both Bargello). His *Putto with Dolphin* (Bargello) was one of the first modern sculptures to have a multiplicity of viewpoints. At Orsanmichele his *Christ with Saint Thomas* cleverly fits two figures into a niche designed for one. ❑

LEFT: a detail from della Robbia's Duomo Cantoria.
ABOVE: Botticelli's *Birth of Venus*.

THE HIGH RENAISSANCE ONWARDS

The Renaissance reached its apotheosis in the towering figures of Leonardo, Raphael and Michelangelo, and the influence of Florentine art continued to inspire artists for many centuries

Verrocchio's pupil, Leonardo da Vinci (from the village near Empoli), Raphael (from Urbino) and Michelangelo, together with two lesser stars, Fra Bartolommeo and Andrea del Sarto, form a culmination to the Italian Renaissance in the years 1495 to 1520, a period known as the High Renaissance. During the 1500s Florence was their centre of activity.

Leonardo da Vinci

Leonardo, the eldest of these, rejected the current Platonic belief that a beautiful body presupposed a beautiful mind, which had made idealisation a prime aim of artists. He took instead the Aristotelian approach that all our knowledge is based on our perceptions, which explains his interest in the ugly and grotesque and preoccupation with science and invention. One of his main aims was to identify the nature of things, and as an illustration of this his portrait of Ginevra da Benci (Vaduz) has an allusion to her name in the background juniper *(ginepro)* bush.

His anatomical studies meant dissecting corpses and demonstrated his concern for the nature of life. He saw movement as the sign of the living. To suggest life in depicting people he realised that the earlier approach with fixed, bounding outlines was static; his solution was to blur them, or rather lose and find the contours in a tonal penumbra. In consequence, the image appeared to breathe, as with the *Mona Lisa* (Paris) or the *Virgin and Child with Saint Anne* (Paris) painted for the Servite friars of Florence. In Florence his now

lost *Battle of Anghiari* was an attempt to create a fluent display of violent movement.

In constant demand, he travelled widely. Always inventive, he is credited with introducing a new painterly manner, with a love of invention – the mark, he said, of a great artist. His *Madonna of the Rocks* (Paris) displays all this, but also the radical concept of pairing Christ with the Angel (the heavenly) and Mary with the infant Saint John (the worldly).

Raphael

Far younger was Raphael who, aged 21, arrived in Florence in 1504 following his apprenticeship with Perugino, a painter of great charm who had been working in Rome. Raphael's *Marriage of the Virgin*, 1504 (Milan), shows his maturity on contact with the great Florentine painters: its assured composition and extreme clarity of action, coupled with a serene sense of poised perfection, became hallmarks of Raphael's Florentine period.

Between 1504 and 1508, when he was summoned to decorate the Vatican, Raphael embarked on a series of Madonna and Childs and Holy Families in which he assessed and absorbed elements of Leonardo's manner, as in the *Madonna del Granducca* (Palazzo Pitti), and developed his own lucid, controlled and balanced way of painting, epitomised in

busiest. Ghirlandaio was prolific in his work for Florence: *The Last Supper* (Ognissanti), *The Adoration* (Santa Trinità), and particularly the *Scenes from the Life of the Virgin* (Santa Maria Novella) demonstrate his abilities, technically and compositionally, and especially his clarity of narrative.

Michelangelo also received training in sculpture with Bertoldo, a former pupil of Donatello. This took place at San Marco under the patronage of the Medici, who introduced Michelangelo to leading Florentine thinkers.

Considering himself as primarily a sculptor, Michelangelo was painter, architect and poet, too. If he had one main artistic tenet it

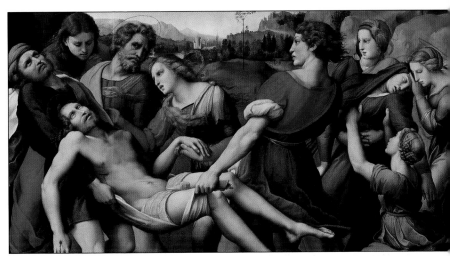

The Madonna of the Goldfinch (Uffizi). With *The Entombment*, 1507 (Rome), Raphael initiated a more dynamic manner, with figures in straining action as they carry the dead Christ, and an assertion of emotion in others. He was pitting himself against Michelangelo, who also was summoned to Rome in 1508.

Michelangelo

Michelangelo had been trained as a painter in Florence under Ghirlandaio, whose workshop, like Verrocchio's, was one of the

was that the human body, preferably male, preferably nude, was the perfect means by which to convey his vision. Thus the *David*, carved in 1504 as a symbol of the city of Florence, with its penetrating gaze and its Platonic ideal muscular body, conveys an archetypal image of bodily power.

As a painter at this early period Michelangelo began to experiment in the *Doni Tondo* (Uffizi) with those complex, twisting poses that resolve three dimensions into two. It was a theme taken up in Rome when from 1508 onwards he was occupied painting the Sistine Chapel ceiling, on which he made the first moves to create space by the volume of the

LEFT: a sketch in charcoal by Leonardo.
ABOVE: Raphael's *Entombment*.

figures rather than using perspective to set a stage to be peopled.

The achievements of Leonardo, Raphael and Michelangelo towards a more painterly style of figure composition with a strong sculptural sense and richness of colour (in part deriving from the growing acceptance of oil paint replacing tempera and fresco) led to a style known as the grand manner.

Both Fra Bartolommeo and Andrea del Sarto demonstrate this. The former, a pupil of Ghirlandaio, took holy orders under Savonarola's influence and developed a powerfully sculptural style that in tonality owed much to Leonardo, but with absolute clarity

of outline, well exemplified by his *Marriage of Saint Catherine* (Accademia). Andrea del Sarto, a student of Piero di Cosimo, evolved a manner that owed much to Fra Bartolommeo, strongly emphasising light and shade, but with a measured sense of gravitas well seen in *The Madonna of the Harpies* (Uffizi).

Mannerism

Leonardo died in 1519; Raphael in 1520. A turning point had been reached. Younger artists could look to Michelangelo, who continued to work up to his death in 1564. His output, however, developed in an idiosyncratic way best exemplified by the Medici

Chapel or New Sacristy in San Lorenzo (1520–34). Michelangelo's architecture here broke many established rules: blind windows cut into their pedimented frames, two scales of pilasters were superimposed, and the altar was out of scale. The sculptural adornment, though never completed, comprised tombs of Lorenzo and Giuliano de' Medici opposite one another. Seated, they wear Roman armour and turn their heads to look at Michelangelo's statue of the Madonna and Child, who face the altar. Below the two Medici are sarcophagi upon which figures of Dusk and Dawn, Night and Day lie uneasily. A chilly intellectualism seems to override the humanity of the images.

This humanity resurfaced in two later carved *pietàs*: the *Florentine pietà*, 1548–56 (Duomo), and the *Palestrina pietà, c.* 1556 (Accademia), where the rough-hewn finish demonstrated a denial of idealisation.

This rejection of the ideal and of the logical that began around 1516 led into the Mannerist period, whose chief initial exponents were Florentine. At its simplest, Mannerist artists worked "in the manner of others", largely Raphael and Michelangelo, but choosing for preference to emphasise those artists' idiosyncrasies. One aim was to find a new direction for art; another to shock the spectator out of a sense of normality; and underlying all this was the rise of Protestantism from 1517, which put into question whether religious painting should be essentially logical or stress spiritual and mystical qualities.

Pontormo, another of Piero di Cosimo's pupils, epitomises these tendencies, especially in terms of spatial ambiguity and dichotomies of scale (see *Joseph in Egypt*, London). This is often coupled with an acidic colour that may derive from Michelangelo in Rome, well demonstrated in *The Deposition* (Santa Felicità) or *The Martyrdom of St Maurice* (Palazzo Pitti).

His contemporary, Rosso Fiorentino, spread this style to Rome and eventually France. *Rosso's Moses and the Daughters of Jethro* (Uffizi) exploited the perspectival ambiguities in Raphael's final works to create an image of disturbing dynamism. Bronzino, the most noted Florentine Mannerist of the mid-century, had studied with

Pontormo and developed a somewhat erotically cold style in his allegories (*Venus, Cupid, Folly* and *Time*, London), and in portraiture gave a sense of distance in which the sitter appeared of less consequence than their clothes (*Eleanora of Toledo*, Uffizi).

Mannerist sculpture

Sculptors, too, picked up elements of Mannerism through an appreciation of Michelangelo, whose *Victory*, 1525 (Palazzo Vecchio), provided a pattern for Bandinelli's dreadful group of *Hercules and Cacus* (before the Palazzo Vecchio). Vastly more successful was Cellini's bronze *Perseus* (Loggia del Lanzi), at once dynamic and elegant; Pierino da Vinci's *Samson and a Philistine* (Palazzo Vecchio) and Danti's *Honour Triumphant over Falsehood*. This last displays a tendency to elongated and perfectly rounded forms, which are traits noticeable in Mannerist painting and which surfaced in Ammannati's bronze figures on the *Fountain of Neptune*.

A sense of virtuosity is an important factor in Mannerism, and possibly the most successful of the groups showing one figure upon another which derive from Michelangelo's Victory is Giovanni Bologna's *Rape of the Sabines* (Loggia dei Lanzi). This forces the spectator to view it from all sides.

The *Mercury* (Bargello) by Bologna is an essay in balance. Rather more sophisticated are his small bronzes of figures that often have poses comprising mixes of frontal and side views that, however, appear totally plausible. The intention was that in turning them, the spectator was constantly impressed and surprised by the changing silhouette.

This sense of surprise was an element of Michelangelo's Medici Chapel. Of similar date is his Laurentian Library (San Lorenzo), whose vestibule, a discomforting space, reverses the norm by recessing columns and advancing the intervening blind-windowed panels. Giorgio Vasari, who is best known as the earliest biographer of the Italian artists, was also a painter and architect. His Uffizi – originally administrative offices, begun 1560 – does a comparable reversal in that small square windows are inserted below, rather than above the larger pedimented ones. Florence's principal gardens, the Boboli Gardens behind the Palazzo Pitti, reveal the Mannerist concern that art should become artifice. They were laid out by Vasari's friend Tribolo (and modified by Ammannati) in a series of groves with a central fountain and the inclusion of sculptures. To the rear was erected Buontalenti's star-shaped Belvedere Fortress.

The Baroque

In 1545 the Council of Trent initiated the Catholic Church's Counter-Reformation, in which artists were exhorted to emphasise an

emotional mysticism for religious subjects, which by 1600 had resulted in the theatrical Baroque style. Its centre was Rome, and Florence's antiquarian climate was at odds with the new style. Nevertheless, Gherardo Silvani's facade to San Gaetano (1645) has a Baroque exuberance of sculpted detail, and his monumental staircase in the Palazzo Corsini, stuccoed by Passardi, is theatrical in intent. Less appealing is the Cappella dei Principi, San Lorenzo, begun 1603, whose oppressive multi-coloured marble veneers contribute to a nightmarish opulence.

The enlargement of the Palazzo Pitti by Parigi (1620–30s), though architecturally

LEFT: Fra Bartolommeo's *Marriage of St Catherine.*
RIGHT: a detail from the *Fountain of Neptune.*

conservative, included enchanting frescos by Pietro da Cortona of Rome, notably that of *The Golden Age*. Cortona's bucolic, gestural manner was echoed in Furini's impressive Allegory on the *Death of Lorenzo il Magnifico*. More tightly constructed were Carlo Dolci's compositions – like *Saint Andrew Adoring His Cross* – which reveal a more classicist painter who excelled in portraiture. In the 1680s, the Neapolitan Luca Giordano frescoed the Palazzo Medici-Riccardi with *Allegory of Navigation*, anticipating the lighter style of the next century.

In Rome Bernini dominated sculptural production, and his dynamic art of movement –

picked up something of the new, French, lightweight manner. Some of this, with its broken forms and unusual viewpoints, is found in Gherardini's fresco *The Dream of St Romuald* (Santa Maria degli Angeli).

Architecturally the century was less distinguished: the Palazzo Capponi by Ruggieri (but perhaps to a design by Carlo Fontana of Rome) has a nobility, and his facade of San Firenze (Chiesa Nuova), amplified later by Rosso, is impressive, but conservative.

Neoclassicism

Throughout Europe, the late 18th and 19th centuries were gripped with the idea of his-

full, twisting forms, coupled with elements of naturalism and antiquity – were later adopted, in part, by Foggini at Florence, whose relief of the *Mass of San Andrea Corsini*, 1685–91 (church of the Carmine), also reflects the more sober work of Bernini's chief rival, Algardi. Foggini was also a talented sculptor of portrait busts, and their painterly manner was picked up by his pupil, Baratta. Both worked well into the next century.

By then, the centres of artistic production in Europe were moving northwards to Paris, Venice and Bavaria. Florentine painters of the 18th century were competent rather than inspired. Gabbiani, a follower of Maratti,

toricism, and in Florence Emilio de Fabris, taking the original Romanesque fabric of the Duomo as a pattern, between 1871 and 1887 added to it a convincing, if over-precise, facade. Likewise, a Moorish style was used by Marco Treves and Vincenzo Micheli for Florence's synagogue. Following Florence's temporary nomination as the capital of Italy after unification, and the consequent population rise, the architect Giuseppe Poggi replanned parts of the city with new, wide streets and conceived the Piazzale Michelangelo.

The growth of archaeology that came with the excavation of Pompeii and other ancient Roman sites led sculptors to neoclassicism.

The chief exponent was the Venetian Antonio Canova, who erected the Alfieri monument in Santa Croce. He influenced Stefano Ricci, who carved the austere memorial to Dante in the same church.

Also in Santa Croce is Lorenzo Bartolini's tomb for the Countess Czartorysky, 1837–44, which, though rooted in the work of Desiderio and Bernardo Rossellino, embodies a stark realism that becomes rather softer in the remarkable cemetery sculptures of 1850–1930. An example is the Laschembach and Guntmausthal memorial (1871) by Ulisse Cambi (Cimitero Porte Sante).

These realist tendencies, allied to an appreciation of colour and subjects of contemporary life, occur with the Macchiaioli painters of the 1860s to '90s. The group in Florence included Silvestro Lega, whose *Canto dello Stornello*, 1867 (Palazzo Pitti), has a lyrical charm; Giovanni Fattori, the most enthusiastic of the group; and Telemaco Signorini, whose subjects offered strong social comment. Fattori's unusual compositions, such as *La Roronda dei Bagni Palmieri*, 1866 (Palazzo Pitti), are paralleled in Impressionism, and the similarity fits with the group's name, for *macchie* refers to patches of paint, like the brush marks of the Impressionists.

Modernism

The major movements of Italian 20th-century art – Futurism, Metaphysical Painting and Arte Povera – belonged to the industrial north; many Italian artists, like de Chirico and Modigliani, drifted to Paris, while others, including Giorgio Morandi of Bologna, remained in their home towns. All, however, contributed to an acceptance of expressive modernism tempered by the Renaissance classical tradition, best seen in Carlo Carra's Novecento group that received some Fascist approval.

More recently, aspects of these traits are seen in Sandro Chia (b.1946, Florence), who plays with a none-too-subtle postmodernist wit in paintings that retain an expressionist form of figurative subject. His richness of colour may be a deliberate rejection of the meagreness of much Arte Povera work of the 1960s and '70s. How far this is Italian, or specifically Florentine, rather than international in spirit, is perhaps in doubt.

This is true, too, of much sculpture. Michelangelo Pistoletti's *Dietrofront* (Porta Romana), a caryatid-like figure, follows trends towards the massive in similar work of the 1920s; and Arnaldo Pomodoro's *Movimento di Crollo*, a split bronze pillar (Frescobaldi Gardens), is typical of much late 20th-century abstraction.

More satisfying is some of the architecture. A house on the Via Scipione Ammirato is perfect Art Nouveau, with its curving, organic forms, metal brackets and iron balcony rails.

Italian modernist architecture stems from 1926 and the founding of Gruppo 7, and, with it, Architettura Razionale.

Florence's classicist leanings led to only a few truly progressive structures, among them Pier Luigi Nervi's stadium of 1932. Most impressive are those by Giovanni Michelucci. His church on the autostrada, organic in form even to its random stone cladding, is wholly satisfying in its grouping.

Perhaps the city's finest public structure is his railway station of 1935. Uncompromisingly of its time, spacious and practical, it makes a fitting entry to the city that gave the world the coherence of the Renaissance. ❑

LEFT: a Baroque ceiling in the Palazzo Pitti.
RIGHT: Santa Maria Novella railway station.

PLACES

A detailed guide to the city, with principal sites
clearly cross-referenced by number to the maps

C haracterised by the huge domed cupola of the cathedral rising out of the dense, rustic-coloured city nestled in the Tuscan hills, Florence is overflowing with history, culture and artistic patrimony. Today the focal point of the Renaissance is very much the city you choose to make of it. Some people hate the place because of its heat, noise and tourists, while the number of expatriates and international students bears testimony to its potentially enduring charm.

Florence's reputation for being a museum city is well deserved and makes negotiating the illogical opening hours a worthwhile, if frustrating, task for the least enthusiastic to the most hardy of art-lovers. However, its lure goes far beyond the sum total of galleries, churches and monuments: in order to experience more than the Florence of the Renaissance, visitors should take the time to appreciate the beauty and ambience of the city by wandering through the many *piazze* and back streets, and along the banks of the Arno and into the surrounding countryside. There is no better time for this than the early evening: as the bustle of the day winds down, the city feels altogether more Italian, especially in the summer when the weather is stifling and the streets packed with tourists.

Despite first appearances, those who linger will discover what a small community Florence really is, for everyone seems to know everyone else, and groups of people fill the pedestrianised streets, swapping gossip and more serious news. Visitors don't have to be excluded from the community: attempting to speak a little basic Italian wins friends and breaks through the Florentine reserve. Regularly frequenting the numerous little bars tucked away in the smaller streets to take a coffee or an *aperitivo* gives an insight into the authentic Italian and Florentine lifestyle.

As for the noise, the heat, the cheating stallholders, pickpockets and rude waiters, surely every city worth its salt has these. The problem has been much exaggerated by those who affect an ennui for the stop on the Grand Tour that has, in their eyes, fallen from fashion. Florence is not so easily dismissed, nor will the discriminating visitor want to leap to easy conclusions about such a complex and rewarding destination. ❑

PRECEDING PAGES: Andrea del Sansovino's terracotta frieze at Poggio a Caiano; Pucci's shopfront, Via de' Tournabuoni.
LEFT: looking through the Palazzo degli Uffizi to the Palazzo Vecchio.

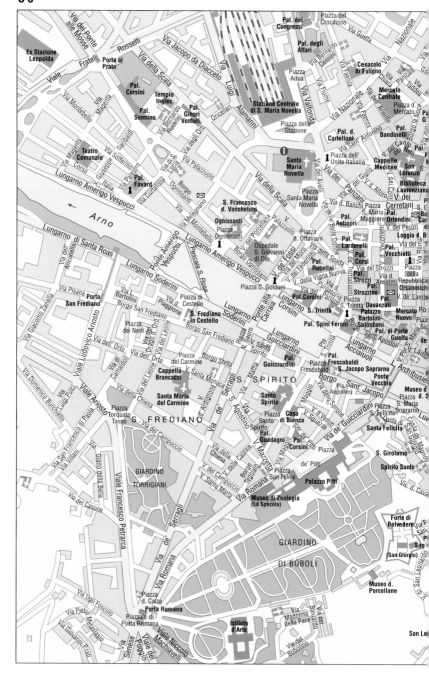

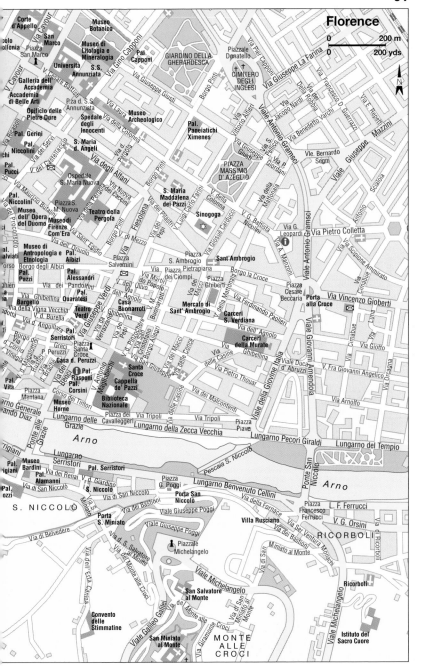

Florence

0   200 m
0   200 yds

VALERIANUS LEGATUS
FUNDAMENTA SACRAVIT

THE DUOMO

One of the largest cathedrals in the world is at
the heart of this impressive area of Florence,
notable for its architecture as well as its art

Traffic has been banned from at least part of the piazza surrounding the Duomo (cathedral), which allows the sheer scale of this truly magnificent, if a little dirty, building, clad in polychrome marble, to be fully appreciated. Next to the Duomo, whose steps are always full of tourists and locals, lie the baptistery and the campanile; all three constructed in the same striking white, green and pink stone.

The Piazza del Duomo and the Piazza di San Giovanni, in which the baptistery sits, are edged by expensive shops and cafés, and filled with street sellers flogging overpriced water, guidebooks, caricatures and tacky models of famous Florentine landmarks. The two main streets which head further into the city centre also lead off from here: Via dei Calzaiuoli and Via Roma.

Standing at the end of Via dei Pecori (behind the baptistery) gives a wonderful view and perspective for photographing the buildings; the illustrious facade of the Duomo is visible, sandwiched between the campanile to the right and the baptistery to the left. From here most of the scaffolding from the current work to construct a visitors' centre and a queuing system is hidden.

Cattedrale Santa Maria del Fiore

The **Duomo ❶** (from Domus Dei, House of God; open Mon–Wed, Fri 10am–5pm, Thur 10am–3.30pm, Sat 10am–4.45pm, Sun 1.30–4.45pm, closed 1st Sat of month; entrance charge) is a symbol of Florentine determination always to have the biggest and the best. It was once the largest in the world, and even now ranks fourth. Being a state church, it was funded by a property tax on all citizens, and is a continuing

LEFT:
the multi-coloured
facade of the Duomo.
BELOW:
a detail from the
baptistery doors.

financial burden on the city and state, requiring constant repair. It took almost 150 years to complete, from 1294 to 1436, though it was not until the late 19th century that the cathedral got its flamboyant neo-Gothic west facade.

The addition makes us appreciate Brunelleschi's genius all the more – his dome draws the eye upwards from the jumble below to admire the clean profile of the cathedral's crowning glory, 107 metres (351 ft) above the ground.

As a tribute to Brunelleschi, considered the greatest architect and engineer of his day, no other building in Florence has been built as tall as the dome since its completion in 1436, when the cathedral was consecrated by Pope Eugenius IV.

Scarcely less tall, at 85 metres (278 ft), is the campanile alongside, begun by Giotto shortly after he was appointed chief architect in 1331 and finished off after his death in

Christ and John the Baptist on the outside of the baptistery.

1337 by Andrea Pisano and then Talenti. Work was eventually completed in 1359. The climb to the top is worth the effort for intimate views of the upper levels of the cathedral and the panoramic city views (open daily 8.30am–7.30pm in summer, 8.30am–4.30pm in winter; entrance charge).

Stark simplicity

By contrast with the polychrome exterior, the cathedral interior is strikingly vast and stark, in keeping with the austere spiritual ideal of Florence during the early Renaissance. At the east end are Luca della Robbia's bronze doors to the new sacristy (1445–69) and the fine wooden inlaid cupboards that line the interior. Here, Lorenzo the Magnificent sought refuge in 1478 after the Pazzi conspirators, in a failed bid to seize power from the Medici, had tried to murder him during High Mass.

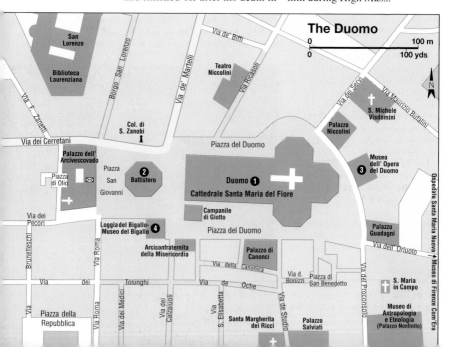

The highlight is the fresco on the underside of the dome, high above the altar, which depicts the Last Judgement. Painted in 1572–9 by Giorgio Vasari and Federico Zuccari, it was intended as the Florentine equivalent to the scenes Michelangelo painted in the Sistine Chapel in the Vatican, and is a truly spectacular sight.

In the north aisle, there is a painting of Dante standing outside the walls of Florence, symbolic of his exile. It was commissioned in 1465 to celebrate the bicentenary of the poet's birth.

Close to it is the famous mural of 1436 depicting the English mercenary, Sir John Hawkwood. It is often cited as an example of Florentine miserliness, for Hawkwood's services to the city were commemorated not by a real bronze statue but by Paolo Uccello's *trompe l'œil* mural. Uccello also painted the fresco clock on the west wall that tells the time according to *ora Italica*, which prevailed until the 1700s, whereby sunset marks the last hour of the day.

There are several memorials in the cathedral but only one man – Filippo Brunelleschi – was granted the singular privilege of burial within its walls, belated recognition of his genius in resolving the problem of the dome. His grave slab can be seen by climbing down the steps at the rear of the Duomo.

The steps lead to a jumble of stonework discovered in 1965, consisting of the remains of Santa Reparata (open Mon–Fri 10am–5pm, Sat 10am–4pm; entrance charge), the church that was demolished to make way for the Duomo, some Roman structures and the gift shop. The slab covering Brunelleschi's tomb bears an inscription comparing him to Icarus. The analogy, as it happens, is apt – for, like the flight of the mythical hero, the dome seems to defy gravity.

The soaring dome

The master plan for the cathedral had always envisaged a central dome (cupola), but no one knew how to erect one of the required height and span without prodigious expenditure on timber for scaffolding. Brunelleschi travelled to Rome to study the prototype of all domed structures – the Pantheon – after which he came up with his master plan: a solution based on classical Roman technology.

Poor Brunelleschi must sometimes have hated the Florentines. Sceptical financiers first made him build a model on the bank of the Arno to prove that his dome would stand up and then appointed the cautious, interfering and incompetent Ghiberti, Brunelleschi's old rival in the competition for the baptistery doors, to supervise the overall construction.

An effective problem-solver, Brunelleschi got rid of Ghiberti by simply walking out of the project,

Map on page 90

Black-and-white marble patterning, a hallmark of Romanesque architecture, adorns the floor of the Duomo's crypt.

BELOW: one of Niccolò Barabino's 19th-century mosaics on the Duomo's facade.

pretending to be ill. Without Brunelleschi, work soon ground to a halt, and he agreed to return only if he was put in sole charge.

Brunelleschi's aesthetic achievement is known to the whole world through countless travel posters. The dome has come to symbolise the city of Florence, an instantly recognisable landmark, rising above a sea of red terracotta roof tiles and seeming to soar as high as the surrounding mountains. To appreciate his engineering achievement it is necessary to climb up to the dome (open Mon–Fri 8.30am–7pm, Sat 8.30am–5.40pm, 1st Sat of the month until 4pm; entrance charge).

The staircase passes between two shells. The inner one is built of brick laid herringbone fashion, providing a virtually self-supporting structure that could be built from above without support from below. This then provided a platform for the scaffolding to erect the outer shell.

The dome was completed in 1436, but the lantern, planned by Brunelleschi, was completed by Michelozzi Michelozzo in 1461,

15 years after the original architect's death. The final touch was the external gallery running round the base. This was begun in 1506 by Baccio d'Agnolo, but work stopped in 1515 with only one side finished, when Michelangelo, whose word was law, described it as a "cricket's cage", implying that the design was rustic and childish. Few visitors will agree with his judgement, which has left the base of the dome with no facing to disguise the raw stonework on seven of its sides.

The baptistery

After visiting the Duomo, the next port of call is the **Battistero** ❷ (baptistery; open Mon–Sat noon–7pm, Sun 8.30am–2pm; entrance charge). In exile, Dante fondly referred to this building as his *"bel San Giovanni"* and described it as "ancient" – a word loaded with meaning. Florentines have always exaggerated its antiquity, asserting that it was originally the Temple of Mars, built by the Romans to commemorate victory over the

If you're thinking of climbing up to the dome, it is probably best to do it early in the day, when you still have some stamina: there are 464 spiralling stairs to negotiate before reaching the top. But once there, the view of the city is fabulous.

BELOW:
the magnificent outline of Giotto's campanile and Brunelleschi's dome.

Etruscan city of Fiesole. In the inter-communal rivalry of the Middle Ages, every Tuscan town claimed to be older than its neighbours, and the baptistery symbolised the Florentine pedigree, its link with the golden classical age.

All the evidence suggests that it was, in fact, built in the 6th or 7th century, albeit reusing Roman masonry. From the 12th century it was taken under the wing of the wool importers' guild, which itself claimed to be the first and most ancient trade association in the city.

The guild paid for the beautiful marble cladding of green geometric designs on a white background. This was widely admired and imitated throughout Tuscany, the prototype of many a church exterior, including that of Florence's own cathedral. The splendid interior was reworked between 1270 and 1300, when the dome received its ambitious cycle of mosaics – illustrating the entire biblical story from Creation to the Last Judgement – and the Zodiac pavement around the font was laid.

Next, the guild turned to the entrances, determined to outdo the great bronze doors of Pisa cathedral. They did so, but not until several decades later. Andrea Pisano's doors, now in the south portal, were completed in 1336, and the 28 panels show scenes from the life of San Giovanni (St John), the patron saint of the city, as well as allegoric themes of the Virtues. They are outstanding examples of the best Gothic craftsmanship, but it was Ghiberti's north and east doors that really set Europe talking 60 years later.

Work stopped on the baptistry during the intervening period due to a series of disasters – including plague, appalling weather, crop failures and famine, as well as bankruptcies and further political turmoil in Florence.

Gates of Paradise

The year 1401 was a watershed date. In the winter of that year the wool importers' guild announced a competition to select a designer for the remaining doors, with the

Map
on page
90

The south doors of the baptistery were the work of Andrea Pisano (c. 1270–1348) – goldsmith, sculptor and architect rolled into one.

BELOW: the double skin of the dome seen on the ascent.

If you look closely at the door frames on the baptistery's east doors, you'll see a self-portrait of the sculptor, Lorenzo Ghiberti: the third head up in the centre of the frame on the left. The similar-looking figure on the right is his father.

BELOW:
Moses receiving the Commandments, as depicted on the baptistery doors.

result that some of the greatest sculptors of the age competed against each other, having been invited to submit sample panels on the theme of the Sacrifice of Isaac. Only those by Lorenzo Ghiberti and Filippo Brunelleschi have survived, and they are now on display in the Bargello *(see page 127)*.

After much deliberation, Ghiberti (c. 1378–1455) was judged the winner in 1403 – though the year scarcely matters since art historians, a little reluctant to award the title of Father of the Renaissance to any one artist, generally consider 1401, the year of the competition, as the starting point of the Renaissance.

Ghiberti's work demonstrates some of the features of the emerging Renaissance style, but it was Brunelleschi's submission that was truly radical, with the use of deep perspective, realism in the portrayal of the human body and allusions to classical sculpture *(see also page 69)*.

Ghiberti finished the north doors, illustrating the Life of Christ, in 1424, having worked on them for more than 20 years. The east doors, hailed by Michelangelo as worthy of being the "Gates of Paradise", took almost all of the rest of his life.

In their original state, with their 10 large panels illustrating the Old Testament, gilded and burnished to a resplendent gold, they must have fully justified Michelangelo's description. The original panels (replaced by resin reproductions) were removed for restoration after flood damage and can now be seen in the Museo dell'Opera del Duomo *(see below)*.

The cathedral museum

The **Museo dell'Opera del Duomo** ❸ (open Mon–Sat 9am–7.30pm, Sun 9am–1.40 in summer, earlier closing in winter; entrance charge) occupies the old cathedral workshop, established in the 15th century to maintain the fabric and commission new works to adorn the building. Here, in the courtyard, Michelangelo carved *David*. The museum contains carvings from the baptistery, Duomo and campanile, brought indoors for protection from pollution and weathering.

The most important of the exhibits are the so-called "Gates of Paradise" by Ghiberti, which, in all their glory, are the focal point of a display area in the courtyard where Michelangelo once worked. With the restoration of all the panels now finished, they can be seen as a whole for the first time in more than 30 years.

Leading off the courtyard are rooms full of weathered stone figures of saints and prophets from niches around the exterior of the Duomo, including several carved for the original facade. This was never completed, and the Gothic statues were removed in 1587. To bring them back together in this

museum, the curators scoured store-rooms, private collections and even Florentine gardens.

Penitence and joy

But these are all curiosities; the great art treasures lie upstairs. Dramatically positioned on the half-landing is Michelangelo's powerful *Pietà*. He began work on it around 1550, intending it to cover his own tomb. Having completed only the expressive body of Christ and the head of Nicodemus (a self-portrait), he broke it up, dissatisfied with the faulty marble and his own work. A servant kept the pieces and a pupil reconstructed it, finishing the figure of Mary Magdalene after the master's death.

The first room upstairs contains two delightful choir galleries *(cantorie)*, made for the cathedral but removed in the 17th century. On the left is Luca della Robbia's marble loft, carved 1431–8; on the right, Donatello's work of 1433–9. Both portray boys and girls singing, dancing, playing trumpets, drums and cymbals in a frenzy of joyous celebration. In stark contrast, Donatello's statue in wood of Mary Magdalene (*c.* 1455) is a striking study of the former prostitute in old age, dishevelled, haggard and penitent.

The room beyond is devoted to early 14th-century bas-reliefs from the base of the campanile, some designed by Giotto, but most carved by Andrea Pisano, who was responsible for the baptistery's south doors *(see page 93)*. They illustrate the Creation of Adam and Eve and the arts, sciences and industries by which the human race has sought to understand and beautify the world since the barring of the Gates of Paradise. Though Gothic in style, they are Renaissance in spirit, a proud celebration of human knowledge and achievement.

The final section of the museum displays pulleys, ropes and brick moulds from the construction of the cathedral's great dome, as well as sketches and scale models made at various dates in an attempt to agree on a design for the incomplete facade.

Map on page 90

Tools of the trade in the Museo dell' Opera del Duomo.

BELOW: the cupola mosaics of the baptistery.

Small but exceptional

On the corner of Via dei Calzaiuoli (almost opposite the baptistery), the **Loggia del Bigallo** ❹ was built between 1352 and 1358 for the charitable Misericordia, which cared for abandoned children left in the loggia, or porch. The organisation still runs an ambulance service and has its headquarters in the square. It later joined forces with the Bigallo, another religious body.

Loggias, typical features of a piazza, were originally built to provide shelter from the sun or the rain, but many now harbour street markets. Although not a market itself, the Loggia del Bigallo – with some fine marble décor typical of the International Gothic style of the 14th century – houses a museum containing the various works of art accumulated over the years by both organisations associated with it.

Recently reopened after a long period of oblivion and known as the **Museo del Bigallo** (open Wed–Mon 10am–6pm; entrance charge), it is almost inconspicuous among the monumental grandeur of the rest of the buildings in the square, but contains some exceptional artworks.

Most famous of these is Bernardo Daddi's fresco of the *Madonna della Misericordia*, in which the earliest-known view of Florence appears (1342). Also worth viewing is Daddi's triptych with the *Madonna and Child and Fourteen Saints*, as well as other works by Domenico Ghirlandaio, Iacopo del Sellaio, Nardo di Cione and sculptor Alberto Arnoldi.

Around the Duomo

Via dell' Oriuolo leads off from the southeast corner of Piazza del Duomo, and a little way down on the left the Via Folco Portinari provides a glimpse of the **Ospedale Santa Maria Nuova**, still one of the city's main hospitals. It was founded in 1286 by Folco Portinari, father of Beatrice, the girl whom Dante made the subject of his early love poetry and his epic *Divine Comedy*. The portico (1612) is by Buontalenti.

Carving on the outside of the Loggia del Bigallo.

BELOW:
the quiet courtyard of Firenze Com'Era.

Further up Via dell' Oriuolo is the **Museo di Firenze Com'Era** (open Fri–Wed 9am–2pm; entrance charge), or "Florence As It Was". It is housed in a former convent with a graceful loggia surrounding three sides of a grassy courtyard.

The museum contains maps and topographical paintings that show how little Florence has changed in any essential respect since the first view of the city was sketched in 1470. Most interesting is the *Pianta della Catena* right at the front – a huge plan of Renaissance Florence in tempura, which is a 19th-century copy of an original engraving now in Berlin. Anyone even half-familiar with the city will enjoy spotting the buildings, many of which still exist.

It might so easily have been otherwise. Another room contains the 19th-century drawings of the city architect, Giuseppe Poggi, who planned to sweep away the "slums" that infested central Florence and replace them with the monumental avenues then in vogue. The Piazza della Repub-blica was built and the 14th-century walls demolished before international opposition halted the scheme. Most of Poggi's plans, which included a suspension bridge over the Arno, ended up as museum curiosities, albeit examples of very fine draughtsmanship.

But the most endearing of the museum's ragbag of city views are the lunettes illustrating the villas and gardens of the Medici, painted by the Flemish artist, Giusto Utens, in 1599. The view of the Palazzo Pitti and Boboli Gardens shows them as they were before the extensions were built by the heirs of Cosimo I.

One block north of Via dell' Oriuolo, in the library complex situated in Via Sant'Egidio, you will find the newly restored **Museo Fiorentina de Preistoria** (open Mon, Wed, Fri and Sat 9.30am–12.30pm, Tues and Thur 9.30am–4pm; entrance charge), of interest to anyone who wants to know about the earliest evidence of human settlement and activity in the Arno valley. ❏

Map on page 90

In the 14th century, unwanted babies used to be left on the porch of the Loggia del Bigallo; if they were not claimed within three days, they would be sent to foster homes.

RESTAURANTS AND CAFÉS

Restaurants

Angels
Via del Proconsolo 29/31
Tel: 055-2398762
www.ristoranteangels.it
D only; L in summer.
€€€
Chic bar and restaurant adjoined to the Grand Cavour hotel which offers good-quality food in a nice ambience. The pasta-based *aperitivo* is filling, whilst the restaurant offers modern cuisine in a smart setting.

Le Botteghe di Donatello
Piazza del Duomo
Tel: 055-216678
www.lebotteghedidonatello.com
L and D daily. €€
Set in Donatello's former workshop, this restaurant offers changing Tuscan dishes, big salads and Neapolitan-style pizzas. Set on the corner of Via dei Servi, it is also equipped with an extensive wine list and offers discounts for students.

Cafés and Gelaterie

Oleum Olivae
Via San Egidio 22r
Tel: 055-2001092
www.oleum.it
L only.
Order a glass of wine and pick your *panino* bread, filling and sauce from the delicatessen – try the pecorino garnished with rocket and walnut sauce. Get there early to avoid the queues.

Perché No?
Via de' Tavolini 194
Tel: 055-2398969
One of the oldest ice-cream parlours in the city and a pioneer of the *semifreddo* – a mousse-like *gelato* which is perfect for colder days.

Scudieri
Piazza San Giovanni 19r
Tel: 055/210733
B, L and T.
A fancy grand café located by the baptistery, perfect for breakfast or a snack, especially a chocolate-based one.

●●●●●●●●●●●●●
Price includes dinner and a glass of wine, excluding tip.
€€€€ over €60, €€€ €40–60, €€ €25–40, € under €25.

PIAZZA DELLA SIGNORIA

The dramas that have unfolded in Florence over the centuries in the city's main square, the Piazza della Signoria, would rival those of the finest theatre

Piazza della Signoria ❶, the main L-shaped square in Florence, evokes strong reactions. Florentines argue furiously about its future, and citizens of neighbouring towns are contemptuous of its lack of grace and architectural unity compared with, say, Siena's harmonious Campo. The buildings, now mainly occupied by banks and insurance companies, seem to belong to some cold northern climate rather than the city that gave birth to the colour and vitality of the Renaissance. However, the piazza – in addition to being virtually an alfresco museum of sculpture – makes an atmospheric setting for the cafés as well as the open-air ballet and concerts in the summer.

The piazza has suffered from the fact that no sooner had the Palazzo Vecchio and the neighbouring Uffizi gallery emerged from the scaffolding that had enshrouded them for a decade or more during an extensive restoration programme than a terrorist bomb caused major structural damage in May 1993. The majority of the art has now been restored and is back on display, although the Loggia dei Lanzi (*see below*) is now undergoing restoration.

Ancient strife

Of course, the controversy surrounding the square's image is not entirely new; the piazza is littered with the symbols of competing ideologies. A plaque near the Neptune Fountain marks the spot where Savonarola was burnt at the stake as a heretic in 1498, whilst statues around the square are loaded with political allusions.

Politicians, as is their wont, have addressed the unsuspecting public from the front of the Palazzo Vecchio since the 14th century – originally from the raised platform, the *ringheria* (which gave rise to the

Map on page 100

LEFT: the Palazzo Vecchio towers above the piazza.
BELOW: a lion standing guard outside the Loggia dei Lanzi.

term "to harangue"), until it was demolished in 1812.

Piazza della Signoria was even born out of strife. The land was owned by the Uberti, supporters of the Ghibelline (imperial) faction, losers to the Guelf (papal) party in the struggles that tore Florence apart in the 13th century. The property of the exiled Uberti was first left to crumble as a sign of the family's defeat, but then chosen as the site of a new palace to house the city government.

One famous resident of the Palazzo della Signoria – as the Palazzo Vecchio was once known – was Dante, who lived there for two months as a representative of the people.

The Palazzo Vecchio

The Palazzo Vecchio dominates the square. Built on the site of the old Roman theatre, its foundation stone was laid in 1299 and the palace was finished by 1322, when the great bell (removed in 1530) was hung in the tower to ring out danger warnings and summon general assemblies.

The name of the building has changed almost as often as power in the city has changed hands. From the Palazzo del Popolo – the People's Palace – it became the Palazzo della Signoria when the *signori*, the heads of the leading families, took over the reins of government. It continued so from 1434, the start of Cosimo de' Medici's unofficial leadership of the city, until the death of his grandson, Lorenzo the Magnificent, in 1492. The years 1494–1537 saw attempts, inspired by the teaching of Savonarola, to establish a republic; the Medici were expelled from the city and an inscription was raised above the palace entrance (where it still remains) declaring Christ to be the only king of Florence.

In 1537, Cosimo I seized control of the city and three years later moved into the palace, which now became the Palazzo Ducale. In 1550, the Pitti Palace became the duke's new official residence, and from that time to this the building has been known as the Palazzo Vecchio, the Old Palace. It is now the

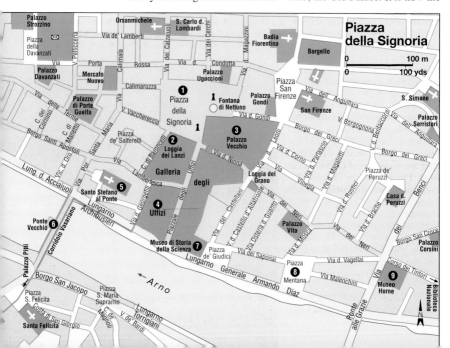

town hall, so this is where the citizens of Florence come to arrange birth and death certificates, pay their fines and get married. It is not unusual to get caught up in a rice-throwing wedding party while viewing the inner courtyards.

A gallery of statues

Before you enter the Palazzo Vecchio, you should take the time to look at the statues outside. The graceful little three-arched **Loggia dei Lanzi** ❷, near the palace on the south side of the square, is named after Cosimo I's personal bodyguards, the lancers, whose barracks were located near by. But it was constructed much earlier – completed in 1382 – to shelter dignitaries from the weather during public ceremonies.

Cosimo considered extending the tall, round arches all around the square, on Michelangelo's advice, to give the piazza a degree of architectural harmony, but the plan was abandoned because it was too costly. Instead, the loggia came to serve as an outdoor sculpture gallery, housing antique statues as well as new works.

The first statue was erected not as an aesthetically motivated decision but as an act of political defiance. Donatello's *Judith and Holofernes* was cast between 1456 and 1460 as a fountain for the courtyard of the Medici Palace. It was brought into the square by the citizens of the newly declared republic of Florence after the expulsion of the Medici in 1494. The symbolism was clear for everyone to read: the virtuous Judith executing the drunken tyrant Holofernes stood for the triumph of liberty over despotism.

Fifty years later, in 1554, another bronze statue depicting a decapitation was erected in the loggia. Cellini's *Perseus* was commissioned by Cosimo I to celebrate his return to power and carried an implied threat – just as Perseus used the head of Medusa to turn his enemies to stone, so opponents could expect exile, or worse. Florentines once believed that images had the magical power to bring good or ill upon the city, and so it was not long before the wisdom of displaying *Judith and Holofernes* began to be questioned. It symbolised death and the defeat of a man by a woman, and so was moved to a less prominent site. However, the statues that remain are equally impressive, in particular Giambologna's *Rape of the Sabines* and Cellini's bronze statue *(see above)*.

Enter David

The appearance of Michelangelo's **David** in its position outside the Palazzo Vecchio was a popular decision that transformed the square and gave it a new focal point. Even now, the pollution-streaked copy (the original is in the Accademia, *see page 157*) has an arresting force and exudes ambiguity. David is both muscular and effeminate, between adolescence and maturity, relaxed but ready to fight, a glorious celebration of the naked human body,

Map on page 100

Benvenuto Cellini's Perseus *in the Loggia dei Lanzi.*

BELOW: the copy of *David* outside the Palazzo Vecchio.

yet apparently distorted with over-large head and limbs.

Moreover, the political symbolism was open to numerous interpretations. Those who wished could see David's bravery before the giant Goliath as a metaphor for Florence, prepared to defend her liberty against all who threatened it; or they could read it more specifically and choose the Medici, the Pope, the Holy Roman Emperor, Siena, or Pisa as the particular enemy.

Neptune Fountain

After the success of David, more works were commissioned on the same monumental scale, but all were greeted with varying degrees of ridicule. Hercules was chosen as a subject because of the legend that Florence was built on swamps drained by the mythical hero. But when the carving by Baccio Bandinelli (1493–1560) was unveiled in 1534, Benvenuto Cellini compared the exaggerated musculature to "an old sack full of melons".

Bartolommeo Ammannati's Neptune Fountain, an allegory of

Ammannati's Neptune Fountain.

Cosimo I's scheme to make Florence a great naval power, was carved in 1563–75 and was immediately nicknamed Il Biancone (Big White One), with deliberately lewd connotations. Neptune looks as uncomfortable as the artist must have felt on hearing his work dismissed in a popular street cry as a waste of a good piece of marble.

The bronze satyrs and nymphs splashing at Neptune's feet are livelier work, in a style typical of the Mannerist art of the period, with elongated necks and limbs. They are also decidedly salacious, and the artist, in a fit of piety later in life, condemned his own work as an incitement to licentious thoughts and deeds.

Near the fountain, standing on its own to the north of the Palazzo Vecchio, is Giambologna's equestrian statue of Cosimo I; this was commissioned by his son Ferdinando and unveiled in 1594. It is imposing but of indifferent artistic quality – the same could be said of Florence under Cosimo's reign, for though he left it powerful, art went into serious decline.

Inside the Palazzo Vecchio – Quartieri Monumentali

Nowhere is the decline that characterised Cosimo I's rule more evident than in the interior of the **Palazzo Vecchio ❸** (open Fri–Wed 9am–7pm, Thur 9am–2pm; entrance charge), completely remodelled when Cosimo moved into it in 1540, having quashed republicanism in Florence and established himself as hereditary duke. It is not all bad, of course; the Cortile (courtyard), designed by Michelozzi Michelozzo in 1453 as the main entrance, is delightful. The little fountain in the centre was designed by Vasari around 1555 – copying the putto and dolphin made for the Medici villa at Careggi by Verrocchio in 1470.

The Politics of the Piazza

One of the most contentious recent debates in Florence centred on work in the Piazza della Signoria. Such is the exaggerated respect for old Florence that the city took 13 years to decide that the piazza needed to be resurfaced. However, Francesco Nicosia, the archaeological supervisor for Tuscany, stepped in and argued that the repaving would cover the Roman baths and ancient buildings that lay beneath the square. He launched a campaign to excavate the piazza and create an underground museum. But the city government did not want another museum, especially one with entrances, exits, air ducts and pavement skylights that would disrupt the piazza. A compromise was reached: the archaeologists could dig, and document everything, but then they would have to cover it back up so the repaving could proceed. Nicosia agreed, but then found a whole town, including a Roman wool-dyeing plant, under the square. He vowed to continue his battle for a museum; city leaders were unmoved. In the end, the square has been repaved – with ugly modern paving stones – much to the relief of all who make a living from its pavement cafés, busking and carriage rides.

The stucco and frescos are also Vasari's work. On the walls are views of Austrian cities, painted to make Joanna of Austria feel at home when she married Francesco de' Medici (Cosimo's son) in 1565. The ceiling is covered in "grotesque" figures – that is, in imitation of the ancient Roman paintings in the grotto of Nero's garden – a colourful tapestry of sphinxes, flowers, birds and playful satyrs.

This courtyard leads through to the main ticket office where, if you have children, you might like to sign them up for one of the "Secrets of the Palace" tours, which take in secret passages and odd corners that are out of bounds to mere adults.

Grown-ups have to be content with the state chambers, starting on the first floor with the Salone dei Cinquecento (Room of the Five Hundred). This was designed in 1495 by Cronaca for meetings of the ruling assembly – the Consiglio Maggiore – of the republic. It was the largest room of its time. The vast space, despite appalling acoustics, is now used occasionally as a concert hall.

Both Leonardo da Vinci and Michelangelo were commissioned to paint the walls and ceilings of the Salone dei Cinquecento, but neither got much further than experimental sketches. It was left to Giorgio Vasari (court architect from 1555 until his death in 1574) to undertake the work, executed with great speed between 1563 and 1565. Nominally the paintings celebrate the foundation of Florence and the recent victories over its rivals, Pisa and Siena. The ubiquitous presence of Cosimo I in all the scenes, however, makes it simply a vast exercise in ducal propaganda.

It is not unusual for visitors to feel uneasy and wonder why Vasari stooped to such overt flattery. Michelangelo's *Victory* is equally disturbing. Brutally realistic, it depicts an old man forced to the ground by the superior strength of a muscular youth. It was carved for the tomb of Julius II in Rome, but Michelangelo's heirs presented it to Cosimo I to commemorate the 1559 victory over Siena. The artist intended it to represent the triumph of reason over ignorance, but in this

Map on page 100

An early caricature? Look for this profile of a man to the right of Palazzo Vecchio's main entrance, just behind the statue of Hercules – it is attributed to Michelangelo.

BELOW: the inner courtyard of the Palazzo Vecchio.

The intricately decorated ceiling in Palazzo Vecchio's Sala d'Udienza.

context it seems part of a gross celebration of war. Even so, artists have frequently sought to imitate Michelangelo's twisted, tortured figures, and it was one of the works most admired by the later 16th-century Mannerists.

Light relief is provided by the Hercules and Diomedes of Vincenzo de' Rossi, a no-holds-barred tussle in which the inverted Diomedes takes revenge by squeezing Hercules' genitals in an agonising grip.

Off the main hall is the study, the Studiolo, of the reclusive Francesco I, built between 1570 and 1575. The beautifully painted cupboards were used to store his treasures and the equipment for his experiments in alchemy. His parents, Cosimo I and the beautiful Eleonora di Toledo, are depicted on the wall frescos.

Next in sequence comes the suite of rooms known as the Quartiere di Leone X, decorated in 1556–62 by Vasari and named after Giovanni de' Medici, son of Lorenzo the Magnificent, who was created a cardinal at the age of 13 and ended up as Pope Leo X.

BELOW: catching up on the news near the Piazza della Signoria.

Second Floor

Above is the Quartiere degli Elementi, with allegories of the elements, including a watery scene reminiscent of the work of Botticelli, once again by Vasari. The corner room, the Terrazza di Saturno, provides fine views east to Santa Croce and south to San Miniato, while in another small room is Verrocchio's original *Boy and Dolphin* taken from the courtyard.

The Quartiere di Eleonora di Toledo, the private rooms of the wife of Cosimo I, includes the chapel with stunning frescos by Bronzino (1540–45), a rare opportunity to study fresco work from close quarters. The sheer range and brilliance of the colour is most striking – colours rarely seen in modern painting: vivid pinks, luminescent blues and almost phosphorescent green.

Eleonora's bedroom is decorated with a frieze based on her initials, and has a lovely marble washbasin; another is painted with domestic scenes – spinning, weaving and the tasks that correspond to the classical idea of virtuous motherhood –

the last with Florentine street scenes and festivities.

A corridor containing the serene death mask of Dante leads to the two most sumptuous rooms of the palace, the Sala d'Udienza and the Sala dei Gigli. Both have gilded and coffered ceilings, decorated with every conceivable form of ornament. The 16th-century intarsia doors between the two depict the poets Dante and Petrarch.

The Sala dei Gigli is named after the so-called lilies (irises, in reality) that cover the walls and are used as a symbol of the city. Donatello's original *Judith and Holofernes* is displayed here, with panels explaining how the bronze was cast and, more recently, restored.

The Cancelleria, a small chamber off to the side (entered through the remains of a 13th-century window), was built in 1511 as an office for Niccolò Machiavelli during his term as government secretary. A portrait by Santi di Tito, depicts the youthful, smiling author of *The Prince*, looking nothing like the demonic figure he was branded when this study of politics and pragmatism was published.

Just off the Sala dei Gigli is another small room, the Sala del Mappamondo (more commonly known as La Guardaroba – the wardrobe), containing a large 16th-century globe showing the extent of the then known world. The room is lined with wooden cupboards adorned with a remarkable series of maps; the 53 panels were painted in 1563 by Ignazio Danti and in 1581 by Stefano Buonsignori.

The Uffizi and the Ponte Vecchio

The Piazza degli Uffizi sits in the centre of the U-shaped building which houses the gallery, lined with statues of Italian personalities such as Dante and occupied by artists and entertainers. A reading of Giorgio Vasari's *Lives of the Artists* (1550), or Browning's poems based on them, is a good preparation for an encounter with the greatest works of the Renaissance, housed in the **Galleria degli Uffizi** ❹ *(see pages 110–13)*. Vasari's anecdotes teach us

Map on page 100

In 1580, the open loggia of the Uffizi administrative building was turned into rooms for the art collections of the Medici; effectively a galleria *enclosed in glass. Today's expression "art gallery" is derived from it.*

BELOW: the Uffizi and Vasari Corridor seen across the Arno.

not to be too adulatory, and to realise that many of the great artists were ordinary men, lustful, greedy and always willing to pander to the whims of their patrons.

When he designed the Uffizi, he incorporated a continuous corridor that runs from the Palazzo Vecchio, via the Uffizi and the Ponte Vecchio, to the Palazzo Pitti on the opposite bank of the Arno. Along this elevated walkway, known as the Corridoio Vasariano, symbolic of their pre-eminent status, Cosimo I and his heirs could walk between their palace and the seat of government without being soiled by contact with people they ruled. In 1737, Anna Maria Lodovica, the last of the Medici, bequeathed the entire collection of the museum and the corridor to the people of Florence.

Leaving the Uffizi, walk back to the river and turn right towards the Ponte Vecchio. Another right turn brings you into Via Por Santa Maria. Modern buildings here indicate that the original medieval buildings were deliberately demolished in World War II to block the approaches to the

Window shopping on the Ponte Vecchio.

BELOW: the Tuscan hills seen behind the Ponte Vecchio.

bridge and hold up the advancing Allies. The first turning right off Via Por Santa Maria leads to **Santo Stefano al Ponte ❺**, founded in around AD 969 and with a fine Romanesque facade of 1233. Now used as a concert hall, it also has a small museum (open Mon–Fri 3.30–7pm, Sat–Sun 10.30am–7pm; free entrance).

The narrow lanes east of this secluded piazza lead to buildings used as workshops for the goldsmiths and jewellers whose creations are sold in the kiosks lining the **Ponte Vecchio ❻**.

The oldest bridge

This bridge, as much a symbol of Florence as the Duomo or Palazzo Vecchio, dates, in its present form, from 1345, replacing an earlier wooden structure that was swept away in a flood. Workshops have always flanked the central carriageway, and in 1565 Vasari's Corridor, linking the Palazzo Pitti and the Palazzo Vecchio, was built high above the pavement along the eastern side.

In 1593, Ferdinando I, annoyed at the noxious trades that were carried on beneath his feet as he travelled the length of the corridor, ordered the butchers, tanners and blacksmiths to be evicted. The workshops were rebuilt and let to goldsmiths, and this traditional use has continued ever since, though no craftsmen work in the cramped but quaint premises any more.

Today, it is not just the shop-owners on the Ponte Vecchio who earn their livelihood from the million-plus visitors that are drawn to the bridge every year. Hawkers, buskers and portrait painters, artists and souvenir vendors all contribute to the festive atmosphere that prevails on the bridge, especially after dark. There is no better place for people-watching or taking in the attractive river views.

Reaching for the stars

Follow the river east along the Lungarno, taking in the view of the opposite bank, to the science museum in Piazza dei Giudici.

The **Museo di Storia della Scienza** ❼ (open Mon, Wed–Sat 9.30am–5pm, Tues 9.30am–1pm, last Thurs June, Aug and 1st Thur July, Sept 8–11pm, winter 2nd Sun of the month 10am–1pm; entrance charge) is the museum attached to the Institute of the History of Science, housed in Palazzo Castellani where recent restorations found evidence of an ancient castle. It is one of the most absorbing museums in Florence and a very welcome change after an over-indulgence in the arts. The exhibits show that Renaissance Florence was pre-eminent in Europe as a centre of scientific research as well as of painting and sculpture – indeed, the humanistic concept of the "universal man" did not recognise any dichotomy between the two.

A great deal of encouragement was given to scientific research by Cosimo II, who, it is said, saw the similarity of his own name to the cosmos as auspicious, and so he announced a grand scheme to master the universe through knowledge. The best mathematicians, astronomers and cartographers were hired from all over Europe and the Middle East, and their beautifully engraved astrolabes and armillary spheres, showing the motion of the heavenly bodies, are well displayed in this museum.

Ironically, though, the most brilliant scientist of his age, and the one whose discoveries and methodology laid the foundations for modern science, suffered greatly as a consequence. Galileo was popular enough when he discovered the first five moons of Jupiter and named them after members of the Medici family. He was appointed court mathematician, and his experiments in mechanics and the laws of motion must have given great pleasure to the Medici court, even if their true significance might not have been understood. Beautiful mahogany-and-brass reconstructions of these experiments, like giant executive toys, are displayed in the museum and demonstrated from time to time by the attendants.

But Galileo fell foul of the authorities when, from his own observations, he supported the Copernican view that the sun, and not the earth, was at the centre of the cosmos. Refusing to retract a view that ran counter to the teachings of the Church, he was tried before the Inquisition in 1633, excommunicated and made a virtual prisoner in his own home until his death in 1642.

As if to exculpate their collective guilt for this unjust treatment, Florence has devoted an entire room of the museum to the man and his work, and many regard him as the greatest Florentine (though he was, in fact, born in rival Pisa).

Map on page 100

Lungarno translates from Italian as "along the Arno". On both sides of the river in Florence, the streets are known as Lungarno This or Lungarno That.

BELOW:
Galileo in a drawing by Ottavio Leoni.

Map
on page
100

*Botticelli was one
of many artists
who ingratiated
themselves with the
Medici by featuring
them in their
paintings. Cosimo il
Vecchio and his
grandsons Giuliano
and Lorenzo the
Magnificent have
starring roles in
the* Adoration of
the Magi.

BELOW: inside the
Museo Horne.

Equally intriguing are the rooms devoted to maps and globes, which demonstrate how rapidly the discoveries of the 15th and 16th centuries were revolutionising old ideas about the shape of the world.

The early 16th-century map by Fra Mauro still defines the world in religious and mythological terms, with Jerusalem at the centre and the margins inhabited by menacing monsters. Only 50 years later, in 1554, Lopo Homem was producing a recognisably accurate map of the world, which had to be extended, even as it was being drawn, to accommodate the newly surveyed west coast of the Americas and discoveries in the Pacific, such as New Guinea.

Further east along the Arno

From the Museo di Storia della Scienza, diagonally opposite is Via dei Saponai, which leads to **Piazza Mentana 8**, the site of the Roman port. Via della Mosca follows the curve of this ancient harbour. At the point where it joins the Via dei Neri, cross to the junction with Via San Remigio to the building on the left that has two plaques high up on the wall. One records the level of the flood reached in 1333, and half a metre (2 ft) above it is the 1966 mark.

Via dei Neri leads to Via Benci and the **Museo Horne 9** (open Mon–Sat 9am–1pm; entrance charge). The best of the art collection assembled by the English art historian, Herbert Percy Horne (1864–1916), is now in the Uffizi, and, although there are no great treasures here, the remaining art includes Benozzo Gozzoli's last work, *The Deposition*, Giotto's golden-backed *St Stephen*, as well as works by Luca Signorelli and others. On the second floor is a diptych thought to be by Barna di Siena; also on display is a book containing 18th-century sketches by Tiepolo.

Latterly Horne's home, the building was first owned by the Alberti family, who then passed it on to the Corsi family in the 15th century. The Corsi were involved in the city's thriving cloth trade; washing and dyeing of fabrics took place underground, the tradings on the ground floor and family life on the upper floors. The *palazzino* has a delightful courtyard, and on view within are all kinds of memorabilia – the remnants of a distinguished life. The kitchen, built on the top floor to stop cooking fumes passing through the whole house, retains its original form – a simple range, chimney and sink – and is used to display Horne's collection of ancient pots and utensils.

Walking further east leads to the impressive-looking **Biblioteca Nazionale** (National Library) in Piazza delle Cavalleggeri, whilst immediately south, the Ponte alle Grazie is a modern bridge which was built to replace the Ponte Rubiconte, first built in 1237 and destroyed in 1944. Upstream, to the east, the modern stone embankment of the Arno gives way to natural grassy banks, trees and reeds. ❑

RESTAURANTS AND CAFÉS

Restaurants

Antico Fattore
Via Lambertesca 1/3r
Tel: 055-288975
www.mega.it/antico.fattore
Closed Sun. €€
A traditional trattoria near to the Uffizi which offers good meat and game dishes as well as the standard Tuscan and Florentine foods such as *trippa* (tripe) and *ribollita* (a soup made from vegetables and bread).

Buca dell'Orafo
Via dei Girolami 28r
Tel: 055-213619
L and D Tues–Sat. €€
A crowded little location which originated as a local hang-out but, to their chagrin, is now overrun with tourists. However, the simple peasant food – based on pasta and pulses – is filling and of good quality.

Frescobaldi
Via de' Magazzini 2/4r
Tel: 055-284724
www.frescobaldiwinebar.it
L and D; closed all day Sun and Mon L. €€–€€€
Tucked away in a nook, this lovely little place makes really flavoursome Tuscan dishes to complement their huge range of local wines. Try the roast pig with a glass of Chianti from the *cantina*. As a bonus they have outside seating in the summer.

Gustavino
Via della Condotta 37r
Tel: 055-2399806
www.gustavino.it
D only; closed Mon. €€€
This is a new and glossy restaurant whose open kitchen allows you to see your meal in preparation. The food is creative without being too elaborate and over-fussy and is served beautifully on large white plates. Look out for the speciality wine and food evenings they run, which can be booked via the website *(see above).*

Trattoria del Benvenuto
Via della Mosca 15r
Tel: 055-214833
Closed Sun. €–€€
This offers reasonably priced food in the centre of the city. It is a basic trattoria, but still popular with locals and tourists alike for its welcoming atmosphere.

Oliviero
Via delle Terme 51r
Tel: 055-212421
www.ristorante-oliviero.it
D only; closed Sun. €€€
Historical restaurant which markets itself as being part of the *dolce vita fiorentina* (the Florentine good life). The menu changes every couple of months and everything is prepared freshly in house – from the pasta to the desserts.

Vini e Vecchi Sapori
Via dei Magazzini 3r
Tel: 055-293045
L and D; closed all day Mon and Sun D. €–€€
Just off Piazza della Signoria, this remains a good bet for Tuscan food. The atmosphere manages to retain something of the Florentine despite the number of tourists who flock to the place.

Cafés

Caffè Italiano (Café)
Via della Condotta 56r
Tel: 055-289020
L and T; closed Sun.
This is an old-fashioned café decked out in wood and offering a range of beverages and light lunches. Relax with a newspaper or read a book over the decent coffee or one their speciality hot chocolates.

Rivoire
Piazza della Signoria 4r
Tel: 055-214412
www.rivoire.it
Closed Mon.
Grand café on the corner of the piazza famed for its chocolate products. Treat yourself to a coffee or *gelato* during the day or a cocktail in the early evening.

RIGHT: a tempting selection at Rivoire.

GLI UFFIZI

An overview of the greatest collection of Renaissance art to be found in the world

Florence's most famous gallery (open Tues–Sun 8.15am–6.50pm; entrance charge) is housed in a U-shaped building whose former use as administrative buildings gave it its name "The Offices". It now holds the highest concentration of Renaissance art in the world, including famous works by Botticelli, Leonardo, Michelangelo and Raphael. The majority of the collection originates from the Medici family, dating from the latter half of the 16th century when Francesco de' Medici decided to convert the second floor into a museum.

The gallery was left to the city at the end of the dynasty line and also contains the **Gabinetto Disegni e Stampe degli Uffizi** (Collection of Prints and Drawings; entrance included), the **Contini Bonacossi Collection** (temporarily closed, normally on request only; tel: 055-2388651; entrance included) and the **Corridoio Vasariano** (Vasari Corridor; closed at present; tel: 055-2654321 for information) which passes over the Ponte Vecchio and connects the Uffizi to the Palazzo Pitti. There are three different entrances into the museum for groups, individuals and individuals with tickets. The frequent long queues make it worthwhile buying tickets with a scheduled entry time in advance (055-294883 or www.florenceart.it).

The main collection is on the second floor, with some important rooms on the first and temporary exhibitions on the ground floor. The paintings are largely arranged chronologically by schools – moving from the predominantly Italian collection to some works by German, Flemish and Dutch masters.

ABOVE: The Botticelli Rooms (10–14) are the most popular exhibit in the Uffizi, containing the world's best collection of work by the artist. Here are the famous mythological paintings which fused ideas of the spiritual and the secular: the *Birth of Venus*, painted around 1485, and *Primavera*, painted around five years earlier. The meaning of the latter remains a subject of fervent discussion, whilst Venus has overtones of the Virgin Mary.

ABOVE: Room 15 exhibits Leonardo da Vinci's early works – including the *Annunciation* (1475) and the unfinished *Adoration of the Magi* (1982) – and also paintings by Perugino and Signorelli.

THE EASTERN CORRIDOR

The two corridors from which the 45 rooms lead off are filled with sculptures, whilst the strip connecting the sides allows magnificent views down the river and towards the Ponte Vecchio. Rooms 2–4 are dedicated to works from Siena and Florence during the Duecento and Trecento (13th and 14th centuries), exhibiting the decorative and iconographic pre-Renaissance style. Notable works are the interpretations of the Madonna by Giotto and Duccio, as well as that of Cimabue, Giotto's master.

Room 7 is dedicated to the Early Renaissance and its founders and leading figures, who include Masaccio and Uccello and, later, Fra Angelico. The Filippo Lippi Room (8) holds the Franciscan monk's lovely *Madonna with Angels*, as well as a number of other celebrated works and is worth visiting for Piero della Francesca's portraits of the Duke and Duchess of Urbino I *(pictured above)*. Room 9 holds works by the Pollaiuolo brothers, whose paintings show no distinctive style but are nonetheless decorative.

After a room of sculpture, the Tribuna (Room 18) is an octagonal room lit from above, with a mother-of-pearl encrusted ceiling, designed by Buontalenti. This room's structure, décor and holding was designed to allude to the four elements and used to exhibit the objects most highly prized by the Medici. It holds a collection of portraits and sculpture, as well as Rosso Fiorentino's super-famous *Putto Che Suona*, or *Angel Musician (pictured opposite)*. The circular route around the room unfortunately renders it somewhat difficult to appreciate the art from a good distance or to linger in front of the portraits.

BELOW: Rooms 5–6 form the International Gothic Rooms, whose paintings exhibit a more conservative and less lavish approach, in keeping with the medieval mindset. Lorenzo Monaco's *Crowning of Mary* provides a good example of this by one of the main practitioners of the era.

ABOVE: The High Renaissance continues in Room 19, which exhibits Perugino and Signorelli's work. These Umbrian artists worked during the 15th and 16th centuries, and the latter's tondo (circular painting) *Holy Family* is reputed to have inspired Michelangelo's version. Room 20 is a break from Italian art, with work by Dürer (including his *Madonna and the Pear* pictured here) and Cranach. The last few rooms on the eastern corridor hold works from the 15th and 16th centuries: the Venetian school in Room 21, followed by Holbein and other Flemish and German realists (22) and more Italian work by Mantegna and Correggio in Room 23. Room 24 contains a collection of miniatures.

THE WESTERN CORRIDOR

The western corridor starts with the Michelangelo room and his vivid *Holy Family* tondo *(below)*. This prelude to Mannerism was produced for the wedding of Angelo Doni to Maddalena Strozzi, and the depth of the figures betrays Michelangelo's penchant for sculpture. Early works by Raphael – such as the glowing *Madonna of the Goldfinch* – and Andrea del Sarto's *Madonna of the Harpies* can be seen in this room. The subsequent room (27) is the last to focus on Tuscan art before moving on to other regions of Italy.

LEFT: Room 28 displays work by Titian, including the erotic *Venus of Urbino (left)*. Rooms 29–30 focus on Emilia-Romagnan art and the Mannerists Dosso Dossi and Parmigianino. Veronese's *Annunciation* is in Room 31, while Tintoretto's sensual *Leda and the Swan* hangs in Room 32. A number of rooms are now dedicated to minor works of the Cinquecento (16th century) before the Flemish art of Rubens and van Dyck in Room 41. The Sala della Niobe has reopened and holds sculpture, whilst Room 43 has works by Rembrandt.

On the first floor are five rooms of paintings as well as the Verone sull'Arno – the bottom of the U-shaped corridor which looks over the Arno and the Piazza degli Uffizi the other side.

The Sala del Caravaggio holds three paintings by the troubled artist whose style is characterised by his realism and use of light *(see his* Sacrificing of Isaac, *right)*. His method inspired the works by other artists contained in the same room and the next three: the Sala di Bartolommeo Manfredi, the Sala di Gherardo delle Notti and the Sala dei Caravaggeschi.

The last room adjacent to the Verone is the Sala di Guido Reni, where three paintings by the classicist artist of the first half of the 17th century are displayed.

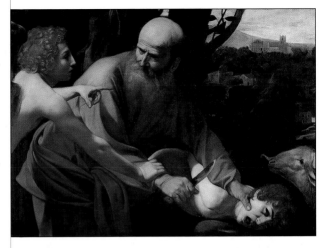

Gabinetto and Contini Bonacossi Collezione

The Gabinetto, recently situated on the second floor, holds a number of important and precious drawings – including works by Renaissance masters (such as Fra Bartolommeo's *Portrait of a Young Woman, right*), some of which are only viewable for academic study purposes. The Contini Bonacossi Collection was recently installed in the Uffizi (moved from its previous home in Palazzo Pitti) and contains paintings, furniture, majolica and coats of arms.

Galleria degli Uffizi

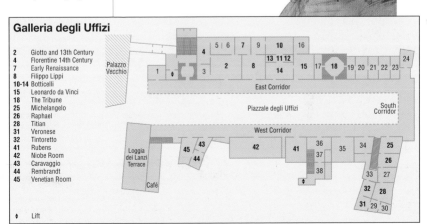

2	Giotto and 13th Century
4	Florentine 14th Century
7	Early Renaissance
8	Filippo Lippi
10-14	Botticelli
15	Leonardo da Vinci
18	The Tribune
25	Michelangelo
26	Raphael
28	Titian
31	Veronese
32	Tintoretto
41	Rubens
42	Niobe Room
43	Caravaggio
44	Rembrandt
45	Venetian Room

Palazzo Vecchio

East Corridor

Piazzale degli Uffizi

South Corridor

West Corridor

Loggia dei Lanzi Terrace

Café

✥   Lift

SANTA CROCE AND THE NORTHEAST

Stars of this section of the city, which still bustles with
Florentines getting on with day-to-day chores,
include the austere Bargello and the serene
Santa Croce, another symbol of civic pride

The densely populated area on the north bank of the River Arno, east of the Palazzo Vecchio, was the workers' quarter of medieval Florence, its narrow alleys packed with the workshops of cloth-dyers and weavers. The human toll in the 1966 flood was greater here than anywhere in the city, and numerous wall plaques set 6 metres (20 ft) up show the level that it reached at its peak. After the flood, many former residents were rehoused elsewhere, but it remains an area of workshops, early-morning markets, low-built houses and pre-Renaissance towers.

Piazza San Firenze ❶, where seven streets meet, is busy with traffic – which everyone manages to ignore as they stop to chat or have a cup of coffee on the way to work. On the west side, a florist's shop occupies one of the most graceful courtyards in the city, that of **Palazzo Gondi ❷**.

The provision of the stone benches running round the base of the palace, called *muriccioli*, for public use was once a condition of planning permission, but the ubiquitous pigeon has now ensured that few Florentines choose to exercise their ancient right to sit in the shade of the palace walls and pass the time of day.

Opposite is the Baroque church of **San Firenze ❸** (1772–5), now partly housing the Tribunale, the city law courts. To the left, **San Filippo Neri** still functions as a church.

Heading north, on the left is the Badia Fiorentina; the entrance is on Via Dante *(see page 131)*.

The Bargello and Via del Proconsolo

Opposite the Badia is the rather grim-looking **Bargello ❹** *(see pages 126–7)*, begun in 1255 as the

Map on page 116

LEFT: the altar in Santa Croce.
BELOW: a *palazzo* fresco on Piazza Santa Croce.

The unfortunate fate of the notorious Bernardo Baroncelli was recorded for posterity by none other than Leonardo da Vinci, who sketched the body as it swung from a Bargello window; a clear warning to other anti-Medici conspirators.

city's first town hall but later used as a court and prison. Bernardo Baroncelli was among those hanged from its walls; he was put to death in 1478 for his part in the Pazzi conspiracy, an ill-judged attempt to wrest power from the hands of the Medici.

From the Bargello, the Via del Proconsolo runs north past the **Palazzo Pazzi ❺**, built in 1458–69, before the anti-Medici conspiracy, and unusually handsome, with roses, moons and ball-flowers decorating the upper windows.

The next building on the right – No. 12 – across Borgo degli Albizi is the **Palazzo Nonfinito** (The Unfinished Palace) – begun by Bernardo Buontalenti in 1593 but still incomplete when it became Italy's first anthropological museum in 1869.

This **Museo di Antropologia e Etnologia ❻** (open Mon, Tues, Thur, Fri and Sun 9am–1pm, Sat

9am–5pm; entrance charge) forms part of the Museum of Natural History – a complex of six sites run by the university. This museum contains native art from the former Italian colonies in Africa, as well as objects collected by Captain James Cook on his last voyage to the Pacific in 1776–9.

There are fascinating exhibits from all over the world, from Peruvian mummies to Arctic clothing (made from whale and dolphin intestines), musical instruments and Polynesian wood-carvings .

Backstreets and ice cream

Leading off Via del Proconsolo is Borgo degli Albizi, at the end of which lies Piazza San Pier Maggiore, a busy little square with the odd market stall below the ruined portico of the church that gave the square its name, and a couple of cheap restaurants and bars. It is also a hang-out for junkies and drunks,

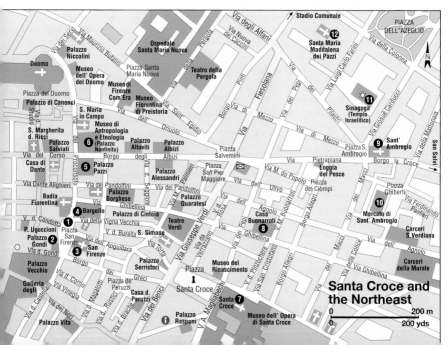

who congregate around the seedy Vicolo di San Piero. This area, and the narrow streets that lead south from it, are different in character to much of the city centre. The low houses and unadorned towers recall the medieval city that existed before wealthy merchants began building grandiose palaces.

Via Matteo Palmieri leads to Via Isola delle Stinche. Here you find the Palazzo di Cintoia, a solid medieval building with *sporti* – massive stone brackets which support the upper storeys, jettied out over the narrow street to increase the living space. The ground floor now houses a smart *osteria* and a pizzeria.

Further along the road, the recently smartened-up **Gelateria Vivoli** is regarded as the home of the world's best ice cream – this is not their own claim, in fact, but that of numerous journalists, whose articles have spread the name and fame of the *gelateria* worldwide. Long queues in summer are commonplace, but these are worth enduring for the alcoholic *zabaglioni* or rich chestnut ice cream – just two of the numerous tempting choices. It is a stand-up only bar, so you might as well buy a tub and move on.

You can continue south to the Via Torta, where the pronounced curve of the street reflects the outline of the Roman amphitheatre (which was still standing when the medieval houses were built up against its walls), and into the **Piazza Santa Croce**.

The football piazza

Here, in Piazza Santa Croce, you can sit and watch young Florentines play football with all the skill and control that will surely make some of them international stars one day. A form of football has been played here since the 16th century – a plaque on the frescoed **Palazzo dell'**

Antella (No. 21), dated 1565, marks the centre line of the pitch. Today, Piazza Santa Croce remains the venue for the violent *calcio in costume* (or *calcio storico*) football game, played on the Feast of San Giovanni (24 June) and three other Sundays in late June or early July.

The square was also used for jousting tournaments between teams from each of the city's wards, and for public spectacles, animal fights and fireworks, mounted by the Medici grand dukes. During the Inquisition, heretics were burnt here, and paintings, mirrors, embroidered clothing and other finery were piled onto great "bonfires of vanity".

The Florentine pantheon

The church of **Santa Croce** ❼ (complex open Mon–Sat 9am–5.30pm, Sun 1–5.30pm; entrance charge), originally a Franciscan foundation, was one of three – with the Duomo and Santa Maria Novella – that were built and funded by the Comune, the city government, as public buildings and sym-

Map on page 116

Vivoli ice cream.

BELOW: flowers and vegetables for sale near the Bargello.

Piazza Santa Croce's statue of Dante.

bols of civic pride. The colour scheme of all three are identical, as are the crowds which flock to the steps both at night and during the day. It was one of the largest churches in the Christian world when built and was used as a burial place for the great and the good of Florence.

Monuments

Monuments to Dante, Petrarch, Boccaccio, Michelangelo and other luminaries attracted 19th-century travellers in great numbers, who came as pilgrims to the shrines of the creators of Western civilisation. Foreigners paid for the unfortunate 1842 neo-Gothic facade and campanile and the lifeless statue of Dante in the square.

But this should not deter, for the interior of Santa Croce (enter on Largo Piero Bargellini) is a splendid example of true Gothic – huge and airy, with a richly painted ceiling and an uninterrupted view of the polygonal sanctuary, whose tall lancet windows are filled with 14th-century stained glass.

A series of tombs in the aisles begins, on the right, with Giorgio Vasari's monument to Michelangelo – an irony here, for the artist who left Florence after refusing to work for the repressive Medici ended up buried beneath the tomb carved by the Medici's chief propagandist.

Next is a massive 19th-century cenotaph to Dante (who is buried in Ravenna), surmounted by an uncharacteristically crabby and introverted portrait of the poet, flanked by neoclassical female figures. Further on is an 18th-century monument to Niccolò Machiavelli and Donatello's partly gilded stone relief of the *Annunciation*.

Beyond lies one of the earliest and most influential funerary monuments of the Renaissance, the tomb of Leonardo Bruni – humanist, historian and eminent politician – by Rossellino (1446–7). It was widely imitated, but rarely so ineptly as in the neighbouring 19th-century tomb of the composer Rossini.

In the floor near by are numerous niello-work tomb slabs covering the graves of Florentine worthies. Con-

BELOW:
Santa Croce's facade.

Map
on page
116

tinuing right, into the south transept, the Capello Castellani is decorated with frescos by Agnolo Gaddi (*c.* 1385), and contains the tomb of the Countess of Albany. She was the widow of Prince Charles Edward Stuart – Bonnie Prince Charlie – who fled to Italy after defeat at the Battle of Culloden in Scotland (1746) and settled in Florence under the spurious title of Count of Albany (Albion being the archaic name for Britain).

Giotto and his pupil

The Cappella Baroncelli contains frescos dating from 1332–8 and once thought to be by Giotto, but now attributed to his pupil Taddeo Gaddi, father of Agnolo. He was no slavish imitator of his teacher's work, but an innovator in his own right. The scene in which the angels announce the birth of Christ to the shepherds is one of the earliest attempts to paint a night scene in fresco.

A corridor to the right leads to the sacristy, with its gorgeous 16th-century inlaid wooden cupboards,

and a souvenir shop whose walls are hung with photographs of the 1966 flood. At the end of the corridor a chapel, usually locked, contains the tomb where Galileo was buried until 1737. He was originally denied burial within the church because his contention that the sun, not the earth, was at the centre of the solar system earned him the condemnation of the Inquisition *(see page 120)*. In 1737, however, he was moved to a place of honour in the north aisle.

Returning to the church, the frescos in the two chapels to the right of the high altar were done by Giotto. The Cappella Bardi, on the left (*c.* 1315–20), shows the life of St Francis, and the Cappella Peruzzi, to the right (*c.* 1326–30), depicts the lives of St John the Baptist and St John the Divine.

These fabulous frescos have been through the wars; they were whitewashed over in the early 18th century, rediscovered only in 1852 and finally restored in 1959. Although fragmentary, they are the best surviving work in Florence of the man

The night scene by Gaddi.

BELOW: the cloister of Santa Croce.

who introduced a new clarity, energy and colour into the art of the fresco and influenced generations of artists to come.

In the north transept, Donatello's wooden *Crucifixion* in the second Cappella Bardi is said to be the one that his friend Brunelleschi dismissed as making Christ look like "a peasant, not a man". You might like to compare this with Brunelleschi's own attempt at the same subject if you visit Santa Maria Novella church *(see page 161)*.

Further up the north aisle, near the west doors, is Galileo's tomb, erected in 1737 in belated recognition of his fundamental contributions to modern science; in the nave floor near by is the tomb slab of his ancestor and namesake, a physician of some standing in 15th-century Florence.

Galileo's tomb, Santa Croce.

Cloisters of serenity

The cloister walk is lined with 19th-century monuments, fascinating for their muddled combination of Christian and pagan classical subjects and only just the right side of mawkishness. It leads to the Cappella de' Pazzi, one of the purest works of the Renaissance, a serene composition of grey stone and white walls, of arches, domes, scallops and blank arcading, and featuring 12 tondi in terracotta of the Apostles by Luca della Robbia.

Brunelleschi planned the chapel in 1430, but the work did not begin until 1443 and was completed after his death in 1446. It shows that even the inventor of Renaissance architecture sometimes faltered, for the fragmentary corner pilasters, squeezed into the angles, are an uncomfortable punctuation of the overall grand design.

The small **Museo dell' Opera di Santa Croce** is housed in the monastic buildings across the first cloister. The second cloister is arguably the most beautiful in all Florence, completely enclosed by hemispherical arches on slender columns, with a medallion in each of the spandrels.

The refectory here contains detached frescos, removed from the church to expose earlier works, and Cimabue's *Crucifixion*. Although it was restored after having been virtually ruined in the 1966 flood, it is still in rather poor condition and serves as a reminder both of the tragic consequences of that event and of just how much great art did, in fact, survive.

Artists in different guises

North of Santa Croce, reached by walking up Via delle Pinzochere, is the **Casa Buonarroti ⑧**, the house of the man we know better by his Christian name, Michelangelo (No. 70 Via Ghibellina; open Wed–Mon 9.30am–2pm; entrance charge). He never lived here, but bought the property as an investment, and his heirs turned it into a museum in 1858. It contains one outstanding sculpture – the *Madonna della*

Galileo: Man of Controversy

Although born in Pisa, astronomer and mathematician Galileo Galilei had strong ties with Florence. His first contact came shortly after he left university, when he taught mathematics in the city. But the real connection came in the early 1600s, when – after hearing about a "spyglass" exhibited by a Dutchman in Venice – he made a series of telescopes, through which he made a number of astronomical discoveries. Among them, he saw four small bodies orbiting Jupiter, which – in an astute attempt to further his career – he named "the Medicean stars". The fawning move worked: Galileo was soon appointed Mathematician and Philosopher to the Grand Duke of Tuscany. He also became a more outspoken proponent of the Copernican system, which theorised that everything revolved around the sun. This, together with his observance of sunspots, and craters and peaks on the moon – which challenged Aristotle's proposition that heavenly bodies were divine and therefore blemish-free – did not sit well with the Catholic Church, which condemned him and sent him into exile, first in Siena and finally in his villa in Arcetri, just outside of Florence. He remained there under house arrest until his death in 1642.

Scala, thought to be his earliest work, carved when he was only 15 years old. It is a remarkably humane and noble relief, in which the Virgin lifts her tunic to comfort the infant Christ with the softness of her breasts whilst Joseph labours in the background.

As for the rest of the museum, it is best enjoyed as a rare glimpse inside a 16th-century *palazzo*, frescoed and furnished in the style of the time. Most of the exhibits are of work once attributed to Michelangelo, or paintings and sculpture inspired by his work. They serve only to highlight the difference between a great artist and the deservedly unknown.

Sant' Ambrogio and the northeast

Via Buonarroti leads north from Michelangelo's house to one of the most bustling areas of Florence, Sant'Ambrogio. Taking its name from the parish church, this is an area of narrow streets filled with dusty junk shops, local bars, grocer's shops and crumbling facades

strung with drying laundry. It is also an area that is becoming increasingly trendy of late, so these same crumbling facades often hide upmarket apartments within.

Just east of the junction of Via Buonarroti and Via Pietrapiana, in Piazza dei Ciompi, is the **Loggia del Pesce**, which was designed by Vasari in 1568. The delicate arcade is decorated with roundels full of leaping fish and crustaceans, but it is no longer used as a fish market. It was moved here in the 19th century when the Mercato Vecchio was demolished to create the Piazza della Repubblica. By day, it is a market for junk and "near antiques". By night it is a rendezvous for prostitutes and their clients.

The nearby church of **Sant' Ambrogio ❾**, at the southeastern end of Via dei Pilastri, was built on the site of a house where St Ambrose stayed whilst visiting the city in AD 393. Despite its 19th-century neo-Gothic facade, the fine church within is 10th century in date and is full of interesting features. One is the splendid marble taberna-

Map on page 116

A bust on Casa Buonarroti.

BELOW: Brunelleschi's Cappella dei Pazzi.

cle in the sanctuary to the left of the high altar. This was designed in 1481 by Mino da Fiesole to house a miraculous communion chalice that was one day found to contain several drops of real blood rather than symbolic wine. Some delightful frescos by Cosimo Rosselli (painted in 1486) tell the story.

Located further to the south, in Piazza Ghiberti, is the **Mercato di Sant' Ambrogio** , the second-largest produce market in the city (the biggest is the Mercato Centrale). It is housed in a somewhat deteriorating cast-iron market hall constructed in 1873, and is a wonderfully lively place to do the shopping in the company of locals.

A synagogue and two masterpieces

From the market, it is a short walk back to Piazza Sant' Ambrogio, up Via dei Pilastri and right up Via Farini, to the **Sinagoga** ⓫ (Tempio Israelitico), the huge synagogue (built in the Hispano-Moresque style between 1874 and 1882) whose green copper-covered dome

is such a prominent feature of the Florentine skyline. Cosimo I founded Florence's ghetto for the city's Jewish community here in 1551; the original place of worship was demolished in the mid-19th century, and a new synagogue built in its place. There is a small museum here which documents the history of the Jews in Florence (synagogue and museum open Sun–Thur 10am–5pm, Fri 10am–2pm; entrance charge).

It is somewhat sobering to think that, had the 19th-century city planners had their way, a significant section of the city from here west to the Piazza della Repubblica would have been demolished and redeveloped as grand avenues.

At the end of the road sits Piazza dell'Azeglio – one of the quieter recreational spaces in Florence. From this point, Via della Colonna leads to Borgo Pinti. A left turn back towards the centre of town at this point passes the entrance to the church of **Santa Maria Maddalena dei Pazzi** ⓬ (open Mon–Sat 9am–noon, 4.45–5.20pm, 6.15–6.50pm,

Florence's synagogue towers above the surrounding rooftops.

BELOW: Hebrew on the synagogue.

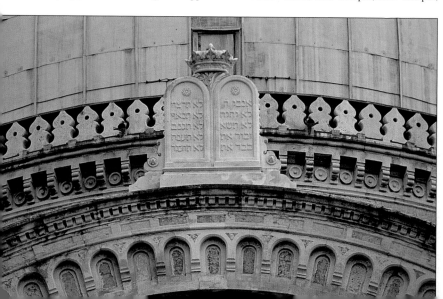

Sun 9am–10.45am, 4.45–6.50pm; donation expected), dedicated to the Florentine nun who was a descendant of the anti-Medici conspirators. She died in 1609 and was canonised in 1685, when the church was renamed in her honour. It was originally run by the Cistercian order, but the Carmelites took over in 1628. In 1926, Augustinian monks moved in, and remain here to this day.

The church originally dates from the 15th century and has a lovely quiet cloister of 1492 formed of square Tuscan columns with flat, rather than rounded, classical arches. The fresco of the Crucifixion in the chapter house – which is entered from the crypt – is one of Perugino's masterpieces, painted in 1493–6. The figures kneeling in adoration of their Saviour are glimpsed, as if through a window, between a series of *trompe l'œil* arches.

The Cross of Christ is set in a delightful landscape of winding rivers and wooded hills, and the whole scene is lit by a limpid blue light. Perugino (*c.* 1445–1523), whose real name was Pietro Van-

nucci, was a founder of the Umbrian School of artists.

Further out of town (2 km/1 mile to the east), at No. 16 Via San Salvi, is the 14th-century church of the former monastery of San Salvi, (open Tues–Sun 8.15am–1.50pm; free entrance). It houses one of the most famous of all Renaissance frescos, Andrea del Sarto's *Last Supper*..

Football stadium

Also a little out of town, to the northeast of Santa Maria Maddalena dei Pazzi, is the huge **Stadio Comunale**, one of the city's few modern buildings of any architectural merit (with the exception of Michelucci's Santa Maria Novella station building), capable of holding 66,000 spectators and designed by Pier Luigi Nervi in 1932. It is the home of the city's football club, Fiorentina.

Along the road leading to it, Viale dei Mille, lies the **Sette Santi Church** – a neo-Gothic, neo-Romanesque fusion which is attractive and different from many of Florence's many churches. ❑

Map on page 116

Luca della Robbia – whose work graces the Cappella dei Pazzi in Santa Croce, as well as many other buildings in Florence – perfected the art of glazed terracotta and kept the technique a secret, known only to his family, who thereby enriched themselves mightily.

BELOW:
Fiorentina celebrate.

RESTAURANTS, CAFÉS AND BARS

Restaurants

Alle Murate
Via Ghibellina 52r
Tel: 055-240618
www.caffeitaliano.it
Closed Mon. €€€€
Part of the Caffè Italiano ownership, this is one of the new generation of Florentine restaurants offering nouvelle cuisine. It offers a creative twist on Tuscan food – there is lots of fish and tender Chianina steak.

Antico Noè
Volta di San Piero 6r
Tel: 055-2340838
Closed Sun. €
Tiny place which offers authentic Tuscan food at cheap prices. Recommended is the *tagliatelle ai porcini* (mushroom tagliatelle).

Aqua al Due
Via della Vigna Vecchia 40r
Tel: 055-284170
www.acquaal2.it
D only. €€
A real dining experience which requires booking ahead due to its popularity. If you have room, try the *assaggi di primi* (five pasta dishes as chosen by the chef) followed by the *assaggi di dolci* (a selection of the dessserts of the day).

Baldovino (Enoteca)
Via San Giuseppe 18r
Tel: 055-2347220
L & D. €€
Following the success of his trattoria *(see below)*, Scotsman David Gardner set up this wine bar with his lawyer wife. It's more intimate and modern than the restaurant below, and the food is marginally superior, with a wide selection of wines.

Baldovino (Trattoria)
Via San Giuseppe 22r
Tel: 055-241773
L & D. €€
This place offers a little bit of everything – great pasta, pizzas, salads, and a few more sophisticated dishes – providing a welcome change from traditional Florentine restaurants. Very popular with tourists.

Caffè Italiano (Osteria)
Via Isola delle Stinche 11/13r
Tel: 055-289368
www.caffeitaliano.it
L and D; closed Mon. €€€€
A smart restaurant set inside the 14th-century Salviati Palace. It offers a changing menu of high-quality Tuscan cuisine in a pleasant atmosphere. Try the huge Florentine *bistecca* to share.

Caffè Italiano (Pizzeria)
Via Isola delle Stinche 11/13r
Tel: 055-289368
www.caffeitaliano.it
D only; closed Mon. €
The tastiest pizza in Florence, with entertainment from the chef often included. Only three varieties – *marinara*, *margherita* and *napoletana* – are offered, and it is worth visiting enough times to try them all. This place is highly recommended – though ask for a table in the back room for a more intimate atmosphere.

Cibrèo
Via del Verrocchio 8r
Tel: 055/2341100
www.cibreo.com
Tues-Sat. €€€€
A justly famous restaurant; elegant yet relaxed, one of the most popular resturants with visitors and Florentines alike. The fare is Tuscan with an innovative twist. Eat much the same food but for a cheaper price in the trattoria section, which is entered from Piazza Ghiberti.

Enoteca Pinchiorri
Via Ghibellina 87
Tel: 055-242777
www.enotecapinchiorri.com
Closed Sun and Mon; D only Tues and Wed.
€€€€
A gourmet paradise and garlanded with awards; hailed by some as one of the best restaurants in Europe and scorned by others as pretentious. The only way to find out is by taking your credit card in hand and diving in. Tuscan food with a French influence and an outstanding wine list. Booking is absolutely essential.

Finesterrae
Via de' Pepi 3/5r
Tel: 055-2638675
D daily. €€-€€€
Mediterranean bar and restaurant with a choice

selection of food from a number of cuisines. Start with tapas, followed by a Moroccan-style *tagine* or pasta dish. The atmosphere is relaxed and sultry, especially in the bar area.

La Giostra
Borgo Pinti 12r
Tel: 055-241341
www.ristorantelagiostra.com
L and D daily. €€€
This is a renowned restaurant run by a Habsburg prince. The crostini are delicious, as are the range of pasta dishes on offer.

Godò
Piazza Edison 3/4r
Tel: 055-583881
B, L and D; closed Sun.
€€–€€€
A little out of town but on the bus route to Fiesole, this restaurant offers wonderful meals throughout the day. The *gnocchi al pomodoro* (gnocchi in tomato sauce) are lovely and the salads generous.

I' Paci (Bar Degustazione)
Via dei Neri 37r
Tel: 055-287252
L and D daily. €
Incredibly cheap little place offering a set and changing menu including pastas and salads as well as appetizers. The staff are very friendly – a real Italian experience in the heart of Florence.

La Pentola dell'Oro
Via di Mezzo 24/26r
Tel: 055-241808
www.lapentoladelloro.it
Closed Sun. €€–€€€
As well as being unique, this is one of the friendliest restaurants in the city. Chef Giuseppe Alessi is more than willing to explain the dishes; the recipes are inspired by medieval and Renaissance cookery.

Il Pizzaiuolo
Via dei Macci 113r
Tel: 055-241171
Closed Sun. €–€€
The pizzas here are neopolitan-style wonders, with lots more on offer, including generous mixed antipasto.

Ruth's
Via Farini 2
Tel: 055-2480888
L and D; closed Fri D. €
Next to the synagogue this little place is one of the few to cater for vegetarians and offers a range of kosher and Middle Eastern-style dishes.

Targa
Lungarno Colombo 7
Tel: 055-677377
www.targabistrot.net
L and D; closed Sun.
€€€
Formerly Caffè Concerto, this bistrot has a delightful riverside setting where the Tuscan food is given a creative edge.

Cafés, Bars and Gelaterie

Caffè Benci
Via dei Benci 13r
L and T.
A small, relaxed café next to the *osteria* of the same name, where drinks and *panini* are served from the early morning to the late evening. Alternatively, pop to the restaurant next door for something more substantial.

Caffè Piansa
Via Borgo Pinti 18r
Tel: 055-2342362
L and T.
A café that is popular with locals, the cheap tasty dishes are great for a quick lunch.

Gelateria dei Neri
Via dei Neri 20/22r
Tel: 055-210034
Wonderfully creamy ice cream in a range of fruit and sweet flavours. In summer try the granitas and *frappés*.

Gelateria Vivoli
Isola delle Stinche 7
Tel: 055-292334
www.vivoli.it
Reputed to be the best gelateria in Florence. Try the amaretto and tiramisu flavours.

The Lion's Fountain
Borgo degli Albizi 34r
Tel: 055-2344412
www.pubflorence.com
Evenings only.
This overpriced but cheery Irish pub also has a range of *panini* and bar snacks.

The William
Via Magliabechi 7/9/11r
Tel: 055-2638357
An English pub just off Piazza Santa Croce. It offers pub grub and a good range of beers and lagers.

PRICE CATEGORIES

Prices for three-course dinner per person with a glass of wine:
€ = under €25
€€ = €25–€40
€€€ = €40–€60
€€€€ = more than €60

LEFT: delicious *porcini* mushrooms.
RIGHT: local sausages are particularly good.

THE BARGELLO

This renowned museum holds Florence's most important sculptures from the Medici and private collections

The *palazzo* was transformed into a museum in 1865, its previous uses as the seat of the city's chief magistrate and later as a prison are reflected by features of the building such as the décor, and the street names of the surrounding area. Entry into the rooms of the museum (open Mon–Sun 8.15am–1.50pm; closed 2nd and 4th Mon, 1st, 3rd and 5th Sun of the month; admission charge) take the visitor through the medieval courtyard whose walls are adorned with emblems of the city wards, magistrates and governors. *Oceanus* by Giambologna is one of the sculptures housed under the vaulted cloisters, which lead off to the right of the staircase into the Sala del Cinquecento. The entrance to this room – which contains a range of Renaissance statues, busts and bas-reliefs in marble and bronze – is flanked by two lions. Of particular note in the room are a number of works by Cellini – a Florentine bronze scupltor of lesser fame – and 16th-century contemporaries such as Ammannati and others complete the collection in this room. An external staircase leads to the second floor and a number of bronze sculptures of birds on display in the loggia, originally made by Giambologna for the Medici Villa di Castello.

ABOVE AND BELOW: the Bargello museum (above in an 18th-century painting by Giuseppe Zocchi) is situated in an impressive Gothic *palazzo* constructed in the mid 13th-century on Via del Proconsolo, the heart of the ancient city.

ABOVE: Donatello's famous version of *David* (from 1430–40) is on display in the Donatello Gallery – a small bronze most renowned for being the first nude since antiquity. It differs dramatically from Michelangelo's masterpiece not just in size and material, but also in its coyness and melancholy, which some view as more faithful to David's youth.

TOP RIGHT: four of Michelangelo's early sculptures are on display in the Sala del Cinquecento: *Bacchus Drunk*, the Pitti Tondo – a depiction of the Madonna and Child shown here – *Apollo-David* and *Brutus*.

ABOVE: in the Donatello room are the bronze panels submitted by Ghiberti and Brunelleschi *(above)* for the Baptistry doors.

THE DONATELLO AND BRONZE GALLERIES

The Salone del Consiglio Generale is often nicknamed the Donatello Gallery. Apart from *David*, other works by Donatello in the room worth paying attention to are *Saint George*, which was designed for the Orsanmichele church, and *Cupid*. The walls and ceiling of the room figure several glazed terracotta works by Luca della Robbia, whilst the adjoining chapel (the Cappella Maddalena) features attractive frescos depicting hell: look out for the figure on the right dressed in maroon thought to be the depiction of Dante. Also on the first floor is a corridor displaying an eclectic group of 5th to 17th century objets d'art, including ivories and Islamic treasures.

Upstairs, the Verrocchio Room displays Tuscan sculpture from the late 15th century, including portrait busts of notable Florentines and an interpretation of David by the artist who lends his name to the room, Andrea del Verrocchio. The adjoining rooms are filled with work by members of the della Robbia family – predominantly Andrea and Giovanni – dominated by the often overbearing large reliefs coloured in yellow, green and blue.

The last major room in the museum is the Bronze Gallery. This has one of the most rewarding displays in the Bargello. The sculptures generally depict mythological tales or Greek history, in the form of both models and more functional articles such as candelabra. The model for Giambologna's *Rape of the Sabines* (on display in the Loggia dei Lanzi) stands out, as do two other of his statues: *Kneeling Nymph* and *Hercules and Antaeus*. Completing the second floor is a collection of medals.

RIGHT: Giambologna's bronze of Mercury is in the Sala del Cinquecento.

PIAZZA DELLA REPUBBLICA

This part of Florence is one of stereotypical contrasts:
although vestiges of the ancient city remain,
these are mixed with 21st-century neon.
Still, the area has its attractions

F raming the western exit dividing the covered walkway that runs along **Piazza della Repubblica ❶** is a triumphal arch bearing a pompous inscription to the effect that "the ancient heart of the city was restored to new life from its former squalor in 1895".

With hindsight, the message has the hollow ring of irony. The plan to develop central Florence was conceived between 1865 and 1871, when the city was, briefly, the capital of Italy. The ancient and "squalid" buildings of the former ghetto – a reminder of feudal, divided Italy – were to be swept away and replaced by broad avenues, symbolic of the new age of the United Kingdom of Italy.

Florence in peril

The site of the Roman forum, at the heart of Florence, was chosen as the appropriate place to begin this transformation. Down came the 14th-century Mercato Vecchio – then still the principal food market in the city – and along with it numerous cafés and taverns with names like Inferno and Purgatorio (names still preserved in the streets southwest of the square). These had been the haunt of artists and writers who later adopted the new café in the square, the Giubbe Rosse.

At this point, enter the interfering foreigner, determined that medieval Florence should be preserved. Was it the cries of "halt" that went up all over Europe that saved the city or simply lack of money to see the scheme through?

In any event, demolition ceased, and the square, with its swish cafés, department stores and billboards, remains a modern intrusion into the heart of the city; useful as a counterpoint to the rest of Florence for, as one turns away and heads for the

Map on page 130

LEFT:
arcades on the Piazza della Repubblica.
BELOW:
caricatures of famous visitors to the café Giubbe Rosse.

narrow medieval streets, the sombre old buildings seem all the more endearing for their contrast to the 19th-century pomp.

By means of Via degli Speziale, which intersects the two main streets, and the lively Via del Corso, you reach the part of the city associated with Dante. In the Corso is **Santa Margherita dei Ricci**, a small church which hosts music concerts in the evenings. A little further on, opposite the Palazzo Salviati (now a bank), an alley leads to the little 11th-century church of **Santa Margherita dei Cerchi ❷** (on the left), which contains a fine 13th-century altarpiece by Neri di Bicci.

The charming Beatrice

This is where Dante is said to have married Gemma Donati and where, some years earlier, he regularly set eyes on nine-year old Beatrice Portinari, a girl whose beauty he considered to be nothing short of divine.

Infatuated, he experienced the most violent passions on the few occasions on which he was able to speak to her, while she, heavily chaperoned and destined to marry a rich banker, regarded him as a figure of fun. Three years after her marriage she died, so that she never read the *Divine Comedy* in which Dante presented her as the embodiment of every perfection.

Nearly opposite the church, on the right, is the **Casa di Dante ❸** (open Wed–Mon summer 10am–5pm, winter 10am–4pm; entrance fee), claimed as the poet's birthplace. The tower is 13th-century, the rest an attractive group of old houses restored in the 19th century and joined together to create a museum of material relating to the poet's work. In fact, there is virtually nothing in the way of original material there.

A right turn leads into the tiny **Piazza San Martino**, with its 13th-

A waiter in Piazza della Repubblica.

century Torre della Castagna, one of the best-preserved of the towers that once filled central Florence, soaring to 60 metres (200 ft) or more until the city government imposed a ban on structures that were more than 15 metres (50 ft) in height.

During the turbulent 13th and 14th centuries, the private armies of warring factions organised hit-and-run attacks on their enemies from towers such as these.

Politics and exile

This particular tower also served, briefly in 1282, as the residence of the *priori*, as they awaited the completion of the Palazzo Vecchio, the new town hall. The *priori* consisted of six members of the leading guilds, the Arte Maggiore, elected to serve two-month terms on the city council.

Dante, a member of the Guild of Physicians and Apothecaries (books were then sold in apothecary shops), was elected to the priorate to serve between 15 June and 15 August 1300. In 1302, he was sentenced to two years' exile on a false charge of corruption during his term of office, part of a mass purge of supporters of the Holy Roman Emperor by supporters of the Pope.

Dante chose never to return to Florence, preferring a life of solitary wandering, during which he wrote his best poetry.

Opposite the tower is the tiny **Oratory of St Martin** (open daily 10am–noon, 3–5pm; free entrance) decorated with fine frescos by followers of Ghirlandaio.

From here, Via Dante Alighieri leads one way to the entrance to the **Badia Fiorentina ❹** (open Mon only 3–6pm; entrance charge; *see page 115*), the church of a Benedictine abbey founded in AD 978 but much altered in 1627–31. The interior is uninspiring, but just inside the door is a delightful painting by Fil-

ippo Lippi, painted around 1485. It shows St Bernard and the Virgin; no ethereal vision, but a warm-blooded woman accompanied by angels whose faces are those of the children of the Florentine streets.

The little-visited cloister, the **Chiostro degli Aranci** (so-named because the monks grew orange trees there), is reached through a door to the right of the sanctuary and up a flight of stairs. This peaceful inner courtyard is adorned with frescos depicting the miracles of St Bernard by Rossellino (*c.* 1434–6); and there are attractive views of the restored 14th-century campanile, Romanesque below and Gothic above.

The other direction, along Via dei Tavolini, leads to Via dei Calzaiuoli. This street, originally Roman, was the principal thoroughfare of medieval Florence, linking the Duomo and Piazza della Signoria. Before being pedestrianised, it was so busy that anyone who stopped to admire a building was likely to be jostled off the pavement into the road, risking injury from an impatient stream of traffic. Now it is a

Map on pege 130

Carrying home the shopping.

BELOW: Dante at work.

bustling shopping street – packed during summer evenings and Sunday afternoon *passeggiate* (strolls) – where mime artists and other performers keep tourists entertained, and the warm nights bring out a range of tarot-card readers, vendors and street life.

Halfway down towards Piazza della Signoria on the right is the two-storey church of **Orsanmichele** ❺ (open daily 8.15am–noon, 4–6pm, closed 1st and last Mon of the month; free entrance). It was built in 1337 on the site of the garden *(ortus)* of the church of San Michele and originally served as an open-arcaded grain market.

In 1380 the arcades were filled in and the ground floor converted to a church, while the upper storey was used as an emergency grain store, to be drawn on in times of siege or famine.

The new aesthetics

A scheme to decorate the exterior was launched in 1339. Each of the major Florentine guilds was allocated a niche, which was to be filled with a statue of their respective patron saints. The Black Death intervened, so that the first statues were not commissioned until the early 15th century, and they illustrate well the contemporary emergence of the new Renaissance aesthetic. Also decorating the exterior of the building are 15th-century enamelled terracotta medallions, bearing the heraldic devices *(stemme)* of the various Florentine guilds, by Luca della Robbia and his workshop.

Donatello's outstanding *Saint George*, hailed as the first truly Renaissance statue, is here represented by a bronze copy of the marble original, now in the Bargello *(see page 127)*. Near to it, on the north side (in Via San Michele) is Nanni di Banco's *Four Crowned Saints* (*c.* 1415), with an interesting frieze below illustrating the work of carpenters and masons, whose guild commissioned the work.

The west face is decorated with elaborate Gothic cartwheel tracery and faces the Palazzo dell'Arte della Lana 6, the Guildhall of the Wool Workers, as might be guessed from

Carving putti, on the outside of Orsanmmichele.

BELOW: the Palazzo di Parte Guelfa.

the numerous Lamb of God emblems that decorate the facade. This building provides access, by means of an overhead bridge, to the splendid Gothic vaulted grain store above the church. It also houses a small museum (opening subject to change and undergoing restoration) which holds mainly statuary from the church and is also used by the Dante Society for talks.

The odd arrangement of Orsanmichele's dark interior was dictated by the form of the building. In place of the usual nave flanked by aisles, the central arcade of the original open market divides the church into two parallel naves of equal size.

The southernmost is dominated by Andrea Orcagna's huge tabernacle (1439–59), encrusted with coloured glass. In the centre, scarcely visible behind cherubs and votive offerings, is a *Madonna* by Bernardo Daddi, painted in 1347 to replace one that appeared miraculously on a pillar of the old grain market. The base of the tabernacle is decorated with scenes from the life of the Virgin.

Mercato Nuovo

The **Mercato Nuovo** ❻ is reached by taking the Via Lamberti and turning left into the Via Calimala. A market has existed here since the 11th century, and the current arcade was built in 1547–51 for the sale of silk and gold. Later it gained the name "straw market" from the woven-straw (raffia) goods sold there by peasants from the countryside. Various cheap and colourful raffia souvenirs are still sold but, as elsewhere in Florence, leather goods and T-shirts now form the bulk of the market's offerings.

One corner of the piazza attracts countless visitors. They come to rub the snout of *Il Porcellino*, the bronze boar copied from the Roman one in the Uffizi, itself a copy of a Hellenic original. The statue you see today is yet another copy; its predecessor was carried off for restoration at the end of 1998. It is said that anyone who rubs the snout is certain to return to the city. Coins dropped in the trough below are distributed to city charities.

Map on page 130

Il Porcellino.

BELOW: rubbing the nose.

The Mercato Nuovo.

The southwestern exit of the market square, past a popular tripe vendor's stall, leads to the Piazza Santa Maria Sovraporta, completely surrounded by medieval buildings. On the right are two 14th-century palaces, and, on the left, the 13th-century battlemented buildings of the **Palazzo di Parte Guelfa** ❼ which houses a library. It was enlarged by Brunelleschi in the 15th century and given its external staircase by Vasari in the 16th.

This palace was the official residence of the political faction that ruled the city from the mid-13th to the mid-14th centuries, when Cosimo de' Medici's pragmatic leadership put an end to the Guelf/Ghibelline feud that had split Florence for the preceding 150 years.

Palazzo Davanzati

In the Via Porto Rossa, just round the corner from the Palazzo di Parte Guelfa, is the **Palazzo Davanzati** ❽, home of a museum that gives a fascinating insight into life in medieval Florence (just

reopening, open daily 8.15am–1.30pm, closed 1st, 3rd and 5th Mon, 2nd and 4th Sun of the month; free entrance).

The palace is much more luxurious inside than would initially appear from the dour exterior; and it could be positively colourful on festive occasions, because the long iron poles on the facade were traditionally used to carry banners and flags during feast days and at carnival time.

Otherwise, the unremitting plainness of the facade, as with most 14th-century Florentine palaces, is relieved only by the typically Tuscan depressed window arches that thicken to a slight point at the apex, and by the coat of arms of the Davanzati family. This family acquired the property in 1578 and owned it until 1838, when the last of the line, perhaps suffering from centuries of inbreeding, committed suicide.

An antiquarian, Elia Volpi, bought the *palazzo* in 1904 and restored it sympathetically as a private museum. This was acquired in

turn by the Italian state in 1951. Most Florentine palaces are still owned by the descendants of the first owners; this one, uniquely, is open to the public.

The vaulted entrance hall was designed mainly for protection, enabling the inner courtyard to be cut off from the street during times of trouble. Later, it was subdivided into three wool shops, much as contemporary aristocratic owners lease the ground floors of their palaces for use as shops, offices and galleries.

Domestic life revolved around the delightful inner courtyard, a peaceful retreat open to the sky but shaded from the sun by the high surrounding walls. A well in the corner by the entrance supplied water to all five floors – a rare luxury at a time when most households depended on the public fountains in nearby piazzas for their water supply.

From here, a graceful external staircase of banded white-and-grey stone rises on corbels and wall brackets to the upper floors.

Splendid interiors

The living quarters, with their gorgeous wall hangings, frescos and painted ceilings, begin on the first floor. The Sala Madornale is above the entrance hall and four holes in the floor enabled missiles to be dropped on would-be intruders.

The Sala dei Pappagalli (Room of the Parrots) is named after the bird motif that covers the walls, in rich reds and blues, imitating, in fresco, fabric wall hangings. The windows, now filled with leaded lights, were originally fitted with turpentine-soaked cloth to repel water and admit some light.

Off to the side of the little child's bedroom is one of several medieval bathrooms. In the main bedroom the sparseness of the furnishings is compensated for by the warmth and splendour of the wall paintings, a running frieze of trees and birds above armorial shields. The bedroom above is even more sumptuously decorated, with scenes from the French romance *La Châtelaine de Vergy*. Antique lace is displayed in a small side room.

Map on page 130

An exquisite vase in Palazzo Davanzati.

BELOW: the interior of the Palazzo Davanzati.

Map
on page
130

An impressive lamp bracket on the Palazzo Strozzi.

BELOW:
a Fiat 500 Bambini.

The top floor was the domain of the women, the usual site of the kitchen so that smoke and cooking smells would not penetrate the living rooms. According to contemporary accounts of household management, far from leading a glamorous life, women were virtual slaves to the kitchen, were found spinning and weaving when they were not preparing meals, rarely leaving the house except for church and festivals.

Even today, it is said that the daughters of the – apparently conservative – Florentine aristocracy are accompanied by a chaperone wherever they go. In some respects, it seems little has changed in the city since Dante first caught a fleeting glimpse of his beloved Beatrice and fed his fertile imagination for decades to come on a few equally brief encounters.

Bankrupt ambition

From Palazzo Davanzati, Via de' Sassetti leads into Piazza Strozzi via a left turn. Here is **Palazzo Strozzi** , one of the last of the hundred or so great Florentine palaces built during the Renaissance, and certainly the largest. Filippo Strozzi watched its construction from the family's house, itself of palatial dimensions, which stands on the opposite side of the piazza.

The construction of the *palazzo* began in 1489; it was still not complete 47 years later, in 1536, when Strozzi died leaving his heirs bankrupt. The massive classical cornice was added as an afterthought towards the end of the construction when Roman-style architecture came into fashion. Original Renaissance torch holders and lamp brackets, carried on winged sphinxes, adorn the corners and facade. The interior, by contrast, has been ruined by the addition of a huge modern fire escape, installed "temporarily" when the building began to be used as an exhibition hall.

By then, anyway, most of the arches of the Renaissance courtyard had been filled in with 19th-century windows to create office space for the various institutions that now occupy the upper floors. A small museum on the left displays the original model made by Giuliano da Sangallo, one of several architects who worked on the palace, and has exhibits explaining its construction.

On the right of the courtyard, the Gabinetto Vieussaux, a public library with an excellent collection of books on the city and its art, is a favourite meeting place of scholars, literati and art historians of every nationality.

Around this area, to the west of Piazza della Repubblica, lies Via Sassetti and Anselmi, large and impressive-looking streets where all the banks are located, as well as a number of very expensive shops (*see also pages 225–7*). ❑

RESTAURANTS, CAFÉS AND BARS

Giubbe Rosse
Piazza della Repubblica
13/14
Tel: 055-212280
www.giubberosse.it
L and D daily. €€€
Florence's famous literary café is still a haunt
of writers and actors.
Panini and a buffet for
lunch with an upmarket
dinner menu.

L'Incontro (The Savoy)
Piazza della Repubblica 7
Tel: 055-27351
www.hotelsavoy.it/
restaurant1.html
L and D daily. €€€€
The Savoy's bar and
restaurant is an elegant
setting in which to enjoy
Tuscan cuisine from a
select menu whilst gazing over the piazza. It is
not cheap, but the food
is delicious and the service is excellent.

Il Paiolo
Via del Corso 42r
Tel: 055-215019
www.ristoranteilpaiolo.it
Closed Sun and Mon L.
€€
Extremely central cosy
restaurant which offers
good-quality Italian food
at lunch and dinner.
Fresh fish and homemade desserts feature
on the menu.

**Ristorante Vecchia
Firenze**
Borgo degli Albizi 67/68r
Tel: 055-2340361
Closed Mon. €€
Situated in a 15th-cen-

tury *palazzo*, the restaurant's atmosphere is intimate, although groups of
students and tourists
can disturb the ambience.

Cafés, Bars and Gelaterie

Chiaroscuro
Via del Corso 36r
Tel: 055-214227
www.chiaroscuro.it
L and T daily.
This café offers coffee
from all over the world,
as well as flavoured hot
chocolates, cocktails, a
buffet lunch and one of
the best *aperitivi* in Florence. The *aperitivo* is
themed – Italian, Mexican, Spanish and Japanese food all have their
night.

Festival del Gelato
Via del Corso 75r
Tel: 055-2394386
Don't let the neon lighting and tourists put you
off a *gelato* from this
place. Every flavour possible features here.

Gilli
Piazza della Repubblica 3
Tel: 055-213896
www.gilli.it
L and T daily.
Gilli claims to be Florence's oldest café. It is
a luxurious chocolaterie
and café in which to
relax with a book and
watch the square.

Paszkowski
Piazza della Repubblica

31/35r
Tel: 055-210236
www.paszkowski.it
Closed Mon.
One of the grand cafés
on the piazza, it is a
good place for coffee
and cake, lunch and
after-dinner drinks
accompanied by live
music.

La Rinascente
Piazza della Repubblica
Opening hours of the
store: 9am–9pm Mon–
Sat, varied Sun opening.
On the top floor of the
department store is a
pleasant café where genteel staff serve coffees
and food throughout the
day. The view over the
cathedral and rooftops of
the city is spectacular.

I Visacci
Borgo Albizi 80r

Tel: 055-2001956
L and T daily; closed Sun
in summer.
Colourful café
which offers drinks
and light lunches
offering more than
pasta, pizza or *panini* –
choose from the
crostini, salads or plates
based on fish or meat.
The ambience is very
relaxed and the staff
friendly.

RIGHT: a famous café in the Piazza della Repubblica.

SAN LORENZO

The powerful Medici family left its mark all over the city – and all over Tuscany. But nowhere is their ancestry more evident than in this area north of the Duomo

osimo I, Duke of Florence and later Grand Duke of Tuscany, consolidated his grip on the newly created Principality of Florence by moving out of the ancestral palace and into the Palazzo Vecchio in 1540. In doing so, he left behind an area of the city that had been home to the Medici for generations, the place from which an earlier Medici dynasty had been content to rule.

Nevertheless, the family connection with the parish remained so strong that every Medici of any consequence would always return, albeit in a coffin, for burial in the family chapel, attached to the church of San Lorenzo.

Under Cosimo de' Medici (later called Cosimo il Vecchio, the elder), Piero the Gouty and Lorenzo the Magnificent, this area of the city was the centre of power from 1434 to 1492. It is now neither beautiful nor especially imposing. The Medici Palace has become simply the familiar backdrop to the everyday life of the city, the nearby streets littered with the debris of the **Mercato Centrale**, the central market (also referred to as the Mercato di San Lorenzo), while the church of San Lorenzo itself is obscured by the canvas awnings of souvenir shops and cheap clothes stalls.

But then again, perhaps the district has always been like this – busy, noisy, a mixed-up jumble of the almost splendid and the almost squalid, home to some of the city's richest and poorest inhabitants. Above all, in the time of the early Medici, it must have seemed as though it were one great construction site, with masons, carpenters and tile-makers busy on the dome of the nearby cathedral and Cosimo de' Medici himself one of the busiest builders.

Map on page 140

LEFT:
the market of San Lorenzo with the church behind.
BELOW:
San Lorenzo's nave.

Eleonora di Toledo, wife of Cosimo I, with their son Giovanni de' Medici.

BELOW: Palazzo Medici-Riccardi.

Via Cavour

Situated at No. 1 on the busy street running between San Marco and the Duomo – Via Cavour – is the Florence Tourist Office. This is a useful place to pick up maps, leaflets on Florence's museums and information on what's on around the city (*see also* www.firenzeturismo.it). The office also gives you a break from studying art and architecture before moving on to the Palazzo Medici further down the road.

Cosimo de' Medici has been described as a man with a passion for building, convinced that what he built would, like the monuments of ancient Rome, last for 1,000 years or more and immortalise his name; and to a large extent this has proved to be true. He commissioned scores of buildings, not just in Florence but as far away as Paris and Jerusalem – cities in which the Medici name was associated with the banking empire founded by his father, Giovanni.

Ironically, and perhaps inevitably, he did not always see the finished product. His own palace, now known as the **Palazzo Medici-Riccardi ❶** (open Thur–Tues 9am–7pm; entrance at No. 3 Via Cavour; entrance charge) – incorporating the name of its later owners – was begun in 1444 but was still not complete when he took up residence there, in 1459, just five years before his death.

Looking at it now, it seems like any other Florentine palace, but it was the prototype, the one that set the standard for many other family homes; if it looks a little dull, that was entirely deliberate. Cosimo carefully cultivated the image of a man of few pretensions, a man concerned with matters of the mind rather than with material finery. Vasari says that he rejected the first palace plans, drawn up by Brunelleschi, because they were too ostentatious, and instead chose his

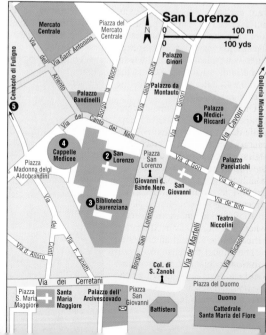

favourite architect, Michelozzo, to design something simpler.

Today, it looks more elaborate than it originally was, because the simple arches of the ground floor, once an open loggia, were given their classical, pedimented windows by Michelangelo in the 16th century. The only real concession to ornament are the Gothic-style windows of the upper floors – recalling those of the 13th-century Palazzo Vecchio – and the much simplified classical cornice.

Inside, the main courtyard deliberately evokes the monastic cloister, for Cosimo was a religious man given to taking retreats in the specially reserved cell of the Dominican priory, San Marco, his own foundation. Antique Roman inscriptions and friezes set into the walls recall that he was also a keen classical scholar, who hired agents to scour Europe and the Near East for ancient manuscripts.

A small garden beyond the courtyard harks back to the medieval, but, like so much of the palace, it looks sparser because it now lacks the antique sculptures and art treasures – including Donatello's *Judith and Holofernes* – that went to the Uffizi and Palazzo Pitti when the Medici moved out.

Only one room, the Medici Chapel – also known as the Cappella dei Magi – retains its 15th-century appearance; it is reached by stairs leading off from a corner of the courtyard. Many of the rest – which are now used for temporary exhibitions – were altered after the Riccardi family bought the palace in 1659, and again, more recently, when they were converted into the offices of the Town Prefecture.

The chapel frescos were commissioned by Piero, Cosimo's sickly eldest son (known as the Gouty) and were painted by Benozzo Gozzoli in 1459.

Piero's liking for rich colours, in contrast to the simple taste of his father, is well reflected in the gorgeous scenes of Benozzo Gozzoli's *Journey of the Magi* (1459), with their retinue passing through an idealised vision of the Tuscan landscape. Many contemporary personalities of the time are depicted in the scene, including, of course, members of the Medici family, identified by ostrich-feather emblems: among them are Lorenzo the Magnificent on the white horse, his father Piero di Cosimo behind him wearing the red beret, and the latter's brother Giovanni. Look, too, for Gozzoli's self-portrait; his name is written around the rim of his cap. The frescos were restored in 1992, and their colours and gold leaf are now extraordinarily vivid.

San Lorenzo

The Palazzo Medici-Riccardi backs onto Piazza San Lorenzo, where the equestrian statue of Giovanni delle Bande Nere by Bandinelli (1540) looks out of place amid the bustle of the modern street market. Above the

Memorial in the courtyard, Palazzo Medici-Riccardi.

BELOW: a holy water stoup in San Lorenzo.

San Lorenzo's unfinished facade.

sea of canvas awnings rises the dome of **San Lorenzo** ❷ (open Mon–Sat 10am–5.30pm; Sun 1.30-5pm; entrance charge), unmistakably the work of Brunelleschi, cousin to his cathedral dome, and partnered by the smaller cupola of Michelangelo.

The facade is rough and unfinished (Michelangelo's design, which can be seen in the Casa Buonarroti, was never built), but the interior is outstanding, a gracious composition of the aptly named grey stone *pietra serena* and white walls. It is one of the earliest and most harmonious of all Renaissance churches, representing a break with French Gothic and a return to an older, classical style.

Giovanni, father of Cosimo de' Medici, commissioned Brunelleschi to design the church in 1419, but the vicissitudes of the Medici banking empire meant that progress was halting, and neither Giovanni nor Brunelleschi lived to see it complete. Thereafter, successive members of the Medici family continued to embellish it, commissioning the greatest artists of their age to add frescos, paintings and – ultimately – their mausoleum. The two great tank-like bronze pulpits in the nave include reliefs by Donatello (*c.* 1460) – the crowded and realistic Deposition and Resurrection scenes – which are among his last and most mature works. They were completed by his pupils after he died.

Beneath Brunelleschi's great soaring dome, in front of the high altar, a massive inlaid marble slab covers the grave of Cosimo de' Medici, buried here in great pomp – despite his characteristic request for a simple funeral – in 1464, after which he was posthumously awarded the title Pater Patriae – father of his country.

On the left, off the north transept, the Old Sacristy (often closed), designed by Brunelleschi, contains the monuments of Cosimo's parents and two grandchildren; frescos on a dome depict the night sky and the positions of the signs of the zodiac as they were when the ceiling was painted in 1442.

Near by, the recently restored Bronzino fresco of the *Martyrdom*

of St Lawrence (1565–9) is a masterful study of the human form in a multitude of contorted gestures, bending to stoke the fire beneath the martyr's gridiron, pumping the bellows and altogether, in their nudity, forming an ironic counterpoint to the notice in the church entrance requesting visitors to "rigorously avoid the wearing of indecent clothes such as miniskirts and shorts".

The *cantoria* (choir gallery) above the cloister entrance, copying the style of Donatello, is no great work, but is one of the few to have survived in its original position. Next to it is another rarity, a modern painting by Pietro Annigoni (1910–88) – along with a work showing Joseph and Christ in a carpenter's workshop against the hills of Tuscany and a blood-red sky, symbolic of Christ's sacrifice, by sculptor Marino Marini of Pistoia, who trained in Florence (he spent much of his working life in Milan).

The Medici Library

The quiet cloister to the north of the church, with its box-lined lawns and pomegranate bushes, gives access by the stairwell in the corner to the **Biblioteca Laurenziana ❸** (open Mon, Fri and Sat 8am–2pm, Tues, Wed and Thur 8am–5pm, closed first 2 weeks of Sept; entrance charge), designed by Michelangelo between 1524 and 1534. The vestibule is almost totally occupied by Ammannati's monumental and extraordinary staircase which leads up to the library itself. It is a dramatic and sophisticated design, which shows Michelangelo trying to cram too many elements into a tiny space, brilliantly inventive but needing a room many times bigger for the ideas to be fully worked out.

By contrast, the interior of the rectangular library is deliberately simple and serene, a scholar's retreat with no visual distractions, lined with lectern-like reading benches. It houses an important collection of classical manuscripts – some of them beautifully illustrated – which was begun by Cosimo de' Medici, including the famous 5th-century Virgil Codex and the 8th-century Codex Amiatinus from the monastery at Jarrow in England.

Medici Chapels

The entrance to the **Cappelle Medicee ❹** (open daily 8.15am–5pm, closed 1st, 3rd and 5th Mon, 2nd and 4th Sun of the month; entrance charge) is in the Piazza Madonna degli Aldobrandini, behind the church of San Lorenzo. The plain entrance to the crypt is paved with simple slabs that cover the graves of cardinals and archbishops, first, second and third wives of Medici princes, and those who luxuriated in grander titles – dukes, grand dukes and electors palatine – the heirs and successors of this merchant family turned rulers of Florence.

A Cappelle Medicee ceiling panel.

BELOW: San Lorenzo's cloister.

Stairs lead upwards from here to the opulent Cappella dei Principi (Chapel of the Princes, currently undergoing some restoration work), so ambitious in its use of costly marbles and semi-precious stones that, from its beginning in 1604, it took nearly 300 years to complete.

The roof of the cupola contains impressive frescos, whilst each of the four great sarcophagi, big enough to contain a score or more burials, is surmounted by a crown, a monument to imperial pretensions and a symbol of nouveau-riche wealth and power.

Scarves for sale in the market.

Two niches contain bronze statues of the deceased dukes, Cosimo II and Ferdinando I. The other three, Cosimos II and III and Francesco I, were planned but never executed. The only details that delight are the 16 colourful intarsia coats of arms, one for each of the principal towns in Tuscany.

A passage off to the left leads to Michelangelo's New Sacristy and his masterful tombs of an earlier generation of the family. On the right, the reclining figures of *Night*

and *Day* adorn the monument to Giuliano, son of Lorenzo the Magnificent, and, on the left, the figures of *Dawn* and *Dusk* sit below the meditative statue of Lorenzo, grandson of the Magnificent. Neither of these two minor members of the Medici family played any significant role in the history of the city, and only the sculpture – which, some would claim, is Michelangelo's greatest work – has kept alive their names.

One of the few Medici worthy of a monument by Michelangelo, Lorenzo the Magnificent himself – the popular and talented poet, philosopher, politician and patron of the great artists of his day – is buried here in near-anonymity in a double tomb with his brother Giuliano. Above the tomb is Michelangelo's *Madonna and Child*, intended as part of an unfinished monument to Lorenzo.

Michelangelo the rebel

Despite the quality of the work he did for them, Michelangelo never really enjoyed working for the

A Lot of Tripe

If you want to "eat as the locals do" in Florence, then the tripe stands around San Lorenzo's Mercato Centrale (and elsewhere) will provide you with a perfect opportunity to do so – *if* you're game. Known as *tripperie*, these small mobile stalls sell not only tripe but just about every other part of the cow that is edible and left over after the butcher has cut up the best bits. The offal is served up either in a little dish with a plastic fork or on a *panino* or roll, to customers ranging from dust-coated builders and local shopkeepers to high-heeled secretaries and suited businessmen. Manna from heaven to the initiated, unspeakable horror to anyone else, the choice of goodies on offer varies, but you can usually find most of the following. *Trippa alla fiorentina* is traditionally stewed tripe with tomatoes and garlic, served hot with parmesan; it is also served cold as a salad. *Lampredotto* are pigs' intestines and are usually eaten in a roll after having been simmered in a rich vegetable stock; *nervetti* are the leg tendons, again cooked in stock, while *budelline* are intenstines cooked in a rich sauce. All this is normally washed down with a glass of rough-and-ready wine, often served in a plastic cup; there are no frills on tripe stands. The *tripperie* are usually open all day, from about 9am to 7pm.

Medici. The New Sacristy was commissioned by Popes Leo X and Clement VII, both of whom were descended, lineally, from Cosimo de' Medici. It was Michelangelo's first commission.

However, Michelangelo resented the manner in which they and their relatives were subverting the old republican political institutions which Cosimo and Lorenzo had guided so adroitly. This is reflected in the sombre mood of the sculpture and the incompleteness of the sacristy – Michelangelo only worked on it by fits and starts in 1520 and again in 1530–3. In the period between these two dates Michelangelo was an active opponent of the Medici.

The Medici family was expelled from the city in 1527, but it soon became apparent that they intended to return and take Florence by force, backed by the army of the Holy Roman Emperor. Michelangelo supervised the construction of fortifications around the hilltop church of San Miniato and established a battery of cannons in the campanile,

enabling the city, briefly, to withstand the seige.

In 1530, however, the city fell to the superior force of the imperial army – the *Night* sculpture is said to be associated with Michelangelo's shock at the city's loss of freedom – and Michelangelo went into hiding in this very sacristy.

The walls of the small room to the left of the altar are covered in pencil sketches thought to have been drawn at that time. These are not normally shown to the public, but a number of Michelangelo's drawings for column bases are visible on the walls either side of the altar, along with graffiti sketched by his pupils. You can try asking at the ticket office to see the sketches; only a limited number of visitors are allowed access at any one time between 9am and noon.

To the northwest of San Lorenzo, at Via Faenza 42, is the **Cenacolo di Fuligno ⑤** (open Mon, Tues and Sat 9am–noon; free entrance) which contains Perugino's well-preserved frescoed version of the Last Supper in the refectory. ❏

The Mercato Centrale

RESTAURANTS AND CAFÉS

Giannino in San Lorenzo
Borgo San Lorenzo 35/37r
Tel: 055-212206
www.gianninoinflorence.com
L and D daily. €€
One of the better restaurants in this area, offering traditional food such as *bistecca alla fiorentina* and *ribollita* as well as a selection of wines. Special themed evenings are worth looking out for.

LOBS
Via Faenza 75/77r
Tel: 055-212748

L and D daily. €€€
Renowned as one of the best fish restaurants in Florence, LOBS offers a range of seafood including swordfish, prawns, octopus and lobster – this last dish should be ordered in advance.

Mario
Via Rosina 2r
Tel: 055-218550
L only; closed Sun. €
Hidden away behind market stalls, this trattoria has a lively atmosphere and is popular with the

local stallholders. Try the *trippa alla fiorentina* (tripe in a tomato sauce) or the *ribollita*.

Nannini
Borgo San Lorenzo 7r
Tel: 055-212680
A good place to stop off for a drink or ice cream or to try *panforte*.

Osteria dell'Agnolo
Borgo San Lorenzo 24r
Tel: 055-211326
www.osteria-agnolo.it
L and D daily. €€
Home-made pasta and a range of pizzas, *calzoni* and desserts make this a good solid, albeit touristy, option near the market.

Trattoria ZàZà
Piazza del Mercato Centrale 26r
Tel: 055-215411
www.trattoriazaza.it
L and D daily; closed Sun. €€–€€€
Set in the piazza behind the central market, this trattoria offers a range of meat-and-fish based dishes. Cosy inside in the winter, and outside seating for the summer.

● ● ● ● ● ● ● ● ● ● ● ●
Price includes dinner and a glass of wine, excluding tip.
€€€€ over €60, €€€ €40–60, €€ €25–40, € under €25.

SAN MARCO

As well as the art treasures in the church of San Marco, this part of the city is home to one of Florence's most famous works – Michelangelo's *David* – held in the Accademia, the world's first school of art

Map on page 148

The area north of the cathedral, now occupied by the buildings of Florence's university, was once very much an extension of the Medici domain. **Piazza San Marco**, where students now gather between lectures, is named after the convent and cloisters on the north side of the square, whose construction was financed by Cosimo de' Medici. Unfortunately the square is ruined by the buses coming and going from the stops on both sides.

An older convent on the site was in ruins when Dominican friars from Fiesole took it over in 1436, and the following year, at Cosimo's request, the architect Michelozzo began to rebuild it.

Fra Angelico showcase

The church of **San Marco ❶**, remodelled subsequently, is decorative, but of more interest are the cloisters and monastic buildings (open Mon–Fri 8.15am–5pm, Sat and Sun 8.15am– 7pm, closed 1st, 3rd and 5th Sun, 2nd and 4th Mon of the month; entrance charge) contain outstanding paintings and frescos by Fra Angelico, who spent much of his life within the walls of this peaceful monastery.

Henry James said of Fra Angelico that all his paintings convey a pas-

sionate pious tenderness and that "immured in his quiet convent, he never received an intelligible impression of evil". That may be true of most of his work, but he did not lack the imagination to conceive the horrors of eternal punishment. In the Ospizio dei Pellegrini (Pilgrims' Hospice), the first room on the right of the cedar-filled cloister, the lively *Last Judgement* is one of the most intriguing of the many altarpieces he painted.

The blessed gather in a lovely

LEFT:
modern decorations hanging in the Spedale degli Innocenti.
BELOW:
Fra Angelico's *Last Judgement*.

garden below the walls of the Heavenly City, but the damned are being disembowelled and fed into the mouth of hell, there to undergo a series of tortures appropriate to their sins: the gluttons are forced to eat snakes and toads, the gold of the misers is melted down and poured down their throats.

Gentler by far is one of his most accomplished works, the *Tabernacle of the Linaiuoli*, commissioned in 1443 by the Flax-Workers' Guild, depicting the Madonna enthroned and surrounded by saints. Across the courtyard in the Sala del Capitolo (Chapter House) is Fra Angelico's great *Crucifixion* (c. 1442). Vasari reports that the artist wept whenever he painted this subject. The angry red sky, throwing into high relief the pallid flesh of Christ and the two thieves, invites comparisons with Van Gogh's work.

In the Refettorio Piccolo (Small Refectory), at the foot of the dormitory stairs, the *Last Supper* is one of two done by Domenico Ghirlandaio (the other is in the convent next to the church of Ognissanti). A small cat occupies the focal position at the bottom of the fresco, adding to the extraordinary naturalism, in which each Apostle is individually characterised, and the tableware and garden scene reveal much about 15th-century style and taste.

Monastic opulence

The Dormitorio is the high point of the museum, consisting of 44 monastic cells under a great open roof. Fra Angelico's *Annunciation* greets visitors at the top of the stairs, and, beyond, each cell contains a small fresco, intended as an aid to contemplation, stripped to the essential religious significance, unlike the gorgeous and crowded paintings commissioned by the guilds and rich patrons.

Cells 1 to 10, on the left, are prob-

San Marco's interior.

BELOW: Fra Angelico's *Crucifixion.*

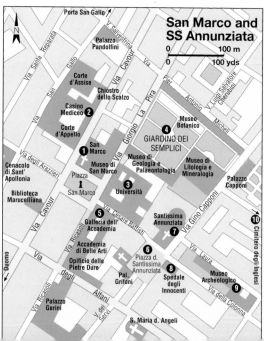

ably the work of Fra Angelico, the rest by his assistants. Cell 7, the *Mocking of Christ*, is typical of his mystical, almost surrealistic style, where, against a black background representing the darkness of night, disembodied hands beat Christ about the head, and others count out the 30 pieces of silver, the price paid to Judas for his betrayal.

Savonarola believed in the futility of earthly deeds and passions and saw only the afterlife as important and, fittingly, Cells 12 to 14 contain his hair shirt, as well as a copy of a contemporary painting of his execution, an event which caused a riot in the city. Having been struck a mortal blow by the executioner, Savonarola's body was raised on a pile of faggots and set on fire. Suddenly, the flames and smoke cleared and the dead Savonarola was seen to raise his hand in blessing. Terrified Florentines fought to escape from the square; many died in the stampede.

The other wing of the Dormitory leads past the Bibilioteca (library), designed by Michelozzo in 1441, a graceful hall built to house the illu-minated manuscripts donated by Cosimo de' Medici to create the world's first public library. The cells that Cosimo reserved for his own retreats are at the end of the corridor.

Around San Marco

Back in Piazza San Marco, Via Cavour, in the northwestern corner, leads past the **Casino Mediceo ❷** (at No. 57), a pretty house ornamented with rams' heads and scallops. The garden (hidden behind a high wall) once contained Cosimo's collection of antique sculpture (now in the Uffizi), which Michelangelo studied ardently as an adolescent. The palazzo now houses Florence's Corte d'Appello, or Court of Appeal.

Just to the right of this, at No. 69, is the elegant **Chiostro dello Scalzo** (open Mon, Thur and Sat 8.15am–1.50pm; free entrance), with frescos by Andrea del Sarto of scenes from the life of John the Baptist.

At the end of the road lies **Piazza Libertà**, an imposing piazza which is now a giant roundabout. Before reaching this, a left turn on Via Salvestri leads to Via San Gallo,

Map on page 148

From the death of Lorenzo in 1492 until his execution for fomenting civil strife in 1498, Savonarola ruled the city with puritanical zeal. He was welcomed as a liberator, but joy turned to revulsion as pleasures – everything from carnival to the possession of mirrors – became a crime punishable by torture.

BELOW:
the *Mocking of Christ*.

Look up when walking through the streets: interesting architectural details abound.

BELOW: fountain in the Piazza della Santissima Annunziata.

where **Palazzo Pandolfini** is on the corner at No. 74. This country villa, designed by Raphael in 1520, is one of his few architectural works to have survived. The entrance provides views of the peaceful gardens, and the facade is decorated with playful dolphins, a pun on the name of the owner, Bishop Pandolfini. Near by is the impressive colonnaded ex-Hospital di Bonifacio which is now the Questura, or police station. Just to the north lies Porta San Gallo, the ancient gate that defended the old road to Bologna, which marks the northernmost point of the walled city.

To the south, Via San Gallo leads to Via XXVII Aprile and the **Cenacolo di Sant'Apollonia** (open daily 8.30am–1.50pm, closed the 2nd and 4th Mon, 1st, 3rd and 5th Sun of month; free entrance). As the dining room of the 14th-century convent of Sant'Apollonia, it was, like most monastic refectories, decorated with a fresco of the Last Supper. But this one is a newly restored masterpiece of early Renaissance art, painted by Andrea del Castagno around 1450.

Note how Judas, separated from the other disciples, has the facial features of a mythical satyr – or, some would say, of the devil himself.

At the end of Via XXVII Aprile lies Piazza dell'Indipendenza, one of the few piazzas with benches on which to relax – it is unfortunately not a very salubrious part of town, however.

The University

On the northeastern side of Piazza San Marco are the buildings now occupied by the administrative offices of the **Università ❸** – originally built as stables for the horses and wild animals kept by Duke Cosimo I. The University contains several small museums at Via La Pira No. 4; the collections housed here were mostly started by the Medici.

There is a fabulous array of fossils in the **Museo di Geologia e Palaeontologia** (open Mon, Tues, Thurs, Fri and Sun 9am–1pm, Sat 9am–5pm; entrance charge). The **Museo di Litologia e Mineralogia** (open Mon, Tues, Thurs, Fri and

Sun 9am–1pm, Sat 9am–5pm; entrance charge) has a collection of exotic rocks, including a 68-kg (151-lb) topaz.

Via Georgio La Pira leads to the **Giardino dei Semplici** ❹ (open Mon–Fri 9am–1pm; entrance charge), a delightful botanical garden begun by Duke Cosimo in 1545. Medicinal herbs were grown and studied here: Semplici refers to the "simples", ingredients used in the preparation of medicine by medieval apothecaries. Today, tropical plants and Tuscan flora have been added to the collection.

On the southeastern side of the square is one of the oldest loggias in Florence (built in 1384). It leads to the **Galleria dell' Accademia** ❺ *(see pages 156–7).*

From the Accademia, Via Ricasoli leads south to its junction with Via degli Alfani and the Conservatorio. Midway down Via degli Alfani, the **Opificio delle Pietre Dure** (opening hours subject to variation; entrance charge) has a small museum devoted to the art of decorating furniture with inlaid semi-precious stone *(pietra dura).*

Santissima Annunziata

A left turn into Via dei Servi takes you to **Piazza della Santissima Annunziata** ❻, one of the loveliest squares in Florence, surrounded on three sides by a colonnade, and recently restored to traffic-free status. In the middle is an impressive bronze statue of Ferdinando I mounted on a horse by Giambologna and his pupil Pietro Tacca. The latter's elaborate bronze fountains flanking the equestrian statue have been recently restored.

The fair held in the piazza on the feast of the Annunciation (25 March) fills it with festive stalls selling home-made biscuits and sweets, and another delightful festival in September – *La Festa della Rifi-*

colona – sees children gather in the square at dusk with candlelit lanterns to commemorate the birth of the Virgin.

To the north is the church of **Santissima Annunziata** ❼ (1516–25), which is still a living church and has not become a tourist haunt. It is a place of worship that is far more typical of the rest of Italy than it is of Florence. Compared to the rational interiors of so many of the city's churches, this one is heavily ornamented. Devout Florentines come in and out all day to pray before the candlelit baldachin that is so cluttered with votive offerings that the object of their veneration is almost hidden; it is an image of the Virgin, said to have been painted miraculously by an angel.

The portico of the church is interesting for its frescos, several of which were painted by Andrea del Sarto. Though damaged, his *Coming of the Magi* is still a rich and colourful scene in which the three kings are accompanied by an entourage of giraffes, camels and splendidly dressed courtiers. The

A moralising plaque on Santissima Annunziata.

BELOW: in the Giardino dei Semplici.

Chiostro dei Morti (Cloister of the Dead) to the left of the church contains more of his frescos and the burial vaults of many leading 16th- and 17th-century artists, including Cellini.

Renaissance orphanage

On the east side of the square is the **Spedale degli Innocenti** , the world's first orphanage, opened in 1445 and still operating as such. The colonnade, built by Brunelleschi beginning in 1419, was the first of the city's classical loggias and the inspiration behind all the others. The portico is decorated with Andrea dell Robbia's famous blue-and-white tondi of swaddled babies.

The **Museum** within (open Thur–Tues 8.30am–2pm; entrance charge) is not much visited and is a quiet, cool retreat in summer. It occupies the upper rooms of the cloister, from which there are views onto the green courtyard and Brunelleschi's slender Ionic columns. Above, the spandrils are decorated with sgraffito – drawings of infants and cherubs scratched into

the plaster when still wet. Many of the frescos in the museum came from nearby churches, removed to expose earlier paintings beneath. Several are displayed with their *sinopia* alongside. These were the sketches roughed out in the plaster using red pigment (obtained from Sinope, on the Black Sea) to guide the artist when the finishing coat of plaster was added and the fresco painted.

The former nursery contains paintings commissioned for the orphanage, nearly all of them variations on the theme of the Madonna and Child. The most remarkable is the radiant *Adoration* by Ghirlandaio. The rich nativity scene in the foreground contrasts poignantly with the scenes of slaughter – the Massacre of the Innocents – in the background.

Archaeological treasures

Heading east from Piazza Santissima Annunziata, Via della Colonna leads to Florence's **Museo Archeologico**  (open Mon 2–7pm, Tues and Thur 8.30am–7pm, Wed, Fri–

A good way of getting around town.

BELOW: one of the roundels from the Spedale degli Innocenti.

Sun 8.30am–2pm; entrance charge), which contains one of the best collections of Etruscan art in Italy.

The museum was badly hit by the 1966 flood, but a long period of restoration work is just about complete, although the reconstructions of Etruscan tombs in the courtyard are still closed. The museum is rarely crowded, and it is a pleasure to browse here peacefully – although the fact that Egyptian treasures have been well restored while the indigenous art of ancient Florence and Tuscany has not is cause for some sadness.

There are now only a few pieces displayed permanently on the ground floor; the most important collections are upstairs. Also on the ground floor is the **Sezione Topografico** – which contains the important Etruscan section divided into regions, and also houses temporary exhibitions.

Etruscan tombs

The Etruscan tomb sculpture on the first floor seems, at first, a mass of hunting and battle scenes taken from the heroic myths of the Greeks. Little by little, though, one discovers the domestic scenes that were carved from real life rather than copied from Hellenic prototypes: banquet scenes, athletic dancers, coffins carved in the shape of Etruscan houses with columns and entrance gates and an arch (see exhibit 5539) that can be paralleled in many a 15th-century Florentine palace. Above the tombs the reclining figures of the dead are obese and garlanded, a wine bowl in their hands, symbolising the eternal feasting and sensual pleasures of the afterlife.

The room devoted to bronze work shows another aspect of the Etruscan culture that the Florentine artists of the Renaissance later inherited: their skill in bronze casting. Here are delicate mirrors inscribed with erotic scenes, cooking pots, military equipment and harnesses, statues and jewellery.

Three of the most important pieces were excavated in the 16th century, when Florentine artists, aware of the brilliant work of their

Etruscan exhibits in the museum.

Map on page 148

BELOW: inside the Archaeological Museum.

Map
on page
148

Elizabeth Barrett Browning.

BELOW: a chariot in the Museo Archeologico.

predecessors, went in search of the finest examples. The fantastical 5th-century BC Chimera, discovered at Arezzo in 1553, was entrusted to Benvenuto Cellini, who repaired its broken foreleg. The statue represents a mythical creature with a lion's body and three heads: lion, goat and snake *(see page 19)*.

The Arringatore (or Orator, c. 1st-century BC) was discovered in Trasimeno in 1566, and the statue of Minerva was found accidentally in Arezzo in 1541; Cosimo I once kept it in his office in the Palazzo Vecchio.

Egyptian teasures

The Egyptian collection resulted from the joint French-Italian expedition of 1828–9. It includes a chariot from a 14th-century BC tomb at Thebes, but equally compelling is the large quantity of organic materials that survived in the arid, oxygen-starved atmosphere of the ancient desert tombs: wooden furniture, ropes, baskets, cloth hats and purses, all looking as fresh as if they had been made only recently, and throw-

ing an illuminating light on the ordinary life of the ancient Egyptians.

The second floor was opened in 1993 and is dedicated to ancient Greek pottery. The interlinking and well-lit rooms contain case after case of vases, dishes, urns and other receptacles of every shape and size. The most important exhibit in this section is the so-called François Vase (named after its discoverer) in Room 2, significant both for its outstanding size and for the detailed illustrations.

In the central corridor is a series of Greek statues in marble; here, two outstanding figures representing Apollo (dated between 530 and 510 BC) demonstrate both the Hellenic origins of Etruscan art and the astounding similarities between the work of the Renaissance and the Etruscan sculptors, though separated by two millennia.

Another recently opened wing of the museum, occupying a long narrow wing to the north of the museum gardens, displays Grand Duke Leopoldo's collections of antique jewellery.

Tree-shaded tombs

From Via della Colonna, Borgo Pinti leads north to Piazza Donatello. Here, marooned on an island in the middle of a major traffic intersection, is the **Cimitero degli Inglesi** ❿, or English Cemetery (open Mon 9am–noon, Tues–Fri 3–6pm; entrance charge).

Opened in 1827, this is the burial place of numerous distinguished Anglo-Florentines, including Elizabeth Barrett Browning, Arthur Hugh Clough, Walter Savage Landor, Frances Trollope (mother of Anthony and author in her own right) and the American preacher, Theodore Parker. Sadly, traffic noise prevents this from being the restful spot it should be, despite the beauty of sheltering cypress trees. ❑

RESTAURANTS AND CAFÉS

Restaurants

Accademia
Piazza San Marco 8r
Tel: 055-217343
L & D daily. €€
Close to the eponymous museum containing Michelangelo's *David*, this restaurant offers both a retreat from culture and a warm setting where pizzas and other food are washed down with the good house wine.

Pugi
Piazza San Marco 10
Tel: 055-280981
www.focacceria-pugi.it
This place is famous among Florentines for their *schiacciate* (flat breads of various kinds). Buy focaccia or pizza by weight as a snack or lunch on the run.

Ristorante da Mimmo
Via San Gallo 57/59r
Tel: 055-481030
http://utenti.lycos.it/damimmo
Closed Sun. €€
Set in a former theatre, with a changing menu – often inspired by southern Italian cooking – this place offers good food and wine at affordable prices.

Lo Skipper
Via degli Alfani 78ar
Tel: 055-284019
L & D Mon–Fri; D only Sat. €€
If you fancy something a little different, try this restaurant run by a nautical club. It offers good Italian food as well as changing dishes inspired by other culinary traditions, such as Mexican and Greek food. It is hidden off the main tourist route.

Taverna del Bronzino
Via delle Ruote 27r
Tel: 055-495220
L & D; closed Sun.
€€€–€€€€
A variety of European cuisines served in an elegant restaurant with a valulted ceiling and patio. Try the *ravioli alla senese* (ricotta-and-spinach-filled pasta parcels) or one of the less Italian but equally divine dishes.

Il Vegetariano
Via delle Ruote 30r
Tel: 055-475030
D Tues–Sun; L Tues–Fri.
€
Il Vegetariano's use of the freshest vegatables in its dishes makes it the main contender for the city's best vegetarian eatery, although admittedly there are few in Florence between which to choose. The atmosphere here is informal and unassuming.

Cafés and Gelaterie

Caffèlatte
Via degli Alfani 39r
Tel: 055-2478878
Mon–Sat B, L & T.
This cosy little café produces healthy homemade cakes, soups and other light snacks from the kitchen behind. Steaming milky lattes (appropriately given its name) are served in huge bowl-like mugs.

Gelateria Carabé
Via dei Ricasoli 60r
Tel: 055-289476
Closed Mon in winter. Not to be missed if you are a fan of ice cream; Sicilian *gelato* made from ingredients shipped in from the island itself.

Robiglio
Via dei Servi 112 (Other branches include Viale dei Mille)
Tel: 055-212784
www.robiglio.it
One of the chain of Robiglio cafés which offer delicious pastries and chocolates as well as lunches. Try the chocolate-filled choux buns.

Zona 15
Via del Castellaccio 53/55r
Tel: 055-211678
Set in a quiet piazza, this bar is a nice place for a leisurely early drink in summer evenings. If you are feeling hungry, it also does a range of modern Tuscan food.

PRICE CATEGORIES
Prices for three-course dinner per person with a glass of wine:
€ = under €25
€€ = €25–€40
€€€ = €40–€60
€€€€ = more than €60

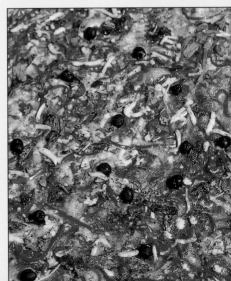

RIGHT: a tempting pizza.

THE ACCADEMIA

Originally the world's first school of art, the gallery is now home to Michelangelo's most famous work, _David_

Michelangelo's _David_ is the main attraction of the Galleria dell'Accademia (open Tues–Sun 8.15am–6.50pm; entrance at No. 60; admission charge includes entry to the Museo degli Strumenti Musicali), but the rest of the art is equally worthy of attention.

The museum was originally part of the world's first art school, the Accademia delle Belle Arti, an institution established by Cosimo I de' Medici and of which Michelangelo was a founding academician. The current gallery was consolidated in the late 18th century by Grand Duke Pietro Leopoldo next to the art school housed in the same row of buildings.

The collection contains sculpture and early Renaissance religious art, and has recently been expanded to incorporate a display of musical instruments. On entry, the Sala del Colosso contains the plaster cast of Giambologna's _Rape of the Sabines_ (on display in the Loggia dei Lanzi – _see page 101_) and a collection of colourful religious art from the early Cinquecento (16th century).

Whilst the exit to the right of the entrance leads to the Museo degli Strumenti Musicali, the Accademia continues through the door to the left. The view of Michelangelo's _David_ from the end of the corridor-shaped Galleria dei Prigionieri is stunning, the domed Tribuna di Michelangelo at its far extent framing the huge statue.

ABOVE: a double bass made by Bartolomeo Castellani in 1792.

ABOVE: Amongst the most notable pieces is Fillipino Lippi's striking _Deposition from the Cross_, which was finished by Perugino on the former's death. Other highlights are _Christ as a Man of Sorrows_ – a poignant fresco by Andrea del Sarto – and Fra' Bartolommeo's Prophets.

Off to the left of the Tribuna di Michelangelo are three small rooms – the Sala del Duecento e Prima Trecento, the Sala dei Giotteschi and the Sala degli Orcagna. These all hold early Florentine works, including works by Taddi and Daddi. The _Tree of Life_ by Buonaguida is one of the best-known and most impressive works in the small collection. Stairs lead to the first floor and four further rooms. The first two contain attractive work from the late 14th century. The following room is dedicated to Florentine painter Lorenzo Monaco, whose work shows the bridge between Gothic and Renaissance art – the key to understanding the Florentine style.

DAVID

Standing at over 4 metres, Michelangelo's *David* is the most famous sculpture in Western art. It was sculpted between 1501 and 1504 as a symbolic commemoration of the start of the republican Florence, through its depiction of the young boy who slew Goliath. Originally placed in front of the Palazzo Vecchio (a copy stands in the former position), the statue was moved to the Accademia in 1873 for reasons of preservation – a decision which was heavily criticised by many at the time. The marble from which *David* was carved was famously rejected as faulty by other artists, but the then 29-year old Michelangelo sought to embrace its faults and patches of discoloration. Recently cleaned up, *David* is celebrated for being of perfect proportions – hailed as a testament to Michelangelo's eye for detail. The artist's attention to minutiae is evident in the muscle contour of the legs and the veins in the arms, which can be appreciated from every angle thanks to the way in which the statue is displayed. The eyes are of particular interest for their heart-shaped pupils – a feature which the visitor could well believe was a computer-generated alteration for the many postcards and souvenirs featuring *David*.

Surrounding *David* in the main room are works by contemporaries, including di Tito and Allori. The first floor is also the location of the Salone del Ottocento a cluttered room of more modern and less attractive sculptures and busts, primarily by Lorenzo Bartolini – and the rooms known as the Sale del Quattrocento *(see left)*. The latter display a holding of 15th-century Florentine paintings, but they are unfortunately often closed. The gallery ends with a small room of International Gothic art.

ABOVE: Botticelli's delightful *Madonna and Child* is in the Sale del Quattrocento Fiorentino, as is Paolo Uccello's masterpiece *Scenes of a Hermit Life*.

SANTA MARIA NOVELLA

A real "mixed bag" of attractions awaits visitors
to the area west of the Duomo, but at its
heart lies the church of Santa Maria Novella
with its magnificent collection of art

n the same colours as the Duomo and Santa Croce and fairly recently restored is the church of **Santa Maria Novella** ❶ (open Mon–Thur and Sat 9.30am–5pm, Fri and Sun 1–5pm; entrance charge), the interior of which was given a major make-over in 2000.

The square in front of Santa Maria could be anywhere in Italy except for Florence. It lies within the 14th-century city walls, but the city's population never grew to fill the space. It remained an undeveloped corner on the western edge of the city, used, from 1568 on, for annual chariot races: the obelisks supported on bronze turtles at either end of the square mark the turning points on the racetrack. In the 19th century the square was peaceful, its new hotels popular with foreign visitors. Henry James, Ralph Waldo Emerson and Longfellow, translator of Dante, all wrote in rooms looking down on the quiet piazza.

Today, the foreigners that come to the square gather on Sunday to drink, play loud music, stroll about the square and complain, in a mixture of English, Italian and various other languages, about their wages, their employers and the problems involved in obtaining a work permit. Although the authorities have made recent efforts to clean up the piazza,

it still retains a slightly scruffy feel, and is the site of a mishmash of tourist hotels, seedy *pensioni*, Chinese restaurants, bus stops and an Irish pub whose revellers spill out on to the square until the small hours. Old ladies scatter bread for the huge flocks of mangy pigeons that infest the square, and gangs of mildly threatening youths stand around.

Romanesque style

Despite its unpromising location, the church of Santa Maria Novella itself

Map on page 160

LEFT:
the impressive facade
of Santa Maria Novella.
BELOW: turtles prop
up the obelisks.

Behind the main altar, the late 15th-century frescos by Ghirlandaio and his pupils (including Michelangelo) are among the most vibrant in Florence. The Life of the Virgin is set in the artist's own time, with details of everyday life and portraits of members of the Tornabuoni family, who commissioned the work. The fresh colours are almost gaudy and the work was dismissed contemptuously by John Ruskin as verging on the vulgar.

BELOW:
Giotto's *Crucifix*.

is rewarding outside with its delicate white marble facade, although more so on the inside. It is also one of Florence's great art churches.

Building began in 1246, starting at the east end. The lower part of the facade, in typically Florentine Romanesque style, was added around 1360. Another 100 years passed before the upper part of the facade was completed; the inscription below the pediment dates it to 1470 and includes the name Ihanes Oricellarius, the Latinised form of Giovanni Rucellai, who commissioned the work from Battista Alberti.

Fear of plague

To the right of the church, the walled Old Cemetery with its cypress trees is lined with the tomb recesses of many a noble Florentine, and the lavishness of the church interior owes much to the wealth of these same families. Frightened into thoughts of eternity by the Black

Death that devastated the city in the 14th century, they donated lavish chapels and works of art in memory of their ancestors. It was here, in this church, that Boccaccio set the beginning of *The Decameron*, when a group of young noblemen and women meet and agree to shut themselves away to avoid contact with the disease, and entertain each other by telling stories.

The basic structure of the church is Gothic, but a toned-down version rather than the florid French style. Pointed arches and simple rib vaults are supported by widely spaced classical columns. The only architectural decoration comes from the alternate bands of white marble and soft grey *pietra serena*. Suspended from the ceiling, and seeming to float above the nave, is Giotto's newly restored *Crucifix* (1290).

The best of the many monuments and frescoed chapels are at the east end. In the south transept (on the

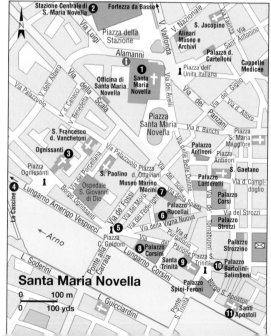

Santa Maria Novella

right) is the Cappella di Filippo Strozzi, with frescos by Filippino Lippi, son of Filippo Lippi and Lucrezia – the nun he seduced while painting the walls of the Carmelite convent in Prato. In style and subject matter, Filippino's work is nothing like that of his father, nor, indeed, that of any of his own contemporaries. His *St Philip*, standing in front of the Temple of Mars with the dragon he has just slain, is full of classical – rather than Christian – allusions, and his crowd-filled scenes and remarkable *trompe l'œil* architecture are brimming with energy.

Wooden crucifix

In the Cappella Gondi, to the left of the main altar, is a wooden crucifix by Brunelleschi, traditionally thought to have been carved to show Donatello how the Redeemer should be represented: Brunelleschi is said to have called Donatello's crucifix in Santa Croce "a mere peasant on the Cross". Brunelleschi's cross, his only sculpture to survive in wood, was carved sometime between 1410 and 1425.

In the north transept, the Cappella Strozzi di Mantova has frescos by Nardo di Cione, painted 1351–7. The *Inferno*, based on Dante's vision, is a maze of demons and tortured souls, while *Paradiso* is crowded with the saved, including portraits of Dante himself and the patrons, members of the Strozzi banking family, being led to heaven by an angel.

Last but not least, one of Santa Maria Novella's most famous frescos, Masaccio's *Trinity* (1428) is to be found on the north aisle wall. This complex, poignant masterpiece exemplifies the early Renaissance artist's pioneering work in perspective and portraiture. Look for Lorenzo Lanzi, Masaccio's patron, kneeling in the foreground of the painting, opposite his wife.

The entrance to the **Cloisters** (open Sat–Thur 9am–2pm; entrance charge) – with more great frescos, all restored since the 1966 flood – is to the left of the church facade. The first is the Chiostro Verde, or Green Cloister, so called after the frescos of Paolo Uccello, which are painted in a green pigment called *terra verde*. Ironically, his major masterpiece, the *Universal Deluge* (c. 1445), was severely damaged by the flood – although it is actually in better condition than most of the others.

On the north side of the cloister is the Cappellone degli Spagnoli (Spanish Chapel), built around 1350 as the chapterhouse and renamed in the 16th century when the entourage of Eleonora di Toledo (wife of Cosimo I) adopted it as their place of worship. The fresco cycle painted by the otherwise little-known Andrea di Buonaiuto (1365–7) – sometimes known as Andrea da Firenze – represents the teachings of St Thomas Aquinas and includes a depiction of the Duomo, complete with a dome which did not then exist – nor did it for another 100 years.

Map on page 160

The Rucellai were a great Florentine family (their name and wealth comes from oricello, *a costly red dye from a lichen imported from Mallorca). They formed a marriage alliance with the Medici in 1461, and symbols of the two families decorate the facade: the ship's sail of the Rucellai stylised to an abstract pattern, and the ring and ostrich feather of the Medici.*

BELOW: Thomas Aquinas depicted on one of the windows.

The Croce del Trebbio *that marks the crossroads of Via delle Belle Donne and Via del Moro (just south of Piazza Santa Maria Novella) is said to mark the scene of the massacre of a group of heretics in 1244.*

BELOW: the station concourse.

Around the square

The church lies by the eponymous railway station, the **Stazione Santa Maria Novella** ❷ (or the Stazione Centrale), the first building that most visitors to Florence see and the first building in Italy to be designed in the Functionalist style. Designed by Michelucci in 1935, the station is perhaps one of the finest modern buildings in Italy. Its clean, functional lines were remarkably avant-garde for the time, and the digital clock at the front is one of the earliest examples of its kind. In spite of this, its appearance was greeted by a joke at its unveiling: "I see the box the station came in, but where is the station?"

On the east side of Piazza Stazione, at the bottom of Via Nazionale, is the Largo Alinari, the new site of the offices and photographic museum of **Alinari** (founded in 1852 and once housed in Palazzo Ruccellai), the firm which supplied 19th-century Grand Tourists with prints, postcards and art books.

It has one of the best photographic collections in Europe and still publishes handsome books whose outstanding black-and-white plates show Florence as it was in the time of George Eliot, the Brownings, Ruskin, E.M. Forster and Henry James.

From here, Via Valfonda leads north to the Viale and the **Fortezza da Basso**, built by Alessandro de' Medici in 1534 as a symbol of the family power. (Ironically, he was assassinated within its walls by his cousin, Lorenzaccio, in 1537.) After the 1966 flood, the fortress was used as a centre for the restoration of damaged works of art. An international exhibition centre, used to stage prestigious fashion shows and other trade fairs, was constructed within the walls in 1978, and the impressive outer walls were smartened up in 1996 for the European summit held in Florence that year.

En route to Ognissanti

From Piazza Santa Maria Novella, there is a choice of routes to Ognissanti, of which Via dei Fossi has most to offer. It has the greatest concentration of art galleries in the city, some specialising in original paintings and others stacked to the ceilings with reproduction Davids, Venuses and female nudes, available in every size from mantelpiece ornaments to monumental pieces for the courtyard or garden.

Alternatively, Via della Scala followed by a left turn has the **Officina di Santa Maria Novella**, at No. 16; the descendants of the 16th-century Dominican friars who founded this pharmacy still make up herbal remedies to cure all sorts of ailments according to recipes laid down by their forbears. The shop is housed in a frescoed 13th-century chapel, and sells fragrant soaps, toilet waters and pot-pourri.

Piazza Ognissanti is open to the river bank, and the hotel buildings on either side frame the view of the plain brick facade of the

church of San Frediano on the opposite bank, and up to Bellosguardo on the hill beyond. Once upon a time the view would have been obscured by the many buildings that were erected across the river at this point, standing on wooden piles, to make use of the water in the processes of washing, fulling and dyeing cloth.

The church of **Ognissanti** ❸ (All Saints) was itself built by an Order of monks, the Umiliati, who supported themselves by wool processing. It was completed in 1239 but in later years came under the patronage of the Vespucci family, merchants who specialised in importing silk from the Orient and whose most famous member, Amerigo, gave his name to the New World. The Vespucci built the adjoining hospital, and several of the family are buried in vaults beneath the frescos they commissioned.

On the south side of the nave (on the right), Ghirlandaio's fresco of 1472 shows the Madonna della Misericordia, her arms reaching out in symbolic protection of the Vespucci family. Amerigo is depicted as a young boy; his head appears between the Madonna and the man in the dark cloak.

Further along the south aisle is Botticelli's *Saint Augustine*, companion piece to Ghirlandaio's *Saint Jerome* on the opposite wall, both painted in 1480 and based on the portrait of Saint Jerome by the Flemish artist, Jan van Eyck, then in the collection of Lorenzo the Magnificent. It is thought that both works were commissioned by Giorgio Vespucci, Amerigo's learned tutor.

In the sanctuary off the north transept, recently discovered frescos by the father and son, Taddeo and Agnolo Gaddi, depict in brilliant colour and realistic detail the Crucifixion and Resurrection of Christ. A similar delight in the real-

istic portrayal of birds, flowers, fruit and trees enlivens a Last Supper of Ghirlandaio (1480) in the refectory of the next-door convent (open Mon, Tues and Sat 9am–noon; free entrance).

A park, market and modern art

At No. 26 Borgo Ognissanti is one of the few Art Nouveau buildings in Florence. It is an excellent example of the style, with exuberant bronze balconies, lamps and window boxes. From here, a 15-minute walk west along the river bank (keeping to the north side) will take you to **Le Cascine** ❹, a pleasant park that runs along the embankment west of the city for 3 km (2 miles) and where Shelley composed his "Ode to the West Wind". Cascina means "dairy farm", and that is what it was until it was acquired by Duke Alessandro de' Medici and laid out as a park by his successor, Cosimo I.

A large market is held here every Tuesday morning, and it is always crowded at weekends with families walking the dog, joggers and roller-

Botticelli's Saint Augustine.

BELOW: a rare example of Florentine Art Nouveau.

Map on page 160

bladers burning up the asphalt. At most times a place of innocent pleasure, it is also the haunt of transvestite prostitutes and is best avoided after dark.

Back towards town, Borgo Ognissanti leads southeast to the **Piazza Goldoni** ❺, the busy meeting point of eight roads. The Via della Vigna Nuova leads past the **Palazzo Rucellai** ❻, halfway up on the left. This, one of the most ornate palaces in Florence, was built around 1446–51 for Giovanni Rucellai, humanist, author and intellectual, and one of the richest men in Europe. In style it blends medieval pairs of lancet windows with classical columns, pilasters and cornices.

Just off Via della Spada, behind Palazzo Rucellai, is the **Museo Marino Marini** ❼ (open Mon, Weds–Sat 10am–5pm; entrance charge), which is housed in the ancient church of San Pancrazio. The museum is dedicated to Marino Marini (1901–80); it contains some 180 of his sculptures, paintings and prints, with recurring themes of horses and riders, jugglers and female figures.

Public fashion, private art

Via della Vigna Nuova emerges in **Via de' Tornabuoni**; these two are Florence's most upmarket shopping streets. The former is home to such names as Armani, Valentino, Coveri and Escada, while the latter is lined with palaces that house the showrooms of Pucci, Ferragamo, Hermès, Gucci and Prada – names that evoke a world of style and craftsmanship that the Florentines believe is another legacy of the Renaissance.

The bridge near here is the **Ponte alla Carraia**, the easternmost of the four ancient bridges across the Arno. When it was built in 1220 it was called the Ponte Nuovo to distinguish it from the older Ponte Vecchio. What we see now is a modern reconstruction. All of Florence's bridges, except for the Ponte Vecchio, were blown up during the Nazi retreat from Florence in 1944 in an attempt to halt the advance of the allies. Even so, it is a faithful reproduction of the graceful 14th-century bridge, perhaps designed by Giotto, which replaced the first timber one.

On the Lungarno Corsini, **Palazzo Corsini** ❽, one of the city's largest palaces, is unmistakable for its villa-like form, with two side wings and classical statues lined along the parapet. Built between 1650 and 1717, it contains the **Galleria Corsini** (admission by appointment only 9.30am–12.30pm, Mon, Wed and Fri; tel: 055-218994), as well as an extensive private art collection which includes works by Raphael, Bellini, Signorelli and Pontormo. The garden is box-hedged and dotted with statues and lemon trees.

Further along, the **Palazzo Gianfiggliazza** (built in 1459) was the

The Palazzo Masetti is now the British Consulate and was, ironically, the home of Bonnie Prince Charlie's widow, the Countess of Albany. She scandalised the Scottish aristocracy by choosing as a second husband the playwright Alfieri, and her salon was the fashionable meeting place of writers and artists, including Shelley and Byron, at the end of the 18th century.

BELOW:
reading by the river.

former home of Louis Bonaparte, King of the Netherlands (he died in 1846).

Santa Trinità bridge

The Palazzo Masetti *(see opposite)* overlooks the **Ponte Santa Trinità**, the most graceful of the four Arno bridges. Some of the original masonry was recovered from the river after 1944, and the quarries of the Boboli Gardens were reopened to enable the bridge to be rebuilt in the original material and to the original design commissioned by Cosimo I from Ammannati in 1567.

The statues of the Four Seasons, carved by Pietro Francavilla for the wedding of Cosimo II in 1593, were also dredged from the river bed and restored to their original position.

Santa Trinità church

A left turn into the elegant shopping street of Via Tornabuoni leads to **Piazza Santa Trinità**. On the right, the battlemented and formidable **Palazzo Spini-Feroni** is one of the city's few remaining 13th-century palaces. It was once the home of the couturier Salvatore Ferragamo, and his boutique (usually full of Japanese tourists and the Florentine great and good) is now on the ground floor. Above the shop, the small but excellent **Museo Ferragamo** (open Mon–Fri 9am–1pm, 2–6pm by appointment; tel: 055-3360456) is a testament to the life and work of one of modern Florence's best-known figures. Some of the most spectacular shoes in the world are on display, as well as memories of his trade and travels.

Opposite the *palazzo*, the noble Baroque facade of **Santa Trinità** ❾, sadly now peeling, has capitals ornamented with cherubs and the Trinity carved in the pediment above the central door. This facade was added in 1593–4 by Buontalenti, but the inner face retains its almost complete 12th-century Romanesque form, indicating the appearance of the original late 11th-century church. The rest of the church, rebuilt in 1250–60, is a simplified form of Gothic, typical of Cistercian austerity.

Map on page 160

Shoes at Ferragamo.

BELOW:
Ponte Santa Trinità.

Map on page 160

From the bridge there are fine views of the Ponte Vecchio. The houses leading up to it were reduced to rubble and used to block the bridge to delay the advance of Allied troops in 1944. Those on the south bank are a more successful evocation of the original jumble of medieval tenements that crowded the embankment than the modern hotels and shops on the north.

BELOW: Ghirlandaio's *Adoration of the Shepherds.*

The life of St Francis

The frescos of the **Sassetti Chapel**, in the choir of Santa Trinità, were painted by Ghirlandaio in 1483 and illustrate the life of St Francis. The scene above the altar, in which Pope Honorius presents St Francis with the Rule of the Franciscan Order, is set in the Piazza della Signoria. Lorenzo the Magnificent and the patron, the wealthy merchant Francesco Sassetti, are depicted on the right.

The altarpiece itself is a delightful painting, also by Ghirlandaio (1485), the *Adoration of the Shepherds.* Joseph turns to watch the arrival of the Magi, clearly bewildered by the extraordinary events in which he has been caught up, but Mary remains serene and beautiful throughout.

Instead of a manger, the infant Christ lies in a Roman sarcophagus; this, along with the scene on the outside wall in which the Sibyl foretells the birth of Christ to the Emperor Augustus, demonstrates the Florentine preoccupation with establishing continuity between their own Christian civilisation and that of the classical world.

Last of the great palaces

The view, on emerging from the church, is of the Roman column on the opposite side of the road, taken from the Baths of Caracalla in Rome and presented by Pius IV to Cosimo I in 1560. It is now surmounted by the figure of Justice.

Behind it is the outstanding **Palazzo Bartolini-Salimbeni** ⓾, built in 1521, and one of the last great palaces to be constructed in the city. It is a curiously feminine building, with a tiny and endearing inner courtyard covered with sgraffito decoration. Today it is considered a gracious work, especially the delicate shell-hood niches of the upper floor.

Nevertheless, it was ridiculed by contemporary Florentines, who thought it over-decorated. The architect, Baccio d'Agnolo, answered his critics by carving an inscription above the door in Latin which translates as "it is easier to criticise than to emulate".

Behind and to the east of the palace is a warren of narrow alleys lined with medieval towers and palaces and, in the little **Piazza del Limbo** (so named because there was once a burial ground for unbaptised babies on the site), one of the city's oldest churches.

Founded by Charlemagne?

The church of **Santi Apostoli** ⓫ (rarely open except for services) is very old, but not as old as the inscription on the facade suggests. This attributes the foundation to "Karolus Rex Romae" – otherwise known as Charlemagne – in AD 786, but the church is Romanesque in style and was most probably built in the 10th century.

The double arcade of dark-green marble columns and Corinthian capitals includes some that were salvaged from the Roman baths of nearby Via delle Terme. ❏

RESTAURANTS, CAFÉS AND BARS

Restaurants

Buca Lapi
Via del Trebbio
Tel: 055-213768
www.bucalapi.com
D only. Closed Sun. €€€
In the cellar of the Palazzo Antinori, this charming restaurant is regarded as serving one of the best *bistecca alla fiorentina* (enormous and beautifully grilled). As expected, being in the basement of the *palazzo* of one of Tuscany's best wine producers, it also has an excellent range of wines.

Coco Lezzone
Via Parioncino 26r
Tel: 055-287178
Closed Sun. €€€
Traditional food of the highest quality using the freshest ingredients in a classic, some say unatmospheric, setting. Peasant dishes of *ribollita* and *pappa ai pomodori* can be followed with traditional *secondi* of roast pork or *bistecca fiorentina*.

Harry's Bar
Lungarno Vespucci 22r
Tel: 055-2396700
L & D; closed Sun. €€€€
Modelled on the original venue in Venice made famous by drinker and writer Ernest Hemingway, Harry's is an American-style restaurant and bar. It is renowned more for

its long list of cocktails than its food, but the latter is often innovative, and fish figures largely on the menu.

Il Latini
Via del Palchetti 6r
Tel: 055-210916
www.illatini.com
Closed Mon. €€
Expect to queue to get into this sprawling noisy restaurant with communal tables. However, the Tuscan food is good and filling and the ambience jovial.

The Lounge
Piazza S. Maria Novella 9/10r
Tel: 055-2645282
www.thelounge.it
L & D daily. €€€€
A chic modern restaurant attached to boutique hotel JK Place; the ambience is modern but perhaps a little lacking in warmth. The food, however, is good.

Trattoria Sostanza
Via Porcellana 25r
Tel: 055-212619
L & D Mon–Fri. €€
Relaxed restaurant with communal seating offering traditional Tuscan *primi* and *secondi* including *tortellini in brodo* (tortellini in broth). Concessions are not made for tourists, and a smattering of Italian would be useful *(see the menu decoder on pages 236–7)*. Hwever, this is a

true Florentine dining experience: substantial and satisfying food.

Cafés and Bars

Caffè Amerini
Via della Vigna Nuova 63r
Tel: 055-284941
This café is smart yet welcoming. A great place for light bites and refreshments, and good to while away a bit of time.

Capocaccia
Lungarno Corsini 12r
Tel: 055-210752
www.capocaccia.com
You need self-confidence to enter this place (one of a chain across Europe's more expensive locations), frequented by the beautiful and trendy of Florence. However, it offers ele-

gant – if perhaps over-fashionable – dining and cocktails as well as sushi *aperitivi*.

Roses
Via del Parione 26
Tel: 055-287090
www.roses.it
L except Sun; sushi D daily except Mon. €€
This is a small bar in a pleasant area of town close to the river. It's good for a quick drink or to eat sushi in the small restaurant.

RIGHT: local cured meats.

OLTRARNO WEST

The attractions of the "other" side of the Arno don' t stop with the Palazzo Pitti – visitors who take the time to explore this part of Florence further will be pleasantly rewarded

Cross south over any of the bridges that span the Arno and you'll be in the district of Oltrarno – meaning simply "beyond the Arno" – first enclosed by walls in the 14th century. Florentines persist in thinking of it as on the "wrong" side of the Arno, although it has gained currency as an up-and-coming area. It contains many ancient and luxurious palaces, as well as some of the city's poorest districts, and has a different, more relaxed atmosphere than the north side of the river.

The southern end of the Ponte Vecchio is actually the more picturesque, for here Vasari's Corridor *(see page 106)* makes several twists and turns, corbelled out on great stone brackets, to negotiate the 13th-century stone tower that guards this approach to the bridge. The corridor then sails over the **Via dei Bardi** and runs in front of **Santa Felicità**, forming the upper part of a portico that shelters the west front. On the opposite side of the busy little **Piazza Santa Felicità** is a charming fountain composed of a 16th-century bronze Bacchus and a late-Roman marble sarcophagus, brought together on this site in 1958.

Santa Felicità ❶ stands on the site of a late-Roman church, thought to have been built in the 3rd or 4th century AD by Eastern merchants at a time when Christians were still liable to persecution. It was rebuilt in the 16th century, and again in 1736, making effective use of contrasting bands of grey and white stone. The frescos in the Cappella Capponi (by Pontormo, 1525–8) include a remarkable Annunciation. The artist captures Mary as she climbs a staircase, one foot in the air, turning to hear the Archangel's scarcely credible message, with a look of genuine disbelief upon her

Map on page 170

LEFT:
Masaccio's *Expulsion from Paradise* in the Capella Brancacci.
BELOW:
Pontormo's Virgin in Santa Felicità.

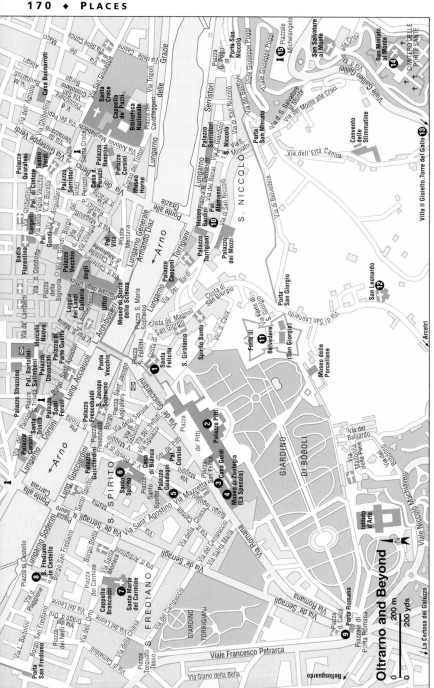

Oltrarno and Beyond

0 ____ 200 m
0 ____ 200 yds

N

Map on page 170

face. Just as accomplished is the altarpiece, a Deposition, in which Pontormo succeeds in recreating, in oils, the vivid colours and translucence of fresco, and the deathly pallor of Christ's flesh.

Via Guicciardini is named after the first historian of Italy, who was born in 1483 in the palace of the same name part-way down on the left. A slice of the fine garden and a relief of Hercules and Cacus can be glimpsed through the gate. Beyond lies the **Palazzo Pitti** ❷ and the **Giardino di Boboli** *(see pages 176–9)*, the extensive gardens behind the Palazzo Pitti. The gardens are most usually accessed through the Palazzo Pitti, but can also be entered from Via Romana 39.

The Casa Guidi

At Piazza San Felice (south of Palazzo Pitti) is **Casa Guidi** ❸ (apartments open April–Nov Mon, Wed and Fri 3–6pm), the house in which the Brownings lived from 1847, shortly after their secret marriage, until Elizabeth's death in 1861.

Beyond lies narrow Via Romana, a one-way street leading into town from Porta Romana and the southern suburbs. Along this road, a little way up on the left at No.17 is Palazzo Torrigiani. This houses the **Museo di Zoologia "La Specola"** ❹ (open Thur–Tues 9am–1pm; entrance charge), whose collection consists of a large number of anatomical wax models, made between 1775 and 1814 by the artist Susini and the physiologist Fontana.

The models were made for the serious purpose of teaching human and animal anatomy. Provided that you can overcome your squeamishness at the site of apparently real human bodies laid out like meat on a butcher's slab, there is much to be learned, and much to enjoy, in this unusual museum. The zoological section has an enormous collection of stuffed or pinned specimens of just about every creature on earth or in the seas.

Antique splendour along Via Maggio

Via Maggio, despite heavy traffic, is a magnificent palace-lined street whose many antique shops are stuffed with rich and expensive treasures – the sheer quantity is an indication of the past wealth of Florence and how much furniture and art has survived. At night, when the lights come on, and before the shutters are drawn, it is possible to glimpse richly frescoed ceilings through the windows of many an upper room – revealing the splendour in which those Florentines fortunate enough to have inherited property pass their daily lives.

Immediately west of the Via Maggio, the scale and atmosphere changes completely. The homes of the aristocracy give way to the homes of the people in the districts of Santo Spirito and San Frediano, adjacent parishes that even have their own dialects and were once

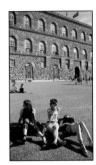
Resting outside the Palazzo Pitti.

BELOW: a Baroque *palazzo* with sgraffito work on Via Maggio.

the areas in which the wool-dyers and leather workers toiled at their noxious trades.

The **Palazzo Guadagni**  ⑤ in Piazza Santo Spirito is one of the few palaces to be built this far west. The pillared upper loggia, open to the air, was an innovation when the palace was built, around 1505. Subsequently, many medieval palaces had an extra storey built in the same style, providing a retreat in which to enjoy the cool evening air above the noise of the city. The top floor now houses an old-fashioned *pensione*.

The convent of Santa Maria del Carmine.

The piazza itself – also home to many furniture restorers' workshops – is an attractive square, planted with trees, with an early morning market on weekdays.

Modelled on Rome

The church of **Santo Spirito** ⑥ was designed by Brunelleschi for the Augustinians and begun in 1436, but he never lived to see it finished. Over time, his plan was modified and compromised – not least by the 17th-century *baldachin* that dominates the eastward view of the nave

BELOW: the facade of Santo Spirito.

and introduces a note of flamboyance into an otherwise measured classical composition. Mentally strip this away and you are left with a building that is secular in inspiration, modelled on Roman civic architecture, and a complete break with the Gothic style that prevailed elsewhere in Europe.

A total of 40 chapels with side-altars and paintings radiate from the aisles and transepts. If Brunelleschi's design had been executed in full, these would have formed a ring of conical-roofed apses around the exterior of the church, clinging like a cluster of limpets to the main structure. The one artistic masterpiece, Filippino Lippi's *Madonna and Saints* (c. 1490), is now in the right transept, and there are many other accomplished 16th-century paintings to enjoy.

Santa Maria del Carmine

From here it is worth taking an indirect route to the church of Santa Maria del Carmine by way of Via Sant' Agostino, left into the Via de' Serragli and right into Via d'

Ardiglione. The latter is the reason for the detour, a simple narrow street which appears to have changed little since Filippo Lippi was born here in 1406. Scarcely wide enough to admit a car, the buildings exclude the city noise, and it does not take much imagination to think oneself back into the 15th century. Halfway down, an aerial corridor links the two sides of the street, and close to it is Lippi's birthplace, No. 30.

At the northern end, a left turn into Via Santa Monaca leads to the church of **Santa Maria del Carmine ❼**. The original church was destroyed by fire in 1771, but by some miracle the **Cappella Brancacci** (open Mon, Wed–Sat 10am–5pm, Sun 1–5pm; entrance charge), with its frescos by Masaccio, was unaffected.

Masaccio lived for only 27 years, and was just 24 when he began work on *The Life of St Peter*, as a pupil of Masolino, in 1425. In 1427, Masaccio was put in sole charge of the work, and the result, painted a year before his untimely death, has been called the first truly Renaissance painting. Masaccio developed the technique of chiaroscuro to highlight the faces of Christ and the Apostles and, for the first time, applied the principles of linear perspective, previously developed in architecture and sculpture, to painting.

However, these alone do not account for the extraordinary power of his work, or the influence it had on leading artists of the 15th century who came to study it. Instead, it is the bold draughtsmanship and the humanity expressed in the faces and animation of the figures, such as Adam and Eve in the powerful *Expulsion from Paradise*.

The frescos' status as one of the city's unmissable sights has been enhanced by comprehensive restoration, though you can consequently expect long queues at the tiny chapel.

San Frediano

Across the spacious Piazza del Carmine, spoilt by its use as a car park, lies **Borgo San Frediano**. This is the principal street of a district full of character, whose tough and hard-working inhabitants are celebrated in the novels of Vasco Pratolini, one of the city's best-known authors.

The district is no longer as rough or as squalid as it was earlier last century, when rag pickers made a living from sifting the nearby refuse dump, and tripe (for sale all over the city) was boiled in great cauldrons in back alleys. Cleaned up, it is now a neighbourhood of small shops selling everything from provocative underwear to fishing tackle.

The church of **San Frediano ❽** looks unfinished because of its rough stone facade, but its fine dome adds a touch of glamour to this part of the city, and it looks over the Arno to the tower of Ognissanti on the opposite bank.

Map on page 170

The nave of Santa Maria del Carmine.

BELOW: the Cenacolo of Santo Spirito.

Map
on page
170

Attractive villas cling to the hillsides above Florence.

BELOW: an evening view over Oltrarno.

At the western end of the Borgo is **Porta San Frediano**, built in 1324 and one of the best-preserved stretches of the 14th-century city walls.

Beautiful view

One of the great joys of being in Florence is the proximity of the surrounding countryside. Other cities are ringed by sprawling suburbs, but in Florence such developments are limited to the north bank of the Arno, leaving the south side, Oltrarno and beyond, surprisingly rural. Natural landscapes, small farms and fine views are available with only 10 minutes' walk from the city centre.

Such is the case with **Bellosguardo**. Its name means "beautiful view", and that is exactly what attracts walkers up the steep paths to this hilltop village south of Florence. The No. 13 bus goes as far as Piazza Torquato Tasso, and from here it takes no more than 20 minutes to walk up to the summit by way of Via San Francesco di Paolo and Via di Bellosguardo.

A plaque in Piazza Bellosguardo records the names of the many distinguished foreigners who have lived in the villas on this hillside, including Aldous Huxley, Nathaniel Hawthorne, the Brownings and D.H. Lawrence. At the very summit, offering the best views over Florence, is the **Villa dell' Ombrellino** – the home, at various times, of Galileo, the tenor Caruso, and Edward VII's mistress Alice Keppel and her daughter, Violet Trefusis (Vita Sackville-West's companion).

Back at the **Porta Romana** ➒, some 5 km (3 miles) to the south (on the No. 37 bus route) lies the **Certosa del Galuzzo** (open Mon–Sun 9am–noon, 3–6pm in summer, 9am–noon, 3–5pm in winter; entrance charge). Sitting like a fortress above the busy arterial road that leads out of town towards Siena (the Via Senese), the imposing complex was founded in 1342 as a Carthusian monastery by Niccolò Acciaiuoli and is the third of six such monasteries to be built in Tuscany in the 14th century. Inhabited since 1958 by a small group of Cistercian monks, it is a spiritual place full of artistic interest.

The main entrance leads into a large rectangular courtyard and the church of **San Lorenzo**, said to be by Brunelleschi, who was also thought to be responsible for the double-arched, graceful lay brothers cloister. Although the church itself is not very interesting, there are some imposing tombs in the crypt chapel.

Sixty-six majolica tondi by Giovanni della Robbia decorate the Chiostro Grande (Main Cloister), around which are the 12 monks' cells. Each of these has its own well, vegetable garden and study room; one is open to visitors.

The **Palazzo degli Studi** houses an art gallery which contains, most notably, a series of fine frescoed lunettes by Pontormo. ❏

RESTAURANTS, CAFÉS AND BARS

Restaurants

Antico Ristoro di' Cambi
Via Sant' Onofrio 1r
Tel: 055-217134
Closed Sunday. €
This restaurant fits perfectly into the heart of the bustling San Frediano area. Traditional in feel and fare, it offers excellent Tuscan cooking and no-nonsense service.

Beccofino
Piazza degli Scarlatti 1r,
Lungarno Guicciardini
Tel: 055-290076
www.beccofino.com
D only Tues–Sat; closed Mon. €€€
A newish restaurant owned by the same couple as Baldovino. The wines are good as are the desserts.

Borgo Antico
Piazza Santa Spirito 6r
Tel: 055-210437
L & D daily. €€
A cosy restaurant where a standard menu is supplemented by an extensive range of daily specials. Try the ravioli for a rich filling pasta dish, or one of the *secondi* from the specials menu.

Cavolo Nero
Via dell'Ardiglione 22
Tel: 055-294744
L & D Mon-Sat. €€€
The "black cabbage" is an elegant place in which Mediterranean food is served. The place is well lit and not one which is on the main tourist trail, though it is well known from its rising popularity with guidebooks.

Napoleone
Piazza del Carmine 24
Tel: 055-281015
www.trattorianapoleone.it
D only. €€
A colourful trattoria in a quiet location across the river. Try the *spaghetti ai gamberi* (spaghetti with prawns).

Osteria del Cinghiale Bianco
Borgo San Jacopo 43r
Tel: 055-215706
www.cinghialebianco.it
D only Mon, Tues, Thur, Fri, closed Wed. €€
A restaurant styled to evoke medieval times in keeping with its location in a 14th-century tower. The pasta and any of the dishes using *cinghiale* (wild boar) are worth trying.

Osteria Santo Spirito
Piazza Santa Spirito 16r
Tel: 055-2382383
L & D daily. €€€
A hip hang-out with colourful décor and noisy music. The food is inventive, and fish figures largely. Try the *orecchiette* for a real pasta experience.

Quattro Leoni
Piazza della Passera, Via Vellutini 1r
Tel: 055-218562
www.4leoni.com
L & D daily. €€
Founded in 1550, this restaurant sits in a quiet square where diners can sit outside in the summer. There are new additions to the Tuscan menu on a daily basis.

Cafés and Bars

Il Caffè
Piazza de' Pitti 9
Tel: 055-2396241
A swish venue sat opposite the Palazzo Pitti, which offers light lunches, dinners and smaller snacks, as well as being better-known as an intimate evening venue.

Dolce Vita
Piazza del Carmine
Tel: 055-284595
www.dolcevitaflorence.com
Evening only.
Trendy bar across the Arno which is frequented for the *aperitivo* and cocktails. Often overcrowded due to its popularity, the *aperitivo* can be a stressful experience.

Hemingway Caffè
Piazza Piantellina 9r
Tel: 055-284781
www.hemingway.fi.it
A café which does hearty American and international-style brunches on a Sunday.

PRICE CATEGORIES

Prices for three-course dinner per person with a glass of wine:
€ = under €25
€€ = €25–€40
€€€ = €40–€60
€€€€ = more than €60

RIGHT: a display outside the Cinghiale Bianco.

PALAZZO PITTI AND GIARDINO DI BOBOLI

The gigantic Palazzo Pitti and the Boboli Gardens were once the royal residence

The Pitti houses seven museums, and provides access to the splendid gardens that became a model for Italian landscaping. The imposing Renaissance palace is built of large, rough-hewn stones; set in its own piazza, it dominates the area to the south of the Ponte Vecchio. The gardens, which lead up to Forte Belvedere, escape being overshadowed thanks to the hill, which allows them to rise to give glorious views over the city to the north and countryside to the south.

A visit to one or two museums combined with the gardens will take up at least half a day, and a three-day ticket offers value for money. Tickets are purchased in the right wing of the palace, and entrance to all the museums is from the internal courtyard. The Appartamenti Reali and the Galleria Palatina (Royal Apartments/ Palatine Gallery) combine luxurious rooms with spectacular works of art. A ticket to the Giardino di Boboli (Boboli Gardens) includes admission to the Museo degli Argenti and the Museo delle Porcellane (Silver Museum/Porcelain Museum). These smaller museums are worthwhile for a second visit or if you have a specific interest. The Galleria d'Arte Moderna and the Galleria del Costume (Gallery of Modern Art/Costume Gallery) are accessed by another joint ticket. The Museo delle Carrozze (Carriage Museum) is closed at present for restoration.

ABOVE: At the end of the Medici reign in 1737, the *palazzo* became the home of the Lorraines, and its elongated cubic form was further extended by the wings which curve round to frame the paved square at its front. Work on the outside was paralleled by alteration to the interior decor, which exhibits the ostentatious tastes of the period of the Lorraines and the Savoys; the next to take up occupancy within its walls. The history of the *palazzo* includes brief tenure by the Bourbons and the Emperor Napoleon before the last ruling monarch, Vittorio Emmanuele III, transferred the house to the public.

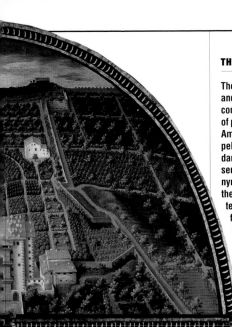

THE GARDENS

The gardens (open daily 8.50am–sunset, closed 1st and last Mon of the month; entrance charge) were commissioned by Cosimo I and created by a range of prolific figures of the day, from Vasari and Ammannati to Buontalenti. One of the most compelling characteristics of Boboli is the shadowy dark-green colour of the cypress and box which serve to highlight the numerous statues of amorous nymphs, satyrs and statuesque deities, as well as the grottoes and fountains. The steps lead up to the terrace behind the palace and in front of Susini's fountain of 1641. The amphitheatre surrounding the fountain occupies the site of a quarry used to obtain much of the stone for the palace, and contains an Egyptian obelisk. A series of terraces leads up the hill to the Neptune Fountain, round to the Rococo Kaffeehaus and up to the statue of Abundance. At the summit lies the Giardino del Cavaliere, or Knight's Garden. This delightful garden – with its low hedges, rose bushes and little cherub fountain – gives open views of San Miniato to the left and the village of Arcetri to the right, rising above a valley dotted with villas and olive groves. This is where the Museo delle Porcellane is located.

The cypress statue-lined avenue known as il Viottolone *(see left)* leads to the Vasca dell'Isola (Island Pool) with its Oceanus fountain (by Giambologna), murky green water, ducks, fish, strange mythical creatures and circular hedge. The route from here to the exit leads past the Grotta di Buontalenti, named after the sculptor who created this cavern in 1583–8. Copies of Michelangelo's Four Slaves (the originals are on display in the Accademia; *see page 157*) are set in the four corners. Finally, on the right as one exits and nestling below the wall of the corridor, is the naked, pot-bellied Pietro Barbino, Cosimo I's court dwarf, seated on a turtle *(see opposite page)*.

ABOVE: the Palazzo Pitti was commissioned in the 15th Century by Luca Pitti, and was designed by Brunelleschi, although he never lived to see the final results. The Medici family took over ownership in 1549 when Eleonora di Toledo, wife of Cosimo I, purchased the *palazzo* when the Pitti family ran into financial strife. She transferred her family from the Palazzo Vecchio to this more tranquil location, though still close to the political heart of the city. This link was strengthened by the Vasari Corridor, which directly connects the residence with Piazza della Signoria by way of the Uffizi and the Palazzo Vecchio. Under the Medici family work on the *palazzo* continued, substantially increasing its size and grandeur. Ammannati was given architectural control, and he constructed the inner courtyard and redesigned the outer façade, which was later further extended.

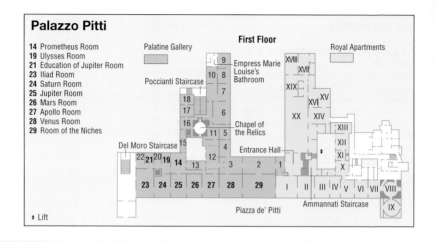

Palazzo Pitti

First Floor

14 Prometheus Room
19 Ulysses Room
21 Education of Jupiter Room
23 Iliad Room
24 Saturn Room
25 Jupiter Room
26 Mars Room
27 Apollo Room
28 Venus Room
29 Room of the Niches

Palatine Gallery

Poccianti Staircase

Empress Marie
Louise's
Bathroom

Royal Apartments

Chapel of
the Relics

Del Moro Staircase

Entrance Hall

Piazza de' Pitti

Ammannati Staircase

Lift

The **Galleria Palatina** on the first floor (open Tues–Sun 8.15am–6.50pm, closed Jan; entrance charge) houses an extraordinary range of paintings collected by the Medici family. In the west wing of the building are the rooms comprising the **Royal Apartments** (same times as the gallery). They are garish and ostentatious, decked out in heavy carpets, wallpapers, fabrics and furnishings, and over-stuffed with treasures. Several of the rooms are named after the colour in which they are themed, and contain paintings and portraits fitting with the mood, followed by the Queen's Apartments, the King's Apartments and a ceremonial room, all filled with exquisite furniture.

ALLEGORICAL FRESCOS

The most important rooms, named after the planets, are frescoed by Pietro da Cortona to allegorise the stages of Prince Ferdinando's education: Sala di Saturno, Sala di Giove, Sala di Marte (during restoration paintings have been moved to the Sala delle Nicchie) and Sala di Venere. These contain works such as Rubens's *The Consequences of War* (Sala di Marte), Raphael's *Portrait of a Lady* (*see left*: Sala di Giove). Other important paintings, such as Raphael's *The Pregnant Lady* (Sala dell'Iliade), Lippi's tondi of the Madonna and Child (*see above*: Sala di Prometeo) and *Sleeping Cupid* by Caravaggio (Sala dell'Educazione di Giove) are found in smaller rooms.

SILVER AND PORCELAIN

On the ground floor, the Museo degli Argenti is in the left-hand corner of the courtyard, whilst the Museo delle Porcellane is situated in the Boboli Gardens (both open daily 8.15am–sunset, closed 1st and last Mon of the month). The former contains much more than silver, ranging from antique vases much loved by Lorenzo the Magnificent to baubles encrusted with semi-precious stones and jewellery. The frescoed rooms alone make a visit worthwhile – in particular the Sala di San Giovanni which formed part of the summer apartments. The frescos by the artist after whom the room is named depict the reign of Lorenzo de' Medici, portrayed as a great patron of the arts. The latter museum displays pottery as well as objets d'art.

The **Galleria d'Arte Moderna** contains mainly Italian works from the neoclassical and Romantic movements, dating from the 18th century to the period after World War 1 (including this fine portrait of *The Artist's Daughter-in-Law* by Giovanni Fattori). The most notable feature of the second-floor collection is its holding of paintings by the Macchiaioli, late-19th century Italian Impressionists. Also situated on the second floor is the **Galleria del Costume** (both open daily 8.15am–1.50pm, closed 1st, 3rd and 5th Mon, 2nd and 4th Sun of the month; entrance charge), whose 6,000-piece holding of clothing, theatrical costumes and accessories are supplemented by frequent special exhibitions.

ABOVE AND RIGHT: one of the finest rooms is the Sala di Apollo, in which are important works by Andrea del Sarto (including his *Lamentation of Christ*, 1522–3, *above*) and another master of the High Renaissance, Titian (notably his *The Interrupted Concert*, c. 1510, *right*).

OLTRARNO EAST

The eastern part of Oltrarno has many attractions, from the Forte Belvedere to the church of San Miniato al Monte, and there are stunning views over the city from Piazzale Michelangelo

From the Ponte Vecchio, the Via dei Bardi leads east to the Piazza dei Mozzi and the **Museo Bardini** ⑩ (also known as the Galleria Corsi; closed for restoration). The great antique-dealer Stefano Bardini built the Palazzo Bardini in 1881 using bits and pieces – doorways, ceilings, stairs – rescued from the demolition of various ancient buildings. He left the palace, and his eclectic art collection within, to the city of Florence in 1923. Particularly fine is the Andrea della Robbia tomb, a Madonna attributed to Donatello, Pollaiuolo's St Michael and a headless Virgin by Giovanni Pisano. There are also fine Persian and Anatolian carpets, Turkish ceramics, a collection of musical instruments, suits of armour and furniture.

A good route up the hill that characterises this part of Oltrarno is via the Costa San Giorgio, a narrow lane that begins at the church of **Santa Felicità** (just south of the Ponte Vecchio) and winds steeply upwards. After a short climb, the granite-flagged lane flattens out at the Porta San Giorgio. This is the city's oldest surviving gate, built in 1260. On the inner arch is a fresco by Bicci di Lorenzo, *Our Lady with St George and St Leonard* (1430). On the outer face is a copy of a 13th-century carving of St George in combat with the dragon (the original is in the Palazzo Vecchio).

The Belvedere

To the right of the gate the sheer and massive walls of the **Forte di Belvedere** ⑪ (open daily 10am–8pm, or sunset if earlier) rise to a great height and cause you to wonder what lies behind. In fact, the interior is almost empty and used now for exhibitions of contemporary and experimental art. Recently

Map on page 170

LEFT:
San Miniato.
BELOW: looking out over the city.

A modern sculpture outside the Belvedere.

restored after a long period of neglect, the Forte di Belvedere offers fabulous views both of the city and of rural Florence.

The fortress was built on the orders of Ferdinando I, beginning in 1590, to Buontalenti's design. It symbolises the Grand Duke's sense of insecurity, for though the structure was explained as part of the city's defences, there was only one means of access – a secret door entered from the Boboli Gardens behind the Pitti Palace. Clearly it was intended for his own personal use in times of attack or insurrection. Now Florentines come to stroll around the ramparts on Sunday afternoons, to walk off lunch and enjoy the extensive views.

Scented alleys

The fort marks the beginning of Via di San Leonardo, a cobbled rural lane that climbs between the walled gardens of scattered villas. Here and there a gate allows a view of the gardens behind, and the wisteria and roses grow so vigorously that they spill over the walls, their abundant and fragrant blossoms tumbling into the lane. On the left is the church of **San Leonardo** ⓬, which contains a fine 13th-century pulpit. Both Tchaikovsky and Stravinsky lived in this lane. Florence was a favourite resort, before the 1917 Revolution, for Russians seeking an escape from the rigours of their own climate.

Cross Viale Galileo and continue along Via di San Leonardo, before taking the first left turn to follow Via Viviani. This road climbs steeply, with the promise of fine views ahead, until it levels out at the Piazza Volsanminiato in the village of Arcetri. Follow the Via del Pian de' Giullari until, after a few metres, the views suddenly open up.

To the right, the only signs of modernity are the receiver dishes of the **Astrophysical Observatory**. On the left is its ancient predecessor, the **Torre del Gallo** ⓭, which was once used for astronomical research, and much restored in the 19th century by Stefano Bardini (of Museo Bardini fame, *see page 181*); he used it as a repository for the larger architectural materials that he rescued from demolished buildings.

On the hillside below the tower is the 15th-century **Villa "La Gallina"**. This contains very fine frescos of nude dancers by Antonio del Pollaiuolo (*c.* 1464–71), but is not normally open to the public.

Galileo's exile

To the right again, the hillside falls away steeply in a series of terraced gardens, vineyards and orchards. Beyond is a typically Tuscan view of a series of low hills covered in sculptural groups of pencil-thin cypress trees, echoing the shape of medieval towers and church campaniles, rising above the red-tiled roofs of villas and simple village homes.

This is a view that Galileo enjoyed, by force, during the last years of his life. He lived at the **Villa il Gioiello**

(No. 42 Via del Pian dei Giullari) from 1631 until his death in 1642, virtually under house arrest, although he was permitted to continue his work and to receive a stream of distinguished admirers. Both the villa and the gardens have been under restoration since the late 1980s, but the city authorities say they will, eventually, be opened to the public.

Choice of routes

At the crossroads in the village of Pian de' Giullari there is a choice of routes. Via Santa Margherita leads to the early 14th-century village church and some far-reaching views up the Arno valley. Via San Matteo leads to the monastery of the same name. An inscription on the nearby house (No. 48) forbids the playing of football in the vicinity – a rule that local children joyfully flout.

The route back to Florence involves backtracking as far as Arcetri and taking the Via della Torre del Gallo downhill to the Piazza degli Unganelli. As the road descends, there are fine views of the city's distinctive cathedral glimpsed across olive groves, a reminder of just how small and rural a place Florence is. Only the occasional sounds of traffic, echoing up the Arno valley, disturb the rural peace – and even this is drowned out by the pleasing sound of church bells at midday or, if you are out on a Sunday, at regular intervals throughout the morning.

Villas of the great

Cypress trees, like beautiful clusters of green pillars from a ruined temple, tumble down the hillside. Many of the villas you will pass have marble plaques recording that they were once the home of philosophers, artists, poets and architects, so many has Florence produced over the centuries. Sunlight warms the scene, and, even in winter, lizards bask on the warm garden walls.

At the **Piazza degli Unganelli**, ignore the main road that bends to the left and look instead for the narrow Via di Giramonte, an unpaved track that leads off to the right between high walls. This cool and shady path follows the sheer walls of the city's 16th-century fortifications and eventually climbs up through trees and oleander bushes to the church of **San Miniato ⓮**. This, in the opinion of many, is one of the most beautiful and least spoilt churches in Italy. St Minias was a merchant from the East (the son of the King of Armenia, according to one story) who settled in Florence but was executed around AD 250 during the anti-Christian purges of the Emperor Decius. A church was probably built on the site of his tomb soon after, but the present building was begun around 1018 and completed around 1207.

Roman origins

Like the cathedral baptistery, the delicate geometrical marble inlay of the facade was much admired by Brunelleschi and his contempo-

Map on page 170

An altar in San Miniato.

To the north of the church is a small graveyard, opened up in 1839, full of rewarding 19th- and early 20th-century monuments. Family tombs, like miniature houses, are supplied with electricity to light the "everlasting lamps" of Etruscan form, and there are numerous highly accomplished figures and portraits in stone and bronze of former Florentine citizens.

BELOW: Piazzale Michelangelo and its stupendous view.

raries, who believed it to be the work of the ancient Romans. Certainly some of the columns of the nave and crypt, with their crisply carved Corinthian capitals, are reused Roman material.

Again, like the baptistery, the Calimala Guild was responsible for the maintenance of the church, and the guild's emblem – an eagle carrying a bale of wool – crowns the pediment. The interior has, remarkably, survived in its original state, except for the 19th-century repainting of the open timber roof and an attempt to line the walls with marble, copying the motifs of the facade. Frescos on the aisle walls include a large 14th-century St Christopher by an unknown artist. The nave floor has a delightful series of marble intarsia panels depicting lions, doves, signs of the zodiac and the date, 1207.

At the end of the nave, between the staircases that lead to the raised choir, is a tabernacle made to house a miraculous painted crucifix (now in Santa Trinità) that is said to have spoken to Giovanni Gualberto, the

11th-century Florentine saint and founder of the Vallambrosan order of Benedictine monks. The tabernacle is the collective work of Michelozzo, Agnolo Gaddi and Luca della Robbia, and was made around 1448.

On the left of the nave is the chapel of the Cardinal of Portugal, who died, aged 25, on a visit to Florence in 1439. The very fine tomb is by Rossellino; the glazed terracotta ceiling, depicting the Cardinal Virtues, by Luca della Robbia; the *Annunciation* above the Bishop's throne by Baldovinetti; and the frescos by the brothers Antonio and Piero Pollaiuolo.

The highlight of the church is the raised choir and pulpit, all of marble and inset with intarsia panels depicting a riot of mythical beasts. The mosaic in the apse, of 1297, shows Christ, the Virgin and St Minias. The combined effect is distinctively Byzantine in feel.

The martyr's shrine

The choir was elevated in order to accommodate the 11th-century crypt below, in which the remains of

St Minias were placed beneath the altar for veneration by visiting pilgrims. The vaulted crypt roof, with frescos of saints and prophets by Taddeo Gaddi, is held up by a forest of pillars and capitals from diverse sources – many of them Roman – with delightful disregard for match and even less for symmetry.

Towering above the church's graveyard is the massive, but incomplete, campanile, built in 1523 to replace the original one that collapsed in 1499. This played a strategic role during the 1530 siege of Florence when the Medici, expelled in 1527, returned to take the city, backed by the army of the Emperor Charles V.

Under Michelangelo's direction, the tower was used as an artillery platform and wrapped in mattresses to absorb the impact of enemy cannon fire. Michelangelo also supervised the construction of temporary fortifications around the church; afterwards they were rebuilt in stone and made permanent. Later they were incorporated into the grand cascade of terraces and staircases laid out by the city architect, Giuseppe Poggi, in 1865–73.

Piazzale Michelangelo

These descend the hillside to the broad **Piazzale Michelangelo** ⑮. This viewpoint, decorated with reproductions of Michelangelo's most famous works, is crowded with visitors at all times of the year who come for the celebrated panorama over the red roofs of Florence to the green hills beyond. Despite the milling hordes and the sellers of tacky souvenirs, the sight is awe-inspiring, and never better than on a clear Sunday in spring at around 11.45am, when the bells of the city's churches all peal to call the faithful to midday Mass, and the surrounding peaks are sharply delineated against the pale-blue sky.

Map on page 170

The best route back to the Ponte Vecchio is the steep descent, through acacia groves and past overgrown grottoes, along the Via di San Salvatore to **Porta San Niccolò**. This imposing gateway (c. 1340) has been restored. Turn left along the Via di Belvedere to Porta San Miniato, now little more than a hole in the wall. A plaque opposite records that members of the Florentine Resistance were shot in August 1944 in a final vindictive act as the Nazis fled the city and the advance of the Allied troops.

From here there is a choice of routes. Continue along the Via di Belvedere for a final taste of rural Florence. The tree-lined lane follows the high walls and bastions of the city's 14th-century defences, marking a sharp division between town and country. It climbs to the **Porta San Giorgio**, from where the Via della Costa San Giorgio leads directly back to the Ponte Vecchio. If it's a more direct route you're looking for, then take the Via di San Niccolò to the Via dei Bardi – lined with medieval buildings – to get back to the bustle of the city. ❑

The view is just as spectacular at night.

RESTAURANTS

Antica Mescita
Via San Niccolò 60r
Tel: 055-2342836
Closed Sun. €
Simple Italian food in a cheery, crowded atmosphere. Part of this *osteria* is set in a former chapel.

Fuori Porta
Via Monte alle Croci 10r
Tel: 055-2342483
www.fuoriporta.it
L & D Mon–Sat. €€
A little *enoteca* near Piazzale Michelangelo whose communal seating adds to the jovial atmosphere. The food is rustic and plentiful.

Golden View
Via dei Bardi 58r
Tel: 055-214502
www.goldenviewopenbar.com
L & D daily. €€–€€€
A modern place with live jazz. It overlooks the Arno and serves Tuscan and European dishes.

Pane e Vino
Via San Niccolò 70r
Tel: 055-2476956
D only; closed Mon. €€
One of the best selections of wine in the city, with good food and an informal atmosphere.

● ● ● ● ● ● ● ● ● ● ● ● ● ● ●

Price includes dinner and a glass of wine, excluding tip. €€€€ over €60, €€€ €40–60, €€ €25–40, € under €25.

FIESOLE

Before there was Florence, there was Fiesole. Although now somewhat eclipsed by the city below, this once-powerful hilltop town of Etruscan origins is fascinating

Perched on a hilltop north of Florence, **Fiesole** is a small place of archaeological importance usually overrun by tourists admiring the views over Florence. Founded perhaps as early as the 8th century BC, Fiesole was colonised by the Romans in around 80 BC and later became the capital of Etruria. The growth of Florence overtook that of Fiesole, but it remained sufficiently important as a competitor to Florence in the 11th and 12th centuries for the two towns to be constantly at war with each other.

Total destruction

In 1125 Florentine troops stormed Fiesole and won what was, perhaps, the easiest victory in a long campaign to dominate the whole of Tuscany. Not content merely to subjugate Fiesole, the Florentines razed the village, sparing only the cathedral complex. With hindsight, this destruction had its benefits. Few buildings were erected in succeeding centuries, and important Roman and Etruscan remains were thus preserved relatively undisturbed beneath the soil.

Much of Fiesole has been declared an archaeological zone, and, despite the snail's-pace progress typical of any process in Italy that involves bureaucracy, excavation

has continued and the results throw new light on the origins and achievements of the Etruscans.

The rejuvenation of Fiesole began in the 19th century. A handful of villas had been built in the 16th and 17th centuries, but the main impetus for growth came with the adoption of Fiesole by the Anglo-Florentine community. The Brownings praised its beauty in their poetry, and here, unlike in Florence itself, there was space for the English to indulge their passion

Map on page 188

LEFT: olive trees and views over Florence.
BELOW: the facade of Badia Fiesolana.

The Teatro Romano, with its numbered seats, could originally accommodate an audience of up to 2,000 people.

for gardening. Standing at nearly 295 metres (1,000 ft) above sea level, Fiesole was considered more salubrious than the furnace of Florence. This belief that the town is cooler than the city below (in fact the difference in temperature is marginal) still attracts refugees attempting to escape from the summer's heat.

The best way to get up to Fiesole from Florence is by taking the No. 7 bus from Santa Maria Novella station, or to go on one of the sightseeing buses. Once through the Florentine suburbs, the bus climbs through semi-rural countryside where villas with trim gardens are dotted among orchards and olive groves. Psychologically, at least, the air feels fresher, and when the bus reaches **Piazza Mino** ❶, Fiesole's main square, there is an atmosphere of provincial Italy which seems miles from urbane Florence down below.

Teatro Romano and archaelogical treasures

Just north of the square is the **Teatro Romano** ❷ (open daily 9.30am–7pm in summer, 9.30am– 5pm in winter, closed Tues Nov–March; combined entrance charge covers the Archaelogical Museum and Bandini Museum), which is still used during the Estate Fiesolana arts festival, in July and August. The larger blocks of stone represent original Roman seats, the smaller ones modern replacements.

The great and noble views from the amphitheatre are as dramatic as anything that takes place on the stage. The theatre, originally built at the end of the 1st century AD, was excavated out of the hillside, which drops steeply away, revealing the beautiful Tuscan landscape. To the left, the River Mugnone cuts a deep valley while, in the middle distance, an endless succession of hills and peaks stretches as far as the horizon,

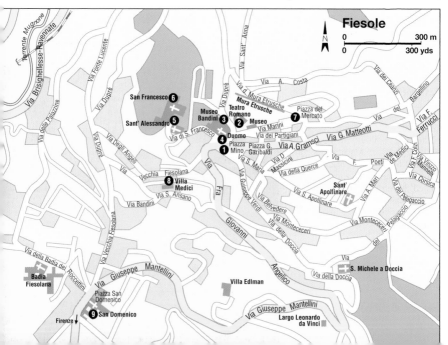

dotted with villas and clusters of cypress trees.

The excellent **Museo Archeo-logico** (open the same hours as the Teatro Romano), next to the theatre, was built in 1912–14. One of the most important archaeological museums in Italy, the building is an imaginative reconstruction of the 1st-century BC Roman temple, whose excavated remains are in the northwestern area of the theatre complex; parts of the original Roman frieze are incorporated into the pediment.

The exhibits on the ground floor consist principally of finds from local excavations and illustrate the historical development of the Florence region from the Bronze Age onwards. The upstairs gallery is used to display early medieval jewellery, coins and ceramics, as well as Etruscan treasures donated by Florentine families. The last room contains a very fine torso of Dionysus and early Roman funerary monuments. The important Costantini collection of pottery from Greece, Magna Graecia and Etruria is also on the first floor.

An underground passage links the main body of the museum to what was once the Costantini collection and is now the bookshop. In this passage is a reconstruction of a Lombardic-era tomb; the skeleton of the deceased (a man aged about 50 who died *c.* AD 650) is surrounded by objects – including a beautiful blue glass-wine goblet – placed there to accompany him to the next world.

Much of the rest of the site is overgrown and neglected, but below the museum, to the right of the theatre, there is a 1st-century AD bath complex with furnaces, hypocaust system and plunge baths. Next, a terrace follows a stretch of 3rd-century BC Etruscan town walls and leads to the ruins of the 1st-century

BC Roman temple built on the foundations of an earlier Etruscan one.

Renaissance collection

Opposite the theatre complex, in Via Dupre, is the **Museo Bandini ❸** (open daily 10am–7pm, 10am–5pm in winter, closed Tues Nov–March; entrance charge), which at the time of writing is temporarily closed for restructuring but due to reopen soon.

It contains the collection of Canon Angelo Bandini, an 18th-century historian and philologist, and features many fine Florentine and Tuscan Renaissance paintings, including works by Taddeo and Agnolo Gaddi, Nardo di Cione and Lorenzo Monaco. There is also furniture, various architectural fragments and a small but remarkable collection of Byzantine carved ivories.

The most striking work is a secular painting, an allegory of the Triumph of Love, Chastity, Time and Piety, painted on wooden panels and once forming part of a wedding chest in which Florentine ladies kept their dowry of fine linen and clothing.

Map on page 188

The Scuola di Musica di Fiesole, housed in Villa la Torraccia in San Domenico, is one of Italy's foremost music schools.

BELOW: a fresco in San Francesco.

The Duomo

The **Duomo di Fiesole** ❹ occupies one end of the Piazza Mino, the town hall, which is currently closed off for works, the other. The Duomo looks uninviting from the outside due to over-restoration in the 19th century, but the interior retains something of its original Roman-esque form. Begun in 1028 and extended in the 14th century, the original nave columns survive (some with Roman capitals), leading to a raised choir above a crypt. The altarpiece by Bicci di Lorenzo (1440) and some 16th-century frescos are outstanding.

A bust in the Medici garden.

City views

The Via San Francesco, west of the Duomo, climbs steeply to the little chapel of **San Iacopo** (opening hours subject to change) and then on up, past gardens and viewpoints, to the church of **Sant' Alessandro** ❺, originally 6th-century and built on the site of earlier Roman and Etruscan temples. The *cipollino* marble columns of the nave are Roman, and there are splendid views over Flo-

BELOW:
the Villa Medici.

rence from a nearby lookout point. The church is now used as an area for temporary exhibitions. Further up, on the summit, is the friary of **San Francesco** ❻, unattractively restored in neo-Gothic style, but with an intriguing small museum of objects brought from the Orient by missionaries.

Back in the main square, you have to decide whether to have lunch in one of the town's over-priced – but picturesque – restaurants, or summon up the energy for further walks in the maze of lanes and footpaths leading east off the square.

Etruscan walls

From the Teatro Romano, Via Marini leads to the **Piazza del Mercato** ❼, which overlooks the valley of the River Mugnone. A little further, on the left, the Via delle Mura Etrusche follows Fiesole's best-preserved stretch of Etruscan wall, composed of monolithic blocks of stone. From here, steep lanes lead back to the main road, Via Gramsci. The first fork left, Via del

Bargellino, leads to an overgrown plot between two houses where two 3rd-century BC Etruscan underground tombs have been preserved. A short way further on, take the right turn for Borgunto to reach Via Adriano Mari, which joins Via Monte Ceceri to return to Piazza Mino in the centre of Fiesole.

The stones of Florence

Along the route there are excellent views of Florence and of the wooded slopes and disused quarries of Monte Ceceri, source of much of the beautiful dove-grey *pietra serena* used by Renaissance architects to decorate the city's churches.

From the southwest corner of the main square, Via Vecchia Fiesolana descends to the **Villa Medici** ❽ *(see page 192)*, one of the first Renaissance country villas, built by Michelozzo in 1458–61 for Cosimo de' Medici, and deliberately sited to make the best of the views.

Take any of the downhill paths from here to reach the hamlet of **San Domenico** ❾ after about 800

metres (½ mile). The church of San Domenico dates from 1406 and contains the recently restored *Madonna with Angels and Saints* (1430), an early work of Fra Angelico, who began his monastic life here before transferring to San Marco.

Directly opposite the church, the Via della Badia dei Roccettini descends to the **Badia Fiesolana**, a monastery that now houses the European University Institute, which was founded in 1976. The huge facade of the Baroque church is built around another exquisite and jewel-like facade of inlaid marble (similar to that of San Miniato). It is all that has survived of the original Fiesole cathedral, rebuilt around 1028 and again in the 15th century when Brunelleschi, it is thought, was responsible for the cruciform plan. The relatively isolated position of the Badia, with views south to Florence, west to the Mugnone Valley and northeast to Fiesole, is superb.

The No. 7 bus can be caught in San Domenico for the return journey to Florence. ❏

Map on page 188

Badia Fiesolana.

LEFT:
the Duomo glimpsed in the distance.

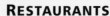

RESTAURANTS

Pizzeria Etrusca
Piazza Mino 2
Tel: 055-599484
L & D; closed Thur in winter. €
Set in the small main piazza near the bus stop, this small pizzeria is a good place to grab a quick slice of pizza before heading back into Florence.

Pizzeria San Domenico
Piazza San Domenico 11
Tel: 055-59182
L & D; closed Mon. €–€€
This is a simple restaurant with a huge selection of pizzas and pastas and friendly service. If you don't fancy a blow-out on the carbohydrates, try

one of the big salads followed by a *coppa della casa* (the house *dolce*) for dessert.

La Reggia degli Etruschi
Via San Francesco 18
Tel: 055-59385
www.lareggia.org
L & D; closed Tues, Mon and Wed L. €€
The patio of this restaurant has a wonderful view over the city of Florence spread out below. The food, if not quite as breathtaking as the view, is nonetheless, good, solid Italian fare.

● ● ● ● ● ● ● ● ● ● ● ● ● ● ●
Price includes dinner and a glass of wine, excluding tip. €€€€ over €60, €€€ €40–60, €€ €25–40, € under €25.

MEDICI VILLAS

All around Florence are country villas, most built for and owned by the Medicis

The style of these Renaissance Tuscan houses is representative of the peaceful period and ideal of gracious living that prevailed over Florence at the time. The villas are generally centred around an inner courtyard and feature porticoes and a loggia, but the centrepieces – often open even if the house is closed – are arguably the gardens. These reflect architectural rigour in their design and feature sculptures and fountains similar to those seen in the Boboli Gardens *(see pages 176–7)*.

Many of the villas are now privately owned or have been transformed into American university campuses, thereby restricting what can be viewed and rendering the opening hours erratic. Most villas are accessible by a short bus ride out of Florence, although some companies organise trips by coach to combine visits.

BELOW: Villa Medici (by appointment only; tel: 055-59164; entrance charge) is easily accessible owing to its situation en route to Fiesole *(see page 191)*, although viewing must be arranged in advance.

ABOVE: an alternative destination is the Villa Medicea della Petraia (open daily 8.15am–sunset, villa by guided tour only, every 45mins from 8.30am, closed 2nd and 3rd Mon of the month; entrance charge). This house was designed by Buontalenti for Ferdinando de' Medici and set on a sloping hill. Also attributed to Buontalenti, the Villa Medicea di Cerreto Guidi (open daily 8.15am–7pm, closed 2nd and 3rd Mon of the month; entrance charge includes admission to the Historical Hunting and Territorial Museum) was used as a fortified hunting lodge, a fact reflected in the small museum's collection of guns.

MEDICI GARDENS

Only the gardens of the Villa di Castello (open daily 8.15am–sunset, closed 2nd and 3rd Mon of the month; secret garden viewable on request; entrance charge) can be seen. The original water effects are no longer evident, but grottoes and statuary abound. Other villas with attractive surroundings include the Villa Demidoff and Parco di Pratolino (*see right*; open 10am–sunset Thurs–Sun, Apr–Sept, Sun only in Mar and Oct; entrance charge) whose Mannerist gardens were restructured into the English Romantic style, and Villa Gamberaia (gardens open daily 9am–7pm, villa on request only) in the easily accessible pretty village of Settignano. The latter now includes facilities

for conferences, and dependencies of the house have been converted into pricey accommodation.

In the direction of Sesto Fiorentino is the Villa Medicea di Careggi (visits on request only) – historically the favoured retreat of the Medici family, which now houses hospital administration buildings. Villa La Pietra and Villa I Tatti have been converted into the Florentine campuses of New York University and Harvard University respectively but can be visited on request.

ABOVE: Villa Medicea Poggio a Caiano (open daily 8.15am–sunset, villa by guided tour only, hourly from 8.30am, closed 2nd and 3rd Mon of the month; entrance charge) is often dubbed the perfect villa. The façade, which was modelled on a Greek temple by Sangallo to satisfy the tastes of Lorenzo, is well preserved.

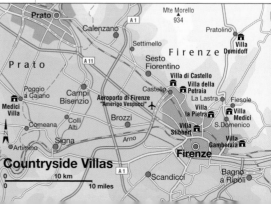

Countryside Villas

EXCURSIONS

Temptingly close to Florence are such alluring
destinations as Arezzo, San Gimignano,
Siena and Lucca, all of which can be
reached easily by public transport

F lorence can be a claustrophobic
city, and there may come a time
when you need to escape. Fortu-
nately, it is well placed for all sorts of
expeditions, to other major art centres
(such as Siena or Lucca), to tourist-
free smaller towns (such as Pistoia or
Vinci), to the coast or to the fabulous
Chianti countryside for a gentle
meander with stops for the odd wine-
tasting and a lazy meal on a vine-clad
terrace. The choice of destination will
probably be dictated by means of
transport; with a car, the possibilities
are endless, but public transport
would probably suggest Lucca,
Arezzo, Siena or Pisa, all of which are
well connected with Florence.

En route to Arezzo

Arezzo is 77 km (48 miles) southeast
of Florence on the A1 autostrada.
There are a few possible stop-offs on
the way, but nothing of great importance for those who feel the time
would be better spent in the city itself.

Heading south on the A1, the Valdarno region (in the Middle Ages a
much fought-over battleground of the
Guelfs and Ghibellines) follows the
Arno's course upstream. **San Giovanni Valdarno** ❶ was fortified as a
bulwark against the Aretines; today,
it is a lively centre with a surprising
display of architectural and artistic
wealth. Masaccio's *Virgin and Child*

is housed in the church of Santa
Maria, and Fra Angelico's *Annunciation* is preserved in the Renaissance
monastery of Montecarlo just outside
the town. The village of Castelfranco
di Sopra, 6 km (4 miles) north, retains
its military character, and many of the
14th-century buildings and streets
have survived. The nearby villages of
Loro Ciufenna and Cennina bear
names derived from the Etruscan
dialect, but a more medieval rusticity
is evident in their alleyways and
ruined castle fortresses.

PRECEDING PAGES:
a golden Tuscan
landscape.
LEFT:
looking over San
Gimignano.
BELOW:
Piazza Grande, Arezzo.

The Arno basin was a lake in prehistoric times, and farmers still unearth remains and bones of long-extinct animals. At **Montevarchi** ❷, 5 km (3 miles) beyond San Giovanni, the **Accademia Valdarnese** (open Tues–Sat 9am–noon, 4–6pm, Sun 10am–noon; entrance charge) is a prehistory museum with an impressive collection of fossilised remains.

Arezzo

And so to **Arezzo** ❸, one of Tuscany's wealthiest cities, known for its gold, art and antiques. Originally an Etruscan city, in 294 BC it became a rest station on the Via Cassia between Florence and Rome. The main Roman site is the amphitheatre, built in the 1st century BC; on the same site, the **Museo Archeologico** (open Mon–Sat 9am–2pm, Sun 9am–1pm; entrance charge) features some of the best examples anywhere of the red-glazed Coralline ware for which Arezzo has long been famous. The

"modern" city is dominated by the Duomo, which has been described as one of the most perfect expressions of Gothic architecture in Italy – although the facade dates only from 1914. Inside, there are clustered columns, pointed arches, beautiful 16th-century stained-glass windows by Guillaume de Marcillat and a fresco of St Mary Magdalene by Piero della Francesca.

The medieval **Piazza Grande**, perfect setting for the Giostra del Saracino (a jousting tournament held each June and September), is dominated on one side by the Loggia di Vasari, built in 1573. But the most impressive building is the round Romanesque apse of the 12th-century church of Santa Maria della Pieve, with its crumbling Pisan-Lucchese facade (on Corso Italia) and adjacent "campanile of a hundred holes". You can see Arezzo's greatest work of art in the otherwise dull church of **San Francesco** in the piazza of the same name. Painted between 1452 and

A group of cypresses beneath a blue Tuscan sky.

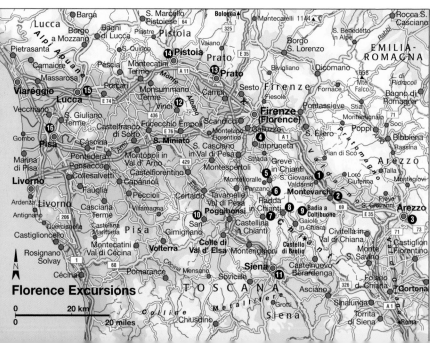

Florence Excursions

0   20 km

0   20 miles

1466, Piero della Francesco's fresco cycle *The Legend of the True Cross* is a powerful and haunting series of paintings which has survived earthquake, fire, lightning and gunfire over the centuries to remain one of the most significant reference points in the history of Italian painting.

The **Museo Statale d'Arte Medioevale e Moderna** (open Tues–Sat 9am–7pm, Sun 9am–12.30pm; entrance charge) is situated diagonally opposite the Duomo in the 15th-century Palazzo Bruni. Its varied collection includes excellent, mostly local majolica, frescos and paintings.

Some great intellectuals lived in Arezzo, including Petrarch, Guido d'Arezzo, the inventor of Western musical notation, and Giorgio Vasari, the 16th-century artist, architect and author. On Via 20 Settembre is the **Casa di Giorgio Vasari** (open Wed–Mon 9am–7pm, Sun 9am–1pm), which he built for himself in 1540; he decorated the ceilings and walls with portraits of fellow artists and friends. From there, walk up to the 13th-century church of **San Domenico** to see a fine Gothic chapel, good frescos and a crucifix by Cimabue.

Chianti wine trail

To take a drive through some of the most stunning countryside Tuscany has to offer, head south out of Florence from Porta Romana on the Via Senese and, when you get to the big roundabout where the Rome autostrada and Siena superstrada converge, take the road marked "Tavernuzze, Impruneta, Greve".

Impruneta ❹ is a pleasant town noted for its production of terracotta (the tiles on Brunelleschi's dome were made here). It was an important early medieval sanctuary where a shrine was erected to house an image of the Virgin Mary, attributed to St Luke. This collegiate church was bombed during the war, but consequently restored, and now houses two beautiful chapels and some marvellous terracottas by della Robbia.

From Impruneta, take the Chiantigiana (SS 222), the road that leads through one of Italy's most important wine-producing areas. Just before Greve on the right, the tiny walled town of **Montefioralle** has been beautifully restored, enclosing narrow streets and stone houses. **Greve** ❺ is the heart of Chianti and a bustling market town; its September wine fair is the biggest in the region. The triangular, arcaded Piazza Matteotti is lined with shops selling wine and olive oil; Falorni, a butcher famous throughout the region, sells wonderful salami here.

A detour off the Chiantigiana takes a circular route along a *strada bianca* (unpaved road) past wine villas and through fabulous countryside. Take a turning to the left just south of Greve signposted **Vignamaggio**. This mellow, pinkish-hued old villa was built by the Gherardini family; the subject of Leonardo da Vinci's famous Mona Lisa is said to have been born here, and it was used as the setting for Kenneth Branagh's

Map on page 198

These grapes will make delicious Chianti wines.

BELOW: cyclists in Greve.

Chianti vineyards overlooked by a beautiful hilltop village.

BELOW: dawn over the hills of San Gimignano.

film *Much Ado about Nothing* in 1992. A shop sells estate-produced wine and olive oil. Continue on this winding road into the hills, and you come first to Casole (where the trattoria serves good, wholesome meals with fabulous views) and then the hamlet of Lamole, before arriving back on the main road. Near **Panzano ⑥** (a partially walled town and an important agricultural centre set in glorious countryside), the Pieve di San Leolino (1 km/½ mile to the south) is a Romanesque building with a pretty portico, and the nearby Fattoria Montagliari (just north of Panzano) sells its own wines, grappa, honey and cheeses.

Castellina in Chianti ⑦, which lies 15 km (9 miles) further south, is a delightful hilltop village whose ancient walls remain almost intact. The castle itself is now a fortified town hall hiding a small **Etruscan Museum** (open Mon–Sat 9am–1pm), surrounded by a warren of atmospheric back streets. The Enoteca Vini Gallo Nero in Via della Rocca is a wine-tasting centre which also offers information on wine tours.

Radda in Chianti

From Castellina you can either continue south and visit the **Fattoria di Fonterutoli** (tel: 0577-73571; www.fonterutoli.com), near the ancient hamlet of the same name, to taste or buy some fabulous wines, or go straight to **Radda in Chianti ⑧**, some 12 km (7 miles) to the east. Here, towards the Monti di Chianti, the terrain becomes more rugged, with Radda perched high on a hill. The streets of this medieval town radiate out from the central piazza, where the **Palazzo Comunale** has a 15th-century fresco of the Madonna with St John and St Christopher in the entrance hall. Just outside Radda are the medieval villages of **Ama** to the south and **Volpaia** to the north; both are home to great wine-producing estates.

Between Radda and Gaiole, the **Badia a Coltibuono ⑨** (open May–Oct, Mon–Fri 2–4.15pm for guided tours; closed Aug), set among pine trees, oaks, chestnuts and vines, is one of the most beautiful buildings in Chianti. The abbey dates from the 12th century but was converted into a private villa in the 18th century. The estate (tel: 0577-749479; www.coltibuono.com) now produces and sells excellent wine, olive oil and honey, and a restaurant serves food in "elegant rustic" surroundings. The only drawback is that the abbey is on every tour itinerary, and so inundated by tour buses.

From Gaiole, a popular retreat for hot Florentines, head south on the SS 484 to **Castello di Brolio** (open daily for guided tours; entrance fee), which is set high in the hills with views that stretch to Siena and Monte Amiata. The castle's past spans Guelf-Ghibelline conflicts, sacking by the Sienese, and German occupation and Allied bombing during World War II. Striking medieval walls surround the castle, which has been in the Ricasoli family since the mid-19th century, when Baron Bettino Ricasoli founded

the Chianti wine industry here. Needless to say, the house wine can be sampled and bought (tel: 0577-7301; www.ricasoli.it).

The quickest way back to Florence is by returning to Gaiole and crossing the hills on the SS 408 to pick up the A1 autostrada near Montevarchi.

En route to Siena: San Gimignano

There is enough to see and do in Siena to warrant an extended stay, but it is also a delightful place for a day trip, and there are some interesting stop-offs on the way. It is only 68 km (42 miles) south of Florence on the SS 2 superstrada (head south out of town via the Porta Romana), and the SITA bus company runs a frequent service (it is quicker than by train).

From Poggibonsi the approach to **San Gimignano ⑩** is memorable as the famous towers come into view behind olives, cypresses and vines. Only 13 of the original 76 towers – the so-called *belle torri* (originally designed as keeps during the Guelf-Ghibelline feuds in the 12th and 13th centuries) – are left standing, but San Gimignano remains Italy's best-preserved medieval city.

The **Romanesque Collegiata** no longer has the status of a cathedral because there is no bishop. The facade is plain, but inside are lavish stripes and vaulted ceilings painted with gold stars, similar in style to Siena's Duomo. The walls are covered in fine frescos, mostly by Sienese artists. Look out for Bartolo di Fredi's vivid Old Testament scenes along the north aisle (Noah and his menagerie are delightful), and Barna di Siena's New Testament scenes covering the south wall. On the west wall are Benozzo Gozzoli's *Saint Sebastian* and Taddeo di Bartolo's gory *Last Judgement*. Off the south aisle lies the Santa Fina Chapel, with Ghirlandaio's flowery depiction of the local saint: legend has it that when

she died in 1253, violets sprang up on her coffin and on the towers.

In the asymmetrical **Piazza del Duomo** lies the **Palazzo del Popolo** with its 54-metre (177-ft) Torre Grossa, completed in *c.* 1300. In the same square the **Museo Civico** (open daily summer 9.30am–7.20pm; winter 10am–5.50pm; entrance charge) contains an excellent collection of Florentine and Sienese masters, including works by Gozzoli, Lippi, Taddeo di Bartolo and Giotto – plus the well-known domestic and profane scenes by Memmo di Filippuccio, an early 14th-century artist. The adjacent Piazza della Cisterna is a lovely triangular piazza with a 13th-century well and lined with medieval *palazzi*; there is an excellent *gelateria* at the top of the square.

Back on the SS 2, just before you reach Siena, you get a good view of the tiny fortified town of **Monteriggioni**. Dating from 1219, this was once the northernmost bastion of Siena, and saw plenty of action during the wars with Florence. Now it perches peacefully on a little hill, its ancient walls broken by 14 towers.

Map on page 198

A Tuscan farmhouse under a full moon.

BELOW: admiring the view, San Gimignano.

Siena

Some people consider **Siena**  to be the most beautiful city in Tuscany. It has hidden gardens, tunnelled passages and secret piazzas, and is often thought of as being the feminine foil to Florentine masculinity. The city's origins are shrouded in myths of wolves and martyred saints; legend tells that it was founded by Senius, son of Remus, and the streets are full of she-wolf symbols.

All roads in Siena lead to the **Campo**, and any tour of the city should start there. The most prominent building on the red-brick, shell-shaped piazza is the Gothic **Palazzo Pubblico**, built in 1310 and surmounted by the slender Torre del Mangia. The tower is flanked by a chapel constructed as a thanksgiving for deliverance from the Black Death.

It houses the **Museo Civico** (open daily 10am–sunset; entrance charge), which is full of Sienese treasures. Look out for Simone Martini's poetic *Maestà* (the enthroned Virgin), his famous *Guidoriccio*, and the civic masterpiece, *The Effects of Good and Bad Government*. Ambrogio Loren-

Siena's Palazzo Pubblico.

BELOW: the Torre del Mangia is one of the city's landmarks.

zetti painted the latter in 1338 as an idealised tribute to the Council of the Nine. A tough climb up the 101-metre (332-ft) tower (the Torre del Mangia) offers unrivalled views of the city (open as above; entrance charge).

The **Duomo** is in Castelvecchio, the oldest part of Siena; depending on your taste, it is either a symphony in black-and-white marble or a tasteless iced cake. Begun in 1220, the interior is an example of creativity run riot: oriental abstraction, Byzantine formality, Gothic flight and Romanesque austerity. The black-and-white walls reach up to starry blue vaults, and on the floor you can see marble engravings (the finest of which are by Matteo di Giovannio) and mosaics, but many of these are covered by hardboard much of the year for preservation purposes.

Within the Duomo is the **Libreria Piccolomini** (open Mon–Sat 9am–7.30pm in summer, 10am–1pm, 2–5pm in winter, Sun 1.30–7.30pm; entrance charge), the most ornate Renaissance room in Tuscany, containing Pinturicchio's frescos. Within the **Museo dell' Opera Metropolitana** (open Mon–Sat 9am–7.30pm in summer; 9am–1pm in winter; entrance fee) are Duccio's *Maestà*, the remarkable statues of saints that originally graced the Duomo facade, and some relics.

Opposite the Duomo's main entrance is the **Ospedale Santa Maria della Scala** (open daily 10am–6pm in summer, 10.30am–4.30pm in winter; entrance charge), which was founded in the 9th century and was held to be one of the most important and advanced hospitals in the world. It closed its doors to patients relatively recently, and has now been turned into a museum. Fascinating frescos by Domenico di Bartolo and others in the main ward and entrance hall depict the daily life and times of the hospital, and bear witness to Siena's long history

of humanism. The **Museo Archeologico** (open daily 10am–6pm in summer, 10am–4.30pm in winter; entrance charge), with significant Etruscan and Roman remains, is housed in the same complex.

In the Gothic **Palazzo Buonsignori**, the **Pinacoteca** (open Tues–Sat 8.15am–7.15pm, Mon 8.30am–1.30pm, Sun 8.15am–1.15pm; entrance charge) contains a collection of Sienese "Primitives"; early Madonnas, Annunciations, saints and various grisly descents into hell. **St Catherine of Siena** (1347–80) is one of Italy's several co-patron saints, and her house, garden and sanctuary, outside the *centro storico* on Vicolo del Tiratoio, can be visited (open daily 9am–12.30pm, 3.30–6pm).

On Via di Città is the **Palazzo delle Papesse**, which is now a centre of contemporary art (Tues-Sun 12am–7pm; entrance charge). It is worth climbing to the rooftop loggia for the wonderful views over the city and the surrounding countryside.

One part of Sienese life can be seen without setting foot in a museum. The *contrade* are the various rival factions of the Palio (Siena's controversial horse race), and each is represented by an animal, fish or bird. All over the city the importance of these factions can be seen in the form of marble or ceramic plaques set into walls, fountains, local churches and tabernacles.

Leonardo country

A gentle meander into the countryside due west of Florence takes in some lovely views, several small towns and Leonardo's birthplace at Vinci.

Head west out of Florence along the SP 66 (in the direction of Pistoia), and turn south at **Poggio a Caiano**, site of an important Medici villa *(see page 193)*. The walled village of **Artimino** is the setting for a huge villa (open by appointment only; tel: 055-8751427) built by Bernardo Buontalenti as a hunting lodge for

Ferdinando I in 1594 and curious for the number of tall chimneys stuck on the roof. Inside is a small Etruscan museum, and the stable block has been beautifully restored to house a hotel. The restaurant specialises in dishes with Medici origins.

A tortuous road leads through olive groves and vines from Artimino to **Vinci** ⑫, where the medieval castle of the Conti Guidi houses the **Museo Leonardiano** (open daily 9.30am–7pm in summer, 9.30am–6pm in winter; entrance charge), which has a vast selection of mechanical models built to the exact measurements of Leonardo's drawings in the Codex Atlanticus notebooks. He is said to have been christened in the 14th-century Santa Croce church next door.

Five km (3 miles) southwest of Vinci is the hill town of **Cerreto Guidi**. Once owned by the Guidi counts, it now produces a good Chianti Putto wine and boasts yet another Medici villa, the **Villa di Cerreto Guidi** *(see page 192)*, built in 1564 for Cosimo I as a hunting lodge. An austere building, it has been rescued from neglect and restored. It contains

Map on page 198

Looking over the Sienese rooftops.

BELOW: the confection that is Siena's Duomo.

some fine portraits of the Medici family and a *pietà* by Andrea della Robbia. Isabella, daughter of Cosimo I, is said to have been murdered here by her husband for her infidelities.

Another 8 km (5 miles) southwest along a country lane will take you to **Fucecchio**, birthplace of Puccini's rascally hero, Gianni Schicchi. The **Palude di Fucecchio**, Italy's biggest inland swamp, covering 1,460 hectares (3,600 acres), offers much for the nature-lover. Some 50 species of migrating birds are protected here, and the same amount again nest in the area: night herons, little egrets, squacco herons and, most recently, cattle egrets. The land is private property, but the Palude centre in **Castelmartini di Larciano** (tel: 0573-84540) organises guided tours.

From Fucecchio, take the back road to **Empoli**, a prosperous, modern market town with a small *centro storico* and a superb Romanesque church, the **Collegiata Sant'Andrea**. The green-and-white-striped facade is reminiscent of Florence's San Miniato, and the small **Museum** (open Tues–Sun 9am–noon, 4–6pm;

The Pulpit of the Holy Girdle on Prato's Duomo.

BELOW: a Henry Moore sculpture in Prato's Piazza San Marco.

entrance charge) contains a surprising amount of precious 13th- and 14th-century Florentine art.

Taking the SP 67 towards Florence, the last stop should be in **Montelupo Fiorentino**, famous for its history of terracotta and ceramic production. The **Museo Archeologico e della Ceramica** (open Tues–Sun 10am–6pm; entrance charge) shows examples of both going back centuries. An annual Festa Internazionale di Ceramica is held here in late June. It celebrates the history of ceramic production with Renaissance music and costume. There are plenty of shops in the town where you can buy modern ceramics. Don't leave without seeing the church of **San Giovanni Evangelista**, with its beautiful painting of *Madonna and Saints* by Botticelli and his assistants.

Prato: old and new

Lucca lies 55 km (34 miles) west of Florence along the A11 autostrada; the other towns mentioned below are all en route. Buses for Lucca leave regularly from the Lazzi bus station in Piazza Adua.

Sixteen km (10 miles) northwest of Florence, **Prato ⓭** is the third-largest city in Tuscany. It is a rich, industrial centre known for the manufacture of textiles. Many examples of Prato's textiles can be seen in the excellent **Museo del Tessuto** (Via Santa Chiara 24; open Mon–Fri 10am–6pm, Sat 10am– 2pm, Sun 4–7pm; entrance charge). There are also numerous factory outlets selling fine fabrics, cashmere and designer clothes.

However, within Prato's modern outskirts lies a *centro storico*, within medieval walls. The **Duomo** is home to what is believed to be the girdle of the Virgin Mary (on public display on only five days per year). Inside, the Chapel of the Holy Girdle (on the left of the main entrance) is covered with frescos by Agnolo Gaddi illustrating the legends surrounding this

most bizarre of holy relics; and built onto the faade of the church is the circular Pulpit of the Holy Girdle, designed by Donatello and Michelozzo. The **Museo dell' Opera del Duomo** (open Mon, Wed–Sat 9.30am–12.30pm, 3–6.30pm; Sun 9.30am–12.30pm; entrance charge) in the cloister contains paintings, sculptures and reliefs by Donatello, Lippi and others.

The church of **Santa Maria delle Carcere** lies behind the Castello dell' Imperatore. Begun in 1485, the church was built by Giuliano Sangallo in typical no-frills Brunelleschian style. The **Castle** (open 10am–sunset; entrance charge) was built by Frederick II Hohenstaufen in the first half of the 13th century; there are good views from its walls.

In Via Rinaldesca is the mid-14th-century frescoed **Palazzo Datini** (open Mon, Tues and Sat 9am–noon, Wed–Fri 9–noon, 4–6pm; entrance charge), former home of Francesco Datini, founder of the city's riches in the wool trade and described as "The Merchant of Prato" in the title of Iris Origo's book; a fascinating description of life in medieval Prato.

On the outskirts is the **Centro per l'Arte Contemporanea Luigi Pecci** (open Mon–Fri noon–7pm, Sat and Sun 10am–7pm; entrance charge), a museum with both permanent and temporary exhibitions of modern art.

Pistoia

Moving west along the autostrada, past the rows of *vivaie* (garden centres), brings you to **Pistoia** ⓭. The fine medieval centre holds enough interest to satisfy the art-hungry, and the shops around Vias Cavour, Cino, Vannucci and Orafi are as glamorous as those in Florence or Lucca. Most of the city's important buildings were constructed in the Middle Ages, when Pistoia flourished as a banking centre. On the **Piazza del Duomo**, the **Cattedrale di San Zeno** (with char-

acteristic green-and-white stripes) dates originally from the 5th century, although it was rebuilt in Romanesque style 700 years later. A blue-and-white Andrea della Robbia bas-relief decorates the porch, and inside are many medieval frescos, Renaissance paintings and, in the Chapel of San Jacopo, a silver altar.

The soaring campanile has three tiers of green-and-white Pisan arches, while opposite is Andrea Pisano's 14th-century octagonal **Baptistery**. The **Museo Civico** (open Tues–Sat 10am–6pm, Sun 9am–12.30pm; entrance charge) in the same square houses an impressive art collection, including a rare 13th-century painting of St Francis and other 15th-century treasures. Pistoia has numerous minor churches which, time permitting, merit a visit for their important artworks and Pisano pulpits.

Lucca

Lucca ⓯ deserves as much time as possible; it is a delightful place, not least for its lack of mass tourism. In Roman times, it was the most important town in Tuscany, and this legacy

Map on page 198

Pistoia's Duomo and campanile.

BELOW: a della Robbia frieze on Pistoia's Ospedale del Ceppo.

The rooftops of Lucca.

BELOW: the facade of San Michele, Lucca.

can be seen today in the grid pattern of the streets, and, more obviously, in the elliptical **Piazza del Anfiteatro**, now lined with shops, bars and restaurants. Like Florence, Lucca's wealth was based on banking and, later, its silk industry. The **Torre Guinigi** (open daily 9am–7.30pm in summer; shorter hours in winter; entrance charge), with oak trees sprouting from the top, was built by one of the wealthiest banking families; a tough climb leads to splendid views over the red rooftops, and is a good way to get your bearings.

Lucca's chief attraction is its particularly interesting and beautiful churches, many of which contain ornate organ cases. **San Michele**, built on the site of the old Roman forum, has one of the most spectacular Pisan Romanesque facades in Italy. The **Duomo of San Martino**, enhanced by its crenellated tower, combines Romanesque and Gothic styles; three tiers of colonnades adorn the facade, while the arches are decorated with superb relief work. Inside the building, the sacristy contains the remarkable tomb of Ilaria del Carretto by Jacopo della Quercia, an outstanding and poignant effigy of Paolo Guinigi's young bride, complete with devoted dog at her feet.

Opera fans should visit Giacomo Puccini's birthplace in Via di Poggio 30. Now a small museum, the **Casa di Puccini** (open Tues–Sun 10am–6pm, closed 1–3pm in winter; entrance charge) contains his piano and various personal effects along with letters, manuscripts and other memorabilia relating to his life and work.

Pisa

Pisa ⑯, home to Italy's most famous landmark, lies 16 km (10 miles) west of Lucca. The best place to begin a tour of Pisa is at the Piazza del Duomo (the **Campo dei Miracoli**), where the Leaning Tower, the Duomo and the baptistery soar above their green lawns. The white marble facing of all three structures emphasises the exquisite harmony of this piazza, which was realised by the people of Pisa themselves, as an expression of their power and pride.

The **Duomo** (open Mon–Sat 10am–7.30pm, Sun 1–7.30pm, closes earlier in winter) was one of the first monumental structures of the Middle Ages, built after a Pisan victory at Palermo in 1063. Buscheto, its architect, combined the ground-plan of an early Christian basilica with a transept – the first sacred building in the shape of a cross in Italy.

Inside, due to the generous use of arches in the aisles, it resembles an enormous mosque. Buscheto was familiar with Islamic architecture, and the ornate marble intarsia decoration on the exterior also reflects Islamic influence; other features are typical of northern Italian Romanesque. This mixture of styles makes it unique. Inside, the marble pulpit (1301–11) by Giovanni Pisano is a masterpiece of Gothic sculpture. The work depicts Old Testament prophets and New Testament Apostles.

Aligned with the cathedral is the **Baptistery** (open daily 8–19.30). Begun in 1153 by Diotisalvi in the same style as the Duomo, the Gothic part (including the loggia) was supervised by Nicola Pisano and later his son Giovanni. Lack of funds meant that the cupola could only be added in the 14th century. In 1260 Nicola Pisano created the first ever free-standing pulpit for the baptistery, one of the most important Late Romanesque works of art in Italy.

The fascinating Sinopia Museum (same hours as the baptistery) on the south side of the piazza has several earlier versions of the frescos discovered during restoration work.

The **Campanile**, or Leaning Tower *(Torre Pendente)*, is one of the best-known structures in the world. Bonnano began work on it in 1173, but the tower soon began to lean, due to the unstable subsoil, and work was abandoned. In 1275, Giovanni di Simone decided to continue building and rectify the inclination as he went. But the tower continued to lean. It does lean to a frightening degree, but work to stabilise it has been a success.

The highlight at the **Museo dell' Opera del Duomo** (same opening hours as the baptistery) is the sculpture collection; there are several fine 12th-century works here, and also masterpieces by Nicola and Giovanni Pisano. More magnificent works of sculpture can be admired in the **Museo Nazionale di San Matteo** (open Tues–Sat 9am–7pm, Sun 9am–2pm; entrance charge).

The sgraffito decoration of the Palazzo della Carovana, the former council chambers of the Pisan Commune, with floral patterns, coats of arms, symbols, and also the church of Santo Stefano dei Cavalieri next door, were based on plans by Vasari; the church is usually only open in the morning. The interior contains several captured standards and sections of ships dating from Pisan naval victories against the Ottomans.

Pisa's only surviving brick *palazzo*, the Palazzo Agostini, is not only famous for its splendid 15th-century terracotta decoration; it also contains the Caffè dell'Ussero which was frequented by the revolutionaries during the Risorgimento. ❏

Map on page 198

A mosaic detail from Lucca's San Martino.

BELOW: Pisa's Campo dei Miracoli.

TRANSPORT

GETTING THERE AND GETTING AROUND

GETTING THERE

By Air

The two main airports that serve Tuscany are Pisa and Florence. Pisa's Galileo Galilei airport handles an ever-growing number of scheduled services as well as charter flights. For most visitors, flights to Pisa are the better option, being more frequent and usually cheaper than flights to Peretola airport (also known as Amerigo Vespucci), which lies 4 km (2 miles) northwest of Florence and serves mainly business travellers. Getting from Pisa to Florence is easy, cheap and fast – by train (www.trenitalia.it) or using the coaches which leave the airport and run to Florence's Santa Maria Novella train station (www.terravision.it). Peretola is just a 15-minute bus or taxi ride away from the centre *(see Getting Around)*.

You could also consider flying to Bologna, Bologna Forli or Perugia; budget airlines operate to the first two.

Finding a Fare

As a general rule, you will get the best deals on the internet, and from so-called "no frills" airlines, such as Ryanair (www.ryanair.co.uk)

and easyJet (www.easyjet.co.uk), which operate a huge number of flights to Italy. It is also possible to buy tickets directly from airlines, which normally offer a choice of tickets: a full economy fare, a restricted fare (with similar restrictions to the old Apex fares – for example a minimum length of stay), or a special fare – the nature (and name) of which will vary from airline to airline.

Europe

British Airways (www.britishairways.com) and Alitalia (www.alitalia.co.uk) operate regular scheduled flights from London to Pisa. These are heavily booked in summer, and advance reservations are essential. Ryanair flies from London Stansted to Pisa three times a day in summer, twice in winter, and charter flights are also available, chiefly through tour operators who specialise in "flight only" packages to Italy. Meridiana (www.meridiana.it) operates regular flights between London Gatwick and Florence and a variety of domestic flights within Italy. Scheduled services fly from Florence to many major European destinations (for example, Paris, Brussels, Frankfurt and Barcelona) and both Florence and Pisa are well served by Alitalia's internal flights to Milan, Rome, Sardinia and Sicily.

United States

As yet, there are no direct flights from North America to Tuscany. The best routes are via London, Brussels, Paris or Frankfurt, but you can get to Florence from almost anywhere now. The alternative is to fly direct to Milan or Rome; the excellent airport train linking Rome's Fiumicino airport with Termini station (in central Rome) and frequent, fast trains to Florence make this a viable option for visitors from the US.

By Rail

The train journey from London to Florence via Paris takes between 16 and 19 hours – 3 hours from London (Waterloo) to Paris (Gare du Nord) on Eurostar, and another 13- or 16-hour journey from Paris (Gare de Lyon or Bercy) to Florence (Santa Maria Novella), depending on the time of day you leave and the connection times. If you enjoy rail travel, it's a pleasant journey, but without a special offer it is not a cheaper option than flying.

For further information on train times and reservations call **Rail Europe** on 08705-848848 (www.raileurope.co.uk). If you wish to take your own car on the train, this number will also give information about **Motorail**, but this only goes as far as the south of

France and again is not a cheap option.

Tickets for Italian trains are issued in the US by **CIT**, 15 West 44th Street, 10th floor, New York NY 10036; tel: 800-CIT-TOUR; www.cit-tours.com. In Canada, contact CIT, 7007 Islington Avenue, Suite 205, Woodbridge, Ontario L4L 4T5; tel: 800-387 0711; www.cittours-canada.com. They will provide details of rail travel, including the availability of special passes restricted to foreigners who purchase the ticket in their home country.

In addition to first and second class, there are some useful special tickets. For people under 26 the Inter Rail Ticket *(Tessera Inter Rail)* is worth considering. It allows unlimited travel for one month in 22 countries of Europe, with a reduction of 50 percent in Italy and 30 percent in the UK.

For more information on rail travel within Italy *see Getting Around, page 210.*

By Road

For those travelling to Italy in their own vehicle, there are several routes to Florence. The best Channel crossing to opt for is the Channel Tunnel from Folkestone to Calais on Eurotunnel (tel: 08705-353535; www.eurotunnel. com) or use one of the Folkestone/Dover to Calais/Boulogne ferry crossings; you can also sail to Ostend from Dover.

The most direct way to drive is to head for Milan via northern France, Germany and Switzerland. The total journey from the Channel port to Florence on this route takes a minimum of 18 hours. The obvious alternative is to head for the south of France and cross into Italy at the northwestern border.

For detailed information on route-planning, mileage, petrol and toll fees, and general advice for motorists, visit the **RAC** website at www.rac.co.uk or the **AA** route-planning service at www.theaa.com.

By Coach

Given the low cost of flights to Tuscany, travelling to Florence by bus is a much less popular option. A regular London to Rome service is operated by **National Express**. The coach departs from Victoria Coach Station and travels via Dover–Paris–Mont Blanc–Aosta–Turin–Genoa–Milan –Bologna–Florence (Via Santa Caterina da Siena) and on to Rome.

The journey as far as Florence takes about 27 hours. Details of bookings can be obtained from National Express, Victoria Coach Station, London SW1; tel: 08705-808080; www.national express.co.uk.

Package Holidays

The **Italian State Tourist Office** (1 Princes Street, London W1B 2AY; tel: 020-7408 1254) can supply free maps and brochures on a wide range of holidays and activities, as well as stays based in Florence, and produces a useful booklet with practical information on unusual travel itineraries.

Italiatour is Alitalia's package-tour operator, offering holidays based on scheduled Alitalia flights from Gatwick to six Italian airports, including Pisa. For brochures and further information, you should contact: Italiatour, 71 Lower Road, Kenley, Surrey CR8 5NH; tel: 0870-7333000; www.italiatour.co.uk

Citalia also offers holidays covering the whole of Italy. Contact them at The Atrium, London Road, Crawley, West Sussex RH10 9SR; tel: 0870-9097555; www.citalia.co.uk. Package deals to Florence, especially weekend breaks, are reasonable.

Magic of Italy (Kings House, 12–42 Wood Street, Kingston-upon-Thames, Surrey KT1 1JF; tel: 0870-8880222: www.magic-travelgroup.co.uk) is an established company which runs good-quality package tours, with a great degree of independence.

GETTING AROUND

On Arrival

The easiest way to get from **Pisa (Galileo Galilei) International Airport** (tel: 050-849111) to Florence is by the coach service (www.terravision.it) whose departures are timed to coincide with flights. The airport also has its own railway station, although departures are infrequent. Trains take 5 minutes into Pisa Centrale and 1 hour for the 80 km (50 miles) to Florence. Tickets can be bought at the information desk inside the airport.

If there is no airport train to coincide with your flight arrival, it is worth taking a taxi or bus (No. 3) into Pisa Centrale station, where the connections to Florence are much more frequent. Car hire is available from the airport, and so are taxis. A toll-free *superstrada* links Pisa airport with Florence.

Peretola (Amerigo Vespucci) International Airport is situated in the northwestern suburbs of Florence (tel: 055-30615) and is connected every 30 minutes by the airport shuttle bus – Vola In Bus – to the Sita bus company depot not far from Santa Maria Novella railway station; the journey time is about 20 minutes and tickets are available on the bus. A taxi into the centre of Florence will cost around €15.

By Air

Alitalia offers a huge range of internal flights from both Florence and Pisa airports. This is supplemented by Meridiana's domestic services, which leave from Florence and are usually slightly cheaper. Other internal airlines, such as Myair (www.myair.com) and Volare (www.volareweb.com; back after going bust) connect a number of Italian cities, but do not stop down in Tuscany.

By Train

The FS (Ferrovie dello Stato), the state-subsidised railway network, is excellent and is a cheap and convenient form of transport for travelling between major cities in Tuscany.

The principal Rome–Milan line stops at Bologna, Florence and Arezzo, while the Rome–Genoa line serves Pisa, Livorno and Grosseto. However, the Florence–Siena route is much faster by coach than by train.

Note that Florence has several train stations: **Santa Maria Novella** is the main station for the city, but the second station, **Rifredi**, is served by several Eurostar trains.

Categories of Trains

Eurocity: these trains link major Italian cities with other European cities – in Germany and Switzerland, for instance.
Eurostar: these swish, high-speed trains have first- and second-class carriages, both with supplements on top of the ordinary rail fare.
Intercity: this fast service links major Italian cities.
Interregionali: these inter-regional trains link cities within different regions (for example Tuscany and Umbria) and stop reasonably frequently.
Regionali: these regional trains link towns within the same region (for example Tuscany) and stop at every station.

Tickets

Seat reservations are mandatory for journeys on the superior trains (Eurostar and Eurocity services) and tickets should be purchased in advance, especially around Easter and in the summer season. Tickets are not dated;

TRAIN INFORMATION

For train information 24 hours a day call 892021 or visit www.trenitalia.it.

you have to stamp (convalidare) your ticket before beginning the journey at one of the small machines at the head of the platforms. Failure to do so may result in a fine.

If you board a train without a ticket, one can be bought from a conductor, though there is a penalty payment of 20 percent extra. You can also pay the conductor directly if you wish to upgrade to first class or a couchette (should there be places available).

Expect long queues for tickets at major stations, but, for a small fee, tickets can also be purchased from many travel agents. There are convenient automatic ticket machines at major stations, which also give timetable information. Payment can be made by cash or credit cards.

There are a wide variety of train tickets and special offers available, which vary constantly and with the season. Some of the more stable are:

• **Group fares**: groups of between 6 and 24 people can benefit from a 20 percent discount.
• **Youth fares**: students between 12 and 26 can buy a yearly Carta Verde (green card). This season ticket entitles them to a 10 percent discount on national trains and a 20 percent discount on international trips.
• **Children's fares**: children under four travel free; children aged between four and 12 are eligible for a 50 percent discount on all trains but must pay the full price of the supplement for Intercity and Eurocity trains.
• **Pensioners' fares**: the over-60s can buy a Carta Argento (silver card). Valid for a year, this "silver card" entitles them to a 20 percent discount on all train tickets.

Railway Stations

The main railway stations in Italy are open 24 hours a day and are integrated with road and sea transport. They provide numerous services, including telecommunications, left luggage, food

and drink, tourist information and porters.

Most large stations have alberghi diurni (day hotels) that provide restrooms, dressing rooms, baths, showers and hairdressers for the convenience of travellers.

In Florence, the train information office at Santa Maria Novella station is next to the waiting room. The train-reservation office is just inside the building (open daily from 6am–10pm), with the international reservations counter off to the side. There is a left-luggage counter where pieces of luggage are left at your own risk, though badly packed or awkwardly shaped packages might be damaged (€3.80 for the first 5 hours, 0.60 for the next 7 hours, 0.2 per hour thereafter).

There is an air terminal at Santa Maria Novella where you can check in for Pisa airport. Beneath the station lie shops and a small supermarket which supplement the bars and pharmacy in the main hall.

By Coach

Coaches are very comfortable and sometimes quicker, though usually more expensive, than trains for local journeys. In addition, numerous sightseeing tours are offered in Florence. City Sightseeing Italy, Piazza Stazione 1; tel: 055-2645363; www.city-sightseeing.it offers two itineraries, one to Fiesole and one to Piazzale Michelangelo. The frequent departures include multilingual commentary and the tickets are valid for 24 hours, allowing you to hop on and off at numerous points around the city.

The main bus companies in Florence are **Lazzi** (Piazza Stazione 3r, Firenze; tel: 055-215155; www.lazzi.it), **Sita** (Via Santa Caterina di Siena; tel: 800-001311; www.sita-on-line.it) and CAP (Piazza Duomo 18, 59100 Prato; tel: 0574/-6081; www.capautolinee.it) for travel in Tuscany and other parts of Italy.

Local Transport

Buses

The bus network, run by ATAF, provides an efficient and fast means of transport in the city and out to suburbs such as Fiesole. It takes a while to master, thanks to the complexity of one-way streets, but there is an excellent booklet published by the ATAF with a comprehensive guide to all routes. Tickets can be bought from tobacconists *(tabacchi)*, newsstands, bars, and from the ATAF offices or automatic ticket machines at main points throughout the city, including Santa Maria Novella station.

You can buy a variety of tickets. With the 60-minute ticket you can make as many journeys as you like during the course of one hour; the *biglietto multiplo* consists of four single 60-minute tickets, and the 3-hour, 24-hour, 3-day, 5-day and 7-day tickets are self-explanatory. All tickets must be stamped in the appropriate machines on board the bus at the beginning of the first journey.

For information and route maps go to the ATAF office at Piazza Stazione (open Mon–Sun 7am–8pm; freefone tel: 800-424500; www.ataf.net); there are also bus maps in city telephone directories.

The No. 7 bus takes you to Fiesole, the No. 13 goes to Piazzale Michelangelo, and the series of small electric buses (the *bussini*) A, B, C and D take intricate weaving routes through the city centre, passing many of the main sights en route.

Taxis

Cabs are white with yellow stripes and are hired from ranks in the main piazzas and at the station. They seldom stop if you hail them in the street. Meters are provided and fares should always be displayed. A tip of 10 percent is expected from tourists.

The Radio Taxi system is fast and efficient, and cabs will arrive within minutes (unless it is rush hour, when you may have to call back several times); tel: 055-4390, 055-4798 or 055-4242.

Walking and Cycling

The main drawbacks to walking in the city are its narrow pavements (frequently blocked by cars or motorbikes) and noisy traffic, although there has been a great improvement in recent years. Cycling is an easy way to get around, and Florence has a wealth of bike lanes. Bicycles can be hired from Alinari (Via Guelfa 85r; tel: 055-280500; www.alinarirental.com) and Florence by Bike (Via San Zanobi 91r; tel: 055-488992; www.florencebybike.it). Motorbikes or mopeds, useful for trips to the countryside, can also be hired from these companies.

Horse-drawn carriages, which can be hired in Piazza Signoria and by the Duomo, are now solely used by affluent tourists. If you take one, be prepared to do some hard bargaining.

Travelling outside Florence

Tuscany is well served by motorways (though tolls are expensive). Siena, Arezzo, Pisa and the coast are all within easy reach. A good map to have is the Touring Club Italiano map of the region. However, if you do not have your own or a hired vehicle, public transport out of Florence is very efficient, and it is possible to reach most other places of interest in Tuscany either by train, coach or bus *(see above)*.

A wide network of bus services operates throughout Tuscany, and fares are reasonable. The main companies are Lazzi and SITA. The latter operates a rapid coach service to Siena, roughly every half an hour in season, which takes just over an hour. Lazzi runs a good service to Lucca and fast trains to Arezzo and Pisa depart regularly from the railway station.

Several companies organise coach excursions of the historic cities and Tuscan countryside. One of the main operators is CIT (Piazza Stazione 51r; tel: 055-284145).

Tourist information for towns and cities outside the "Provincia di Firenze" (the Province of Florence) is not available in the city. You should apply to the local branch of the APT, the tourist office. In smaller towns, the *comune*, or town hall, holds tourist information.

Driving

Florence has introduced a partial city-centre driving ban (at least for non-residents), and it makes sense not to drive, or to leave the car in the car parks on the edge of the historic centre.

State highways in Tuscany include the No. 1 "Aurelia", which runs north–south, to the west of Pisa. The national motorways (autostrade) are the A11, the "Firenze–mare", and the A12, the "Sestri Levante–Livorno". Both of these are toll roads. The two superstrade (Florence–Siena and the new Florence–Pisa–Livorno) are toll-free.

Car Hire

You can rent cars from major rental companies (Hertz, Avis, Europcar, etc.), but the smaller local firms offer cheaper rates, although cars can only be booked on the spot. Generally, booking from the UK as part of a fly-drive package is much cheaper than hiring on arrival. Even with four or five people sharing, hiring a car can be fairly expensive. Rates generally allow unlimited mileage and include breakdown service. Basic insurance is included but additional cover is available at fixed rates. Most firms require a deposit equal to the estimated cost of the hire. They often take and hold a credit card payment, which serves as the charge on return of the car.

In Florence, cars may be hired from the following outlets and

also at Pisa and Florence airports. Most of the car-hire companies have offices on or near Borgo Ognissanti.
Avis, Borgo Ognissanti 128r; tel: 055-213629.
Auto Europa, Via il Prato 47r; tel: 055-2657677.
Maxirent, Borgo Ognissanti 155r; tel: 055-2654207.
Hertz, Via Maso Finiguerra 33r; tel: 055-282260.

Licences and Insurance

Drivers must have a driving licence issued by a nation with a reciprocal agreement with Italy. The pink EU licence does not officially need an Italian translation. All other licences do need a translation, obtainable (free) from motoring organisations and Italian tourist offices.

Obtain a Green Card (international motor-insurance certificate) before travelling. For minimum cover, certificates can be purchased at ferry terminals in Britain and at the customs office at any border. You should also take out breakdown insurance, which offers compensation for the hire of replacement vehicles and transport home if you break down. Not being able to present this documentation on request can result in a fine.

Rules of the Road

These generally follow the norm for continental Europe: traffic travels on the right-hand side of the road and seat belts are compulsory. There are, however, a few local differences.
Road signs: ALT is a stop line painted on the road at junctions; STOP is for a pedestrian crossing. Italy uses international road signs on the whole.
Side mirrors: these are compulsory on the left-hand side of the car, for both right- and left-hand drive vehicles. Drivers may be required to have one fitted.
Precedence: at crossroads, motorists must give precedence to vehicles on their right, except on recently built roundabouts,

when those already on the roundabout have priority. Trams and trains always take precedence from left to right. If a motorist approaching a crossroads finds a precedence sign (a triangle with the point downwards) or a stop sign, he or she must give precedence to all vehicles coming from both the right and left.
Parking: Outside cities and towns, parking on the right-hand side of the road is allowed, except on motorways, at crossroads, on curves and near hilly ground not having full visibility.

Rush Hours

The busiest time in Florence is 8am–1pm. There is a lull in the afternoon until 3pm, and traffic is heavy again 4–8pm. On country roads and motorways, heavy traffic into the cities builds up in the mornings and again in the evenings around 7pm. In summer, roads to the coast on Saturday mornings are especially busy, and, on late Sunday afternoons, long queues can form on routes into the cities, with people returning from a day or weekend away.

Motorway Tolls

Charges for driving on motorways (www.autostrade.it) in Italy can be considerable. Within Tuscany, there is a charge on the A11 from Florence to Pisa of about €4 for cars; from Florence to Lucca, €3.50. For more information on tolls, charges and routes, as well as traffic, contact **Centro Servizi Firenze–Ovest**, tel: 055-4200444.

Breakdowns and Accidents

In case of a breakdown, dial 116 from the nearest telephone box. Tell the operator where you are, the registration number and type of car, and the nearest Automobile Club d'Italia (ACI) office will be informed for immediate assistance. They are very efficient.

On motorways, telephones are 2 km (just over 1 mile) apart, with special buttons to call for

the police and medical assistance. Both have to be contacted if an accident involves an injury.

If your car breaks down, or if you stop or block the road for any reason, you must try to move your vehicle right off the road. If this is impossible, you are required to warn other vehicles by placing a red triangular danger sign at least 50 metres (150 ft) behind the vehicle. All vehicles must carry these signs, which can be obtained on hire from all ACI offices at the border for a deposit.

Petrol Stations

In Florence, petrol stations and garages open at night include:
AGIP, Via Antonio del Pollaiuolo. Self-service.
Tamoil, Via Senese. Self-service.
Texaco, Viale Guidoni. Self-service.

At self-service stations you need €10 and €20 notes.

Parking

Parking is a major problem in Florence; the safest place is in one of the costly private underground car parks found all over the city. Somewhat cheaper, but still equipped with surveillance cameras, are the city car parks (www.firenzeparcheggi.it). **Parcheggio Parterre**, Via Madonna delle Tosse 9 (near Piazza Libertà; tel: 055-5001994) and the **Parcheggio Piazza Stazione**, Via Alamanni 14 (under the railway station; tel: 055-2302655) are both open 24 hours a day.

Street parking is almost impossible as most central areas are strictly no-parking. Public street parking is marked by blue stripes on the road, and these must be paid for by the hour. There are now some parking metres in the city. Do not leave your car on a space next to a *passo carrabile* or a *sosta vietato* sign or in a disabled space (marked in yellow). If your car gets towed away, contact the *vigili urbani* (the traffic police) at tel: 055-32831, or call the central car pound, tel: 055-308249, quoting your number plate.

A CCOMMODATION

SOME THINGS TO CONSIDER BEFORE YOU BOOK THE ROOM

Choosing a Hotel

As might be expected in a city which caters for millions of visitors every year, the quality and range of accommodation is extremely varied. You can choose between anything from a grand city *palazzo* (a historic family-run establishment) or a small *pensione*-style hotel, to numerous budget places that are either simple but comfortable or just plain inadequate.

Visitors should also consider staying just outside the city, in one of the many grand country villas, or opting for the increasingly popular *agriturismo* – farm-stay holidays, which are often self-catering. It is also possible to rent an apartment or villa, or arrange a private home stay (bed and breakfast is a new concept in Italy; breakfast is often not provided).

Although Florence is well provided with accommodation, hotels usually need to be booked well in advance. There is also a huge variation in what you get for your money in the city – the star ratings refer to facilities rather than atmosphere.

Many hotels with restaurants insist on a half- or full-board arrangement, particularly in the high season.

The APT website (www.firenze

turismo.it) has wonderful listings of hotels in Florence and is worth using. Hotels can be booked at the **ITA office** *(Informazioni Turistiche Alberghi)* at the train station (open daily 8.30am–7pm). There is also a tourist-information desk at Peretola airport which is open from 7.30am–11.30pm daily.

The cheapest hotels in Florence tend to be situated around the Santa Maria Novella station area and the most expensive along the banks of the Arno. In the upper price bracket, the essential decision is between a historic centrally located *palazzo* in the city or a beautifully appointed villa in the hills. One thing to look for, especially in the summer, is a hotel with a garden or terrace; it can make all the difference after a long, hot day's sightseeing to be able to sip an *aperitivo* in the open air, and even the more modest establishments often have some kind of outside space.

Villas and Apartments

Prices vary enormously, depending on the season and the luxuriousness of the accommodation. In general, prices range from a simple four-person villa in the low season for about €400 per week to a magnificent secluded villa for about €2,000 in the high season.

The following agency is one of the many that deal with rentals:
• **Milligan and Milligan**, Via Alfani 68, tel: 055-268260; www.italy-rentals.com.
• Apartments are also listed with links on www.firenze.net

Residences

Serviced apartments, or residences, are an attractive alternative to hotels, but must be taken for a minimum of one week. Again, prior booking (several months in advance for the summer season) is essential. Two of the best have been converted from historic palaces; they are the **Residence Palazzo Ricasoli**, Via delle Mantellate 2; tel: 055-352151; www.ricasoli.net and **Residence La Fonte**, Via S. Felice a Ema 29; tel: 055-2220115.

Private Home Stays

This is a fairly new development in Florence, but is a good way of experiencing closer contact with the locals while paying modest prices. Private homes are carefully graded from simple to luxurious, with prices varying accordingly. Contact **ABBA** *(Associazione Bed & Breakfast Affittacamere)* at Via P Maestri 26, 50135 Firenze; tel: 199-113539; www.abba-firenze.it

Youth Hostels and Camping

A list of youth hostels is available from ENIT (Ente Nazionale Italiano per il Turismo or the Italian national tourist office) and places can be booked through them or through local Tuscan tourist offices. Alternatively, contact the Associazione Italiana Alberghi per la Gioventu, Via Cavour 44, 00184 Rome; tel: 06-4871152; www.ostellionline.com In Florence, the main youth hostel is on the north edge of town, just below Fiesole: **Villa Camerata**, Viale Augusto Righi 2–4, 50137 Florence; tel: 055-601451. There is also a new hostel with excellent facilities near the station: **Hostel Archi Rossi**, Via Faenza 94r; tel: 055-290804; www.hostelarchirossi.com. Further

out towards the stadium is the **7 Santi Hostel**: Viale dei Mille 11, tel; 055-5048452.

The closest campsite to town is the **Italiani e Stranieri** at Viale Michelangelo 80 (tel: 055-6811977), open all year round. The **Camping Panoramico in Fiesole** (tel: 055-599069) is also open all year and has lovely views. There is also a campsite at the **Villa Camerata** *(see above)*. For information on all sites write to **Federazione Italiana Campeggiatore**, Via Vittorio Emanuele II, 50041 Calezano, Florence; tel: 055-88239; www.federcampeggio.it

Hotels

The selection of Florence hotels listed below are arranged corresponding to the areas in the

Places section. The price indication refers to the cost of a standard double room, usually with breakfast. Note that many hotels in Florence lower these rates at less crowded times of the year, and it can sometimes pay to bargain a little. Websites offering last minute deals can also give good offers if you are willing to be flexible: try www.laterooms.com which also has a link to a sister site for apartments.

The hotels below are divided by area, and each is given a price rating. The price categories below are per night for a double room during the high season:

€ under €100
€€ €100–150
€€€ €150–250
€€€€ over €250

THE DUOMO

Bellettini
Via de' Conti 7
Tel: 055-213561
Fax: 055-283551
www.hotelbellettini.com
Close to San Lorenzo market, this is a friendly hotel with rooms decorated in simple Florentine style. Good and generous breakfasts. €€

Brunelleschi
Piazza Santa Elisabetta 3
Tel: 055-27370
Fax: 055-219653
www.brunelleschi.it
Comfortable four-star hotel located in a tiny central piazza and partly housed in a church with a 6th-century tower. €€€€

Guelfo Bianco
Via Cavour 29
Tel: 055-288330
Fax: 055-295203
www.ilguelfobianco.it
Comfortably furnished rooms in two adjacent 15th-century houses just north of the Duomo. The family rooms are very

spacious and there is a little internal courtyard. €€

PIAZZA DELLA SIGNORIA

Alessandra
Borgo SS Apostoli 17
Tel: 055-283438
Fax: 055-210619
www.hotelalessandra.com
A centrally located *pensione* with rooms that range from the quite grand and atmospheric

with antique furniture, to the more ordinary without bathroom. €€
Fiorino
Via Osteria del Guanto 6
Tel: 055-210579
Fax: 055-268929
www.hotelfiorino.it
A basic and unpreten-

tious hotel near to the Galleria degli Uffizi and the river. Not grand but in a good, central location. €€
Hermitage
Vicolo Marzio 1, Piazza del Pesce
Tel: 055-287216

TRANSPORT

ACCOMMODATION

ACTIVITIES

A – Z

LANGUAGE

Fax: 055-212208
www.hermitagehotel.com
A delightful hotel directly above the Ponte Vecchio with a lovely roof garden overlooking the city. Some of the (rather small) rooms have wonderful river views, although for

sleeping you may prefer to stay in the quieter ones at the back. **€€€**
Relais Uffizi
Chiasso de' Baroncelli 16
Tel: 055-2676239
Fax: 055-2677909
www.relaisuffizi.it
This tiny new hotel is tucked away behind the

Galleria degli Uffizi with spectacular views over Piazza della Signoria and the Palazzo Vecchio. It has both comfortable and stylish rooms. **€€**
Torre Guelfa
Borgo SS Apostoli 8
Tel: 055-2396338

Fax: 055-2398577
www.hoteltorreguelfa.com
Part of this hotel includes the tallest privately owned tower in Florence. The bedrooms are prettily furnished with smart bathrooms, and there is a grand salon. **€€**

SANTA CROCE AND THE NORTHEAST

Grand Cavour
Via del Proconsolo 3
Tel: 055-266271
Fax: 055-218955
www.hotelcavour.com
A recently modernised luxury hotel in the historic 14th-century Palazzo Strozzi-Ridolfi. It is in a quiet location and has fine views over the city from the intimate roof garden. **€€€**
J&J
Via di Mezzo 20
Tel: 055-26312
Fax: 055-240282
www.jandjhotel.com
Housed in a former convent near Sant' Ambrogio, this smart and discreet hotel has an interior designer's touch throughout. Breakfast is served in the cloister in summer.

The rooms are very comfortable; some of them are enormous. **€€€**
Liana
Via Alfieri 18
Tel: 055-245303
Fax: 055-2344596
www.hotelliana.com
A quiet, pleasant and slightly faded hotel some way north of the centre in the former British Embassy building (the Consulate is now in a palazzo overlooking the Arno). The rooms range from the simple to the quite elegant "Count's Room". Private car parking is available. **€€**
Monna Lisa
Borgo Pinti 27
Tel: 055-2479751
Fax: 055-2479755

www.monnalisa.it
A small but in part characterful hotel set in a 14th-century palazzo, furnished with paintings and antiques. The quieter rooms, overlooking the delightful courtyard garden, are the best. It is best to avoid the charmless rooms in the new extension. Private parking is available. **€€€**
Hotel Plaza & Lucchese
Lungarno della Zecca Vecchia 38
Tel: 055-26236
Fax: 055-2480921
A comfortable and efficiently run hotel overlooking the Arno, some 10 minutes' walk to the east of the Ponte Vecchio. The rooms are decent and

some of them have lovely views. **€€€**
Regency
Piazza Massimo d'Azeglio 3
Tel: 055-245247
Fax: 055-2346735
www.regency-hotel.com
This is a grand hotel in a 19th-century palazzo with a highly regarded restaurant and an elegant garden set between the two wings. The rooms are elegant and comfortable with good facilities. Private parking is available for guests. **€€€€**

PIAZZA DELLA REPUBBLICA

Beacci Tornabuoni
Via de' Tornabuoni 3
Tel: 055-212645
Fax: 055-283594
www.bthotel.it
A lovely hotel, set in a 14th-century palazzo in the city's most prestigious shopping street. Private parking is available. Comfortable and classically furnished rooms. **€€€**

Firenze
Via del Corso/Piazza Donati 4
Tel: 055-214203
Fax: 055-212370
A reasonable hotel with clean rooms whose main advantage is its location. All the rooms have private bathrooms. **€–€€**
Helvetia & Bristol
Via dei Pescioni 2
Tel: 055-26651
Fax: 055-288353

www.royaldemeure.com
A small but grand hotel, with antiques and paintings. Sumptuous rooms, a winter garden and a gourmet restaurant. **€€€€**
Hotel Savoy
Piazza della Repubblica 7
Tel: 055-27351
Fax: 055-2735888
www.hotelsavoy.it
A luxury hotel on the

central piazza. Comfortable rooms with contemporary and elegant Italian décor. **€€€€**

SAN LORENZO

Botticelli
Via Taddea 8
Tel: 055-290905
Fax: 055-294322
www.hotelboticelliflorence.com
This is a new hotel at
the back of the central
market. It is both com-
fortable and appealing,
with all mod cons fea-
turing alongside original
architectural features
such as vaulted ceilings
and the odd fresco here
and there. **€€**

Casci
Via Cavour 13
Tel: 055-211686
Fax: 055-2396461
www.hotelcasciflorence.com

Situated north of the
San Lorenzo market
area, this frescoed Quat-
trocento *palazzo* is family-run with a welcoming
atmosphere. All of the
attractive bedrooms are
air-conditioned. **€–€€**

Centro
Via dei Ginori 17
Tel: 055-2302901
Fax: 055-212706
www.hotelcentro.net
A historic place to stay
situated near the Via
Cavour and the Palazzo
Medici-Riccardi. This
ancient *palazzo* was
once Raphael's resi-
dence and has now been

renovated to provide spa-
cious, light rooms. **€€**

Residenza Johanna 1
Via Bonifacio Lupi 14
Tel: 055-481896
Fax: 055-482721
www.johanna.it
One of a set of great-
value-for-money resi-
dences across the city.
Set in a residential area
to the northwest of the
centre, the rooms are
comfortable and nicely
decorated, but there are
few hotel frills; not all of
the rooms have
attached baths. A do-it-
yourself breakfast kit is
provided in each room. **€**

Hotel Relais Collodi
Via Taddea 6
Tel: 055-291317
Fax: 055-2654059
www.relaishotel.com
A small family-run hotel
just to the north of San
Lorenzo. It is nicely furnished and has some
good offers on its rates
throughout the year.
€–€€

SAN MARCO

Andrea
Piazza Indipendenza 19
Tel: 055-483890
Fax: 055-461489
www.andrea.hotelinfirenze.com
Situated on a monu-
mental square, this
imposing three-star
hotel has decent rooms
and a great view of the
Duomo. **€€**

Le Due Fontane
Piazza Santissima Annunziata
14
Tel: 055-210185
Fax: 055-294461
www.leduefontane.it
This is a small modern
hotel located on a quiet
and characterful square.
The rooms are comfort-

able and decently fur-
nished. Private parking is
available. **€€**

Loggiato dei Serviti
Pza della Santissima Annunziata 3
Tel: 055-289592
Fax: 055-289595
www.loggiatodeiserviti.it
A fabulous place to stay
and truly part of the historic fabric of the city.
The Loggiato dei Serviti
was designed for the
Servite fathers. San
Gallo's gracious 16th-
century *palazzo* is set on
a lovely traffic-free piazza
and looks out onto
Brunelleschi's Ospedale
degli Innocenti. Antiques
adorn the vaulted inte-
rior, and the rooms are
beautifully and individu-
ally decorated. This is
one of Florence's most
refined small hotels. **€€€**

Morandi alla Crocetta
Via Laura 50
Tel: 055-2344747
Fax: 055-2480954

www.hotelmorandi.it
This is an informal and
quiet hotel with only 10
rooms, housed in an ex-
convent. The peaceful
rooms are comfortable
and furnished with a
few antiques. Several of
the rooms have their
own private terraces.
€€–€€€

Orto dei Medici (Ex Splendor)
Via San Gallo 30
Tel: 055-483427
Fax: 055-461276
www.ortodeimedici.it
This small yet imposing
palazzo near San Marco
has been restored and
converted into a hotel
but is now unfortuantely
showing signs of wear
and tear. Even so, this
can still be an atmos-
pheric and attractive
place to stay. The public
rooms have frescoed
ceilings, rich in stucco-
work. There is also a
plant-filled terrace. **€€**

Residenze Johlea I and Johlea II
Via San Gallo 80/76
Tel: 055-4633293 & 055-461185
Fax: 055-4634552 & 055-461185
www.johanna.it
Excellent-value places to
stay, part of a well-priced
chain, not too far from
the centre. These two
residences are set in the
pleasant area around the
church of San Marco.
They retain an authentic
Tuscan feel, have com-
fortable rooms and are
equipped with modern
conveniences. *(See also
the Residenza Johanna 1
near San Lorenzo
above.)* **€–€€**

SANTA MARIA NOVELLA

Alba
Via della Scala 22
Tel: 055-282610
Fax: 055-288358
Comfort at reasonable prices. Cheerful, brisk and conveniently central.

Albion
Via Il Prato 22r
Tel: 055-214171
Fax: 055-283391
www.hotelalbion.it
Set in a stylish neo-Gothic *palazzo*, the hotel is a showcase for modern art. Bicycles are available for guests. €€

Aprile
Via della Scala 6
Tel: 055-216237
Fax: 055-280947
www.hotelaprile.it
More appealing than most hotels near the station, this is an ex-Medici palace complete with frescos, a pleasant breakfast room and a garden. Rooms range from simple to quite grand, and prices vary accordingly. €€

Hotel Baglioni
Piazza dell' Unità Italiana 6

Tel: 055-23580
Fax: 055-23588895
www.hotelbaglioni.it
This classic hotel retains its air of discreet elegance while providing extremely comfortable rooms. The rooftop restaurant has fabulous views of the city skyline. Popular with the business community. €€€

Excelsior
Piazza Ognissanti 3
Tel: 055-264201
Fax: 055-217400
www.westin.com
Old-world grandeur combined with modern conveniences in this former Florentine address of Napoleon's sister, Caroline; polished service, luxurious rooms and fine views of the Arno from the roof garden. Private parking. €€€€

Goldoni
Borgo Ognissanti 8
Tel: 055-284080
Fax: 055-282576
www.hotelgoldoni.com
A central hotel in a historic *palazzo* near the river, not far from the train station. €€

Grand
Piazza Ognissanti 1
Tel: 055-288781
Fax: 055-217400
www.westin.com
Recently refurbished sister hotel to the Excelsior and just as luxurious in terms of *fin-de-siècle* grandeur (with a corresponding price bracket). €€€€

Kraft
Via Solferino 2
Tel: 055-284273
Fax: 055-2398267
www.krafthotel.it
Ideally placed for music-lovers, this recently refurbished hotel is a stone's throw from the Teatro Comunale and has the only rooftop pool in the city. €€€€

Mario's
Via Faenza 89
Tel: 055-216801
Fax: 055-212039
www.hotelmarios.com
Most of the hotels in Via Faenza near the Mercato Centrale are scruffy, but Mario's is an exception. Decorated in rustic Tuscan style with comfortable bedrooms (the back

is quieter) and a pretty breakfast room. €–€€

Montebello Splendid
Via Garibaldi 14
Tel: 055-27471
Fax: 055-2747700
www.montebellosplendid.com
A comfortable and traditional hotel in a residential area west of the centre of town and near the station. There is a conservatory restaurant and pleasant garden. Private parking. €€€–€€€€

Palazzo Vecchio
Via Cennini 4
Tel: 055-212182
Fax: 055-216445
www.hotelpalazzovecchio.it
Opposite the station, this surprisingly pleasant hotel has undergone major renovation and is comfortable and modern with good facilities. Free car parking. €–€€

OLTRARNO WEST

Annalena
Via Romana 34
Tel: 055-222402
Fax: 055-222403
www.hotelannalena.it
Excellent-value antique-furnished rooms in a gracious 15th-century former convent, originally built as a refuge for widows of the Florentine nobility. An atmospheric hotel near the Giardino di Boboli with views over a pretty garden. €–€€

Boboli
Via Romana 63
Tel: 055-2298645
Fax: 055-2337169
www.boboli.com
This simple but appealing two-star hotel has decent rooms. It is conveniently situated for visiting the Palazzo Pitti, Giardino di Boboli and the Oltrarno district. €

Classic Hotel
Viale Machiavelli 25
Tel: 055-229351

Fax: 055-229353
www.classichotel.it
An attractive, pink-washed villa set in a shady garden on a tree-lined avenue just above the Porta Romana. The rooms are spacious and comfortable with antique furniture. €€

La Scaletta
Via Guicciardini 13
Tel: 055-283028
Fax: 055-289562
www.lascaletta.com

Set in a convenient position near to the Palazzo Pitti, this family-run *pensione* has an attractive roof garden. However, some of the rooms are rather dowdy and not all have bathrooms. Half-board is available. **€–€€**

Lungarno
Borgo San Jacopo 14
Tel: 055-27261
Fax: 055-268437
www.lungarnohotels.com
Smart, comfortable modern hotel very popular for its superb position on the river and views of the Ponte Vecchio from the front rooms. Restaurant specialising in fish, and private parking. **€€€–€€€€**

Pitti Palace
Via Barbadori 2

Tel: 055-2398711
Fax: 055-2398867
www.vivahotels.com
Small, traditional hotel just south of the Ponte Vecchio, popular with English-speaking visitors, largely because the co-owner is American. Private parking. **€€–€€€**

Sorelle Bandini
Piazza Santo Spirito 9
Tel: 055-215308
Fax: 055-282761
This hotel, rich in rather faded atmosphere if somewhat lacking in comfort, is situated at

the top of a *palazzo* on lively Piazza Santo Spirito. Delightful loggia. **€€**

Torre di Bellosguardo
Via Roti Michelozzi 2
Tel: 055-2298145
Fax: 055-229008
www.torrebellosguardo.com
Set in the hills just above Porta Romana, this atmospheric, quiet and roomy hotel consists of a 14th-century tower attached to a 16th-century villa. It has frescoed reception rooms and highly individualistic and charm-

ingly decorated bedrooms, with antiques and quirky details. Secluded swimming pool, delightful grounds with lily pond. **€€€**

Villa Belvedere
Via Benedetto Castelli 3
Tel: 055-222501
Fax: 055-223163
www.villa-belvedere.com
Exceptionally friendly, modern hotel on the hill just above Porta Romana. Sunny rooms, gardens with a pool and tennis court and lovely views over Florence. **€€**

OLTRARNO EAST

Silla
Via de' Renai 5
Tel: 055-2342888
Fax: 055-2341437
www.hotelsilla.it
An old-fashioned *pensione* to the southeast of the Ponte Vecchio looking over a leafy *piazza* onto the River Arno. It has a pleasant breakfast terrace. **€€**

Villa Cora
Viale Machiavelli 18
Tel: 055-2298451
Fax: 055-229086
www.villacora.it
Nineteenth-century villa on the tree-lined avenue leading up to Piazzale Michelangelo. Lavish public rooms; bedrooms vary enormously in style from grand to more live-

able. Extensive gardens, private parking, pool and good restaurant. Free limo service. **€€€€**

Villa Liberty
Viale Michelangelo 40
Tel: 055-6810581
Fax: 055-6812595
www.hotelvillaliberty.com
Situated in a chic residential area of Florence, winding up towards Piaz-

zale Michelangelo, this early 20th-century villa is homely and is set in a lovely garden. **€€**

FIESOLE

Pensione Bencistà
Via Benedetto da Maiano 4
Tel/fax: 055-59163
www.bencista.com
Set on the Florence road just south of Fiesole, this delightful 14th-century villa lives up to its name which means "stay well":

one immediately feels at home here. The interior of the sprawling building is full of antiques and rustic furnishings. There are cosy reception rooms, fine hillside views, and breakfast is served alfresco on the lovely terrace. Half-board is obligatory. No credit cards are accepted. **€€**

Villa Bonelli
Via Francesco Poeti 1
Tel: 055-59513
Fax: 055-598942
www.hotelvillabonelli.com
This friendly and welcoming family hotel lies

on a steep but clearly signposted road not far out of town. The restaurant offers good, solid Tuscan fare. **€–€€**

Villa San Michele
Via Doccia 4
Fiesole 50014
Tel: 055-5678200
Fax: 055-5678250
www.villasanmichele.com
Four km (2½ miles) to the northeast of Florence, this hotel is one of the finest in Tuscany. As befits a building supposedly designed by Michelangelo, this monastery has harmo-

nious lines and heavenly views, particularly from the loggia and restaurant. The antique-filled interior is beautifully tiled and vast grounds, a pool and piano bar complete the picture. The plush suites have jacuzzis.
€€€€

OUTSIDE FLORENCE

Arezzo

Val di Colle
Località Bagnoro
Tel: 0575-365167
A meticulously restored
14th-century house, 4
km (2½ miles) from the
centre of Arezzo. Antique
furniture rubs shoulders
with modern art. €€

Artimino

Paggeria Medicea
Viale Papa Giovanni XXIII 3
59015 Florence
Tel: 055-8718081
Fax: 055-8751470
www.artimino.it
Nestling between olive
orchards and vineyards
near Carmignano, 18 km
(11 miles) northwest of
Florence, this grand
hotel occupies the for-
mer servants' quarters
of a restored Medici villa.
The hotel's gourmet
restaurant, Biagio Pig-
natta, serves "Florentine
Renaissance speciali-
ties". €€–€€€

Candeli

Villa La Massa
Via della Massa 24
Tel: 055-6261
Fax: 055-633102
www.villalamassa.com
Situated 7 km (4 miles)
north of Florence, this
cluster of beautifully converted 17th-century vil-
las radiates elegance. In
addition to a piano bar
and riverside restaurant,
there are facilities for
swimming and tennis
and a free shuttle bus
into the city centre. €€€€

Castellina in Chianti

Belvedere di San Leonino
Località San Leonino
Tel: 0577-740887

Fax: 0577-740924
www.hotelsanleonino.com
Imposing 15th-century
country house with a
pool surounded by olive
groves and vineyards. €

Gaiole in Chianti

Castello di Spaltenna
Tel: 0577-749483
Fax: 0577-749269
www.spaltenna.it
Formidable fortified
monastery, now a
luxurious hotel with an
excellent restaurant.
Supremely comfortable,
individualistic rooms.
€€€€

Galluzzo

Relais Certosa
Via Colle Romole 2
Tel: 055-2047171
Fax: 055-268575
A former hunting lodge
(once attached to the
Carthusian monastery)
now turned into a wel-
coming residence, with
spacious grounds and
tennis courts. €€€

Greve in Chianti

Villa San Giovese
Piazza Bucciarelli 5
Panzano
Tel: 055-852461
Fax: 055-852463
A restored villa in Chianti
offering additional rooms
in a converted traditional
farmhouse. Noted
restaurant and wines.
Closed Jan–Feb. €€

Lucca

Piccolo Hotel Puccini
Via di Poggio 9
Tel: 0583-55421
Fax: 0583-53487
www.hotelpuccini.com
A small, friendly hotel
just round the corner
from Puccini's house
and crammed with

mementoes of the
maestro. Excellent value
and helpful staff. €
Universo
Piazza del Giglio 1
Tel: 0583-493678
Fax: 0583-954854
Large, slightly faded
Victorian hotel where
Ruskin always stayed.
Good fish restaurant. €€

Mercatale Val di Pesa

Salvadonica
Via Grevigiana 82
Tel: 055-8218039
Fax: 055-8218043
www.salvadonica.com
This feudal estate has
been sensitively con-
verted into a rural hotel.
Tiled floors, beamed ceilings and a setting amidst
olive groves add to the
charm. Has tennis
courts and a swimming
pool. Single-night stays
are possible only accord-
ing to availability. €€

Pistoia

Il Convento
Via San Quirico 33
Tel: 0573-452651
Fax: 0573-453578
Tranquil and comfortable
hotel, once a Franciscan
monastery. Has a lovely
garden, pool, restaurant
and even a chapel. Five
km (3 miles) from town.
€€

San Gimignano

L'Antico Pozzo
Via San Matteo 87
Tel: 0577-942014
Fax: 0577-942117
Old townhouse, carefully
restored and simply but
tastefully furnished. €€

Siena

Antica Torre
Via Fieravecchia 7

Tel/fax: 0577-222255
A tiny, atmospheric
hotel, essentially a
conversion of a 17th-
century tower. Early
booking is advised. €€
Palazzo Ravizza
Pian dei Mantellini 34
Tel: 0577-280462
Recently refurbished
town house with lovely
gardens and a good
restaurant. Well-chosen
antiques and fabrics in
the bedrooms; welcom-
ing public rooms. €€

Trespiano

Villa Le Rondini
Via Bolognese Vecchia 224
Tel: 055-400081
Fax: 055-268212
www.villalerondini.it
Situated 4 km (2½
miles) to the northeast
of the city, this secluded
villa is notable for its
wonderful setting; from
the pool, set in an olive
grove, there are lovely
views down over the
city.The pool and
restaurant are open to
non-residents. A bus
links the hotel with the
centre of town. €€€

Vicchio

Villa Campestri
Via di Campestri 19
Tel: 055-8490107
Fax: 055-8490108
www.villacampestri.it
An imposing Renais-
sance villa in a wonder-
ful, rural setting in the
Mugello area some 35
km (25 miles) north of
Florence. Impressive
public rooms, excellent
food and a relaxed
atmosphere. Bedrooms
in the main villa are quite
grand; those in the
annexe less so. Pool,
horse riding. €€–€€€

ACTIVITIES

THE ARTS, SPECIALIST HOLIDAYS, NIGHTLIFE AND SHOPPING

CULTURE

Art and Architecture

Florence is a treasure trove of architectural history, with churches and civil buildings dating from the Romanesque through the Gothic to the Renaissance periods. Tuscany as a whole abounds with examples of all these styles, but Florence is the most important centre.

Renaissance art is, of course, what Florence is most famous for. The most outstanding collections are in the Uffizi gallery, the Palatine Gallery in the Palazzo Pitti, The Bargello and the Accademia, but there are countless less important museums with fine examples of the period in the city.

Works of art from the Late Renaissance and Mannerist periods, the baroque, the neoclassical and Romantic and, to a lesser degree, the 20th century are exhibited at most galleries and museums.

Sightseeing

Details of important museums and art galleries, together with opening hours and entrance fees, are included in the *Places* section of this book. Note, however,

that museum opening hours are notoriously unreliable, and strikes, union meetings and "staff shortages" frequently result in the closure of all or part of a museum without notice. Opening hours also change with the season. Information on many of the museums can be found at www.polomuseale.firenze.it and www.firenzemusei.it

Special Tickets

To avoid queueing at the Uffizi, it is well worth booking in advance, which you can do by phoning the gallery directly, tel: 055-294883 or try www.florenceart.it. There is a small booking service fee per person, but the ability to collect your tickets at the museum and walk straight in, instead of standing in line for an hour, is well worth it. There is a special entrance ticket (a "Carnet") which gives a 50 percent discount into Florence's *Musei Comunali* (Municipal Museums), the Cappella Brancacci, the Museo Marino Marini and the Museo Stibbert. However, these museums are among the least expensive in Florence, so it may not be worth the price if you do not intend to visit them all. There is a *Biglietto Cumulativo* for entrance to the museums of Palazzo Pitti; it costs around €10

and is valid for three days.

Members of the EU and other countries with reciprocal arrangements under 18 and over 60 years of age are entitled to free entrance into state museums. Be sure to carry identification to take advantage of this. There are no discounts for students. A free monthly publication, Florence Today, is published in Italian and English and lists current exhibitions. It also has informative articles about museums and places of interest. Firenze Spettacolo is a monthly events magazine and covers exhibitions and museums. A section of it is in English.

The Friends of Florentine Museums Association (Via degli Alfani 39) has 12,000 members. It arranges museum visits from 9am–11pm in the summer, sometimes with concerts, to allow Florentine workers to visit museums during the tourist season, and for tourists to get a further insight into Florentine culture. In response to popular demand, the authorities have extended the opening hours of museums in summer. Many have special evening opening times. Contact the Florence tourist office for details.

Entrance fees for museums and galleries range from

€2.50–8, with the Uffizi, the Accademia and the Palatine Gallery among the most expensive. State museums (such as the Uffizi) are closed on Monday, while other museums' closing days vary.

Every year, Florence offers a free museum week (La Settimana dei Beni Culturali), when all the state museums offer free admission to visitors. Look out for this in December or May.

Events

Like most Italian cities, Florence has its fair share of events and festivals – some religious, others cultural or commercial – throughout the year. The following are the main events held in the city or close by:

Easter Day: Scoppio del Carro, the Explosion of the Cart (actually fireworks on a float). An ancient ritual accompanied by processions of musicians and flag-throwers in Renaissance costume.

Ascension Day: Festa del Grillo, Festival of the Crickets, in the Cascine Park. Children bring or buy crickets in cages.

End of April: Flower Show in the Parterre, near Piazza Libertà – a riot of colour and heady scents.

May and June: Maggio Musicale Fiorentino festival of opera, ballet, concerts and recitals.

Sunday in mid-June, Arezzo: Giostra del Saracino – the Saracen's Joust. Another ancient pageant accompanied by colourful processions.

16–17 June, Pisa: Luminaria di San Ranieri – a spectacular event, with thousands of candles being lit on the buildings along the Arno. Boat race on the second day.

24 June: San Giovanni – Florence's patron saint's day and a public holiday in the city. The calcio in costume football game is played in Piazza Santa Croce; other matches are also played around this time.

Last Sunday in June, Pisa: Il Gioco del Ponte – a kind of

medieval tug-of-war played out on the Ponte di Mezzo.

2 July, Siena: the first of the Palio horse races takes place in Siena. The second is on 15 August.

July: Florence Dance Festival – a three-week festival of dance in outdoor venues in Florence.

25 July, Pistoia: Giostra del Orso – Joust of the Bear in Piazza del Duomo. A mock battle is staged between a wooden bear and 12 knights in costume.

Late July–mid-August, Torre del Lago: Puccini Opera Festival – the shores of Lake Massaciuccoli provide an evocative setting for a series of Puccini operas.

Specialist Holidays

Language Courses

There are numerous language schools in Florence. The reputable ones are run by Florence University or are organised by long-established centres, such as the British Institute. These are some worth looking in to:

Centro di Cultura per Stranieri, Università degli Studi di Firenze, Via Francesco Valori 9, 10132 Florence; tel: 055-454016; www.unifi.it/unifi/ccs

Koinè Center, Via de' Pandolfini 27, 50122 Florence; tel: 055-213881; www.koinecenter.com

Machiavelli, Piazza Santo Spirito 4, 50125 Florence; tel: 055-2396966; www.centromachiavelli.it

Scuola Leonardo da Vinci, Via Bufalini 3, 50122 Florence; tel: 055-261181; www.scuolaleonardo.com

Art Tours

Prospect Music and Art Tours (36 Manchester Street, London, W1U 7LH, tel: 020-7486 5704; www.prospecttours.com) is a specialised upmarket company which runs sophisticated art tours to Tuscany.

Art Courses

Università Internazionale dell'Arte (Villa Il Ventaglio, Via

delle Forbici 24/26, 50134 Florence; tel: 055-570216; www.uiafirenze.com) offers various art-appreciation courses, which include specialisation in museum collections, conservation and restoration, design and graphic design.

Istituto d'Arte di Firenze (Piazzale di Porta Romana 9, 50125 Florence; tel: 055-220521; www.isafirenze.it) offers courses in drawing, design, photography, painting, watercolours, sculpture, restoration, ceramics and jewellery-making.

British Institute (Piazza Strozzi 2, 50123 Florence; tel: 055-26778200; www.britishinstitute.it) conducts art and language courses. This is the centre with the best reputation for such courses in Florence. It also has an excellent English and Italian library at Palazzo Lanfredini (Lungarno Guicciardini 9, tel: 055-26778270) to which one can have temporary membership.

Istituto per l'Arte e Restauro (Palazzo Spinelli, Borgo Santa Croce 10, 50122 Florence, tel: 055-246001; www.spinelli.it) This art-restoration school has a reputation for being the best in Italy and offers restoration courses in Italian.

Fashion Institutes

Centro Moda, Via Faenza 111, 50123 Florence; tel: 055-36931; www.pittimmagine.com

Polimoda, Via Pisana 77, 50143 Florence; tel: 055-7399628; www.polimoda.com

Cookery Courses

Scuola di Arte Culinaria "Cordonbleu" (Via di Mezzo 55r, 50121 Florence; tel: 055-2345468; www.cordenbleu-it.com) offers courses in English, French and Italian.

Judy Witts Francini (Via Taddea 31, 50123 Firenze, tel: 055-292578; www.divinacucina.com). At the other end of the scale, Judy Witts offers personalised, informal courses which can last for anything from a single day up to

and include a shopping trip to the nearby central market.

Music, Opera and Dance

To keep up-to-date with events, buy *Firenze Spettacolo*, the monthly listings magazine (although it is in Italian, the listings themselves are quite straightforward, see www.firenze spettacolo.it also). Alternatively, check the entertainment pages of *La Nazione*, the regional newspaper, or the Firenze section of *La Repubblica*. If you read Italian well, then get *Toscana Qui*, and *Firenze Ieri, Oggi, Domani*.

The **Maggio Musicale** music festival, held from the end of April to the end of June, is a big event, with top names in opera, music and ballet (Jonathan Miller and Zubin Mehta have long been associated with the festival) performing in various theatres throughout the city. The main venue is the Teatro Comunale, Corso Italia 16, which these days prefers to style itself the Teatro del Maggio Musicale Fiorentino. Information can be found and tickets can be booked online at www.maggiofiorentino.com, or in person at the box office or other vendors, or by tel: 119-112211 or 0039-0424-600458 from abroad.

The **Estate Fiesolana** – Fiesole's summer festival of concerts, opera, ballet and theatre – is held in the town's Roman amphitheatre, but has somewhat diminished in importance over the past years.

Outside this festival, many concerts are held throughout the summer in cloisters, piazzas, churches or even in the Boboli Gardens. These are of varying standard, but the settings are often highly evocative. More information can be gathered from tourist offices.

The opera and ballet season at the **Teatro Comunale** (Corso Italia 16, 50123 Florence; tel: 055-217935) opens around the middle of September and runs

through to Christmas. International performers and scenographers appear regularly, particularly in operatic productions.

The principal venue for quality chamber-music concerts in Florence is the **Teatro della Pergola** (Via della Pergola 18-32, 50100 Florence; tel: 055-2479651; www.pergola.firenze.it), which is a superb example of a 17th-century theatre (inaugurated in 1656). These concerts, featuring world-famous chamber groups and singers, are generally held at weekends and are well publicised.

The **Teatro Verdi** (Via Ghibellina 99, 50122 Florence; tel: 055-212320; www.teatroverdifirenze. it) is also the venue for a wider range of entertainment, from light opera and ballet to jazz and rock concerts, while the Orchestra Regionale Toscana's lively concert series runs from December to May.

The **Fiesole Music School** in San Domenico also organises a series of concerts (tel: 055-597 8527; www.scuolamusica.fiesole.fi.it).

To find out what rock, jazz and Latin American music is on offer, check in the latest issue of the *Spettacolo* listings magazine.

MaggioDanza is the resident ballet company at the Teatro Comunale, and they perform throughout the year; the most interesting productions are likely to be between September and December or during the *Maggio Musicale* festival from April until June.

The **Florence Dance Festival**, held in late June/early July and again in December, features both well-known international and national names along with up-and-coming dancers and choreographers (tel: 055-289276; www.florencedance.org for information).

There are also numerous smaller dance events during the year; for information about these and other visiting companies see the Dance section in *Firenze Spettacolo*.

Theatre

Florence is home to numerous theatres and theatre companies, ranging from the classical season at Teatro della Pergola to contemporary and fringe productions at some tiny venues. To find out what plays are on, buy *La Repubblica* newspaper or look in the appropriate section of *Firenze Spettacolo*; most productions are in Italian.

The main theatre is the state-subsidised **Teatro della Pergola** *(see above)* – some of the best-known Italian actors and directors appear regularly here.

The **Teatro Metastasio** in Prato (some 30 km/19 miles west of Florence) is another place to see high-quality drama productions (tel: 057-46084; www.metastasio.net).

Cinema

There are a number of cinemas in Florence, including the recently opened Warner Village on the outskirts of town. Almost all films are dubbed into Italian, but there are a few cinemas that occasionally show original versions, screenings by organisations such as the British Institute *(see page 221)* and the odd film festival or special season which will use subtitles rather than dubbing. The main cinema for foreigners is the **Odeon** (Piazza Strozzi, tel: 055-214068), which shows recent films in English on Mondays, Tuesdays and Thursdays and is packed with foreign students and expatriates.

During the summer a number of films are shown in the open air – details of where and when can be sought from the tourist offices.

NIGHTLIFE

The Scene

Italians enjoy going out, and Florence has a good number of

bars, often with live music. Nightclubs are not as popular and tend to be located out of town, although in the summer more open up to cater for the tourists and foreign students. There are also a number of English, Irish and Scottish pubs in the city – these often show sport on Sky. To keep up with the ever-changing scene, buy *Firenze Spettacolo*, pick up a free copy of *Vivi Firenze* (www.vivifirenze.it) or look at the listing in *La Nazione* or *La Repubblica*.

Bars and Live Music

The following places are all in Florence. Some places are closed on Monday.

Astor
Piazza del Duomo 20r; tel: 055-284305
Cocktail bar with dance floor; largely frequented by Americans.

Be Bop
Via dei Servi 76r.
Cocktail bar with live music: country, blues and jazz.

Il Caffè
Piazza Pitti 9; tel: 055-2396241
Chic and refined: a cosy spot to chat to friends, during the day or evening.

Caffè Cibreo
Via del Verrocchio 5r; tel: 055-2345853
Annexe to the famous restaurant, this beautiful and intimate wood-panelled bar is ideal for anything from a morning coffee to a late-night *digestivo*. Snacks come from the Cibreo kitchen. Closed Sunday and Monday.

Caffèdeco
Piazza della Libertà 45
This stylish, Art Deco-style bar is popular with jazz-lovers.

Caruso Jazz Café
Via Lambertesca 14–16r; tel: 055-281940.
Relaxed café with art exhibitions and live music Wednesday—Friday. Closed Sunday.

Dolce Vita
Piazza del Carmine; tel: 055-280018; www.dolcevitaflorence.com
Fashionable bar in the bohemian Oltrarno quarter.

Hemingway
Piazza Piattellina 9r; tel: 055-284781
Beautifully decorated café where you can have a drink and a snack, or sample the superb chocolates. Comfy chairs and books to browse.

Jazz Club
Via Nuova dei Caccini 3; tel: 055-2479700
Relaxed basement bar with live music daily. Small fee to become a member.

Moyo
Via dei Benci 23r; tel: 055-2479738
New swanky cocktail bar in the Santa Croce area with outside seating and delicious cocktails.

Nova Bar
Via dei Martelli
Pleasant bar during the day, turns into a noisy cocktail bar with dance floor in the evening.

Piccolo Caffè
Borgo Santa Croce 23r; tel: 055-2001057
This small café is primarily a gay men's bar, but is a friendly place which provides welcome relief from unwanted attention for women as well.

Il Rifrullo
Via San Niccolò 55r; tel: 055-2342621
The long bar groans with munchies during cocktail hour and there is an open fire in the back room. The expert barman mixes great cocktails. Open daily.

Tabasco
Piazza Santa Cecilia 3; tel: 055-213000
Men only; this was the first gay bar in Italy.

I Visacci
Borgo Albizi 80r; tel: 055-2001956
Art café with friendly staff, relaxed music and a good selection of wines and cocktails.

Nightclubs

Central Park
Via Fosso Macinante 1, Parco delle Cascine; tel: 055-353505
Possibly the trendiest disco in Florence. Open Thursday to Saturday.

Dolce Zucchero
Via Pandolfini 36–38r; tel: 055-2477894
One of the few discos in the city centre, it operates a drinks card whereby you pay on exit.

Escopazzo Garden
Lungarno Colombo 23r; tel: 051-676912
Popular with celebrities. You are advised to check the nature of the night's entertainment before turning up. Closed Monday.

Maracanà
Via Faenza 4; tel: 055-210298; www.maracana.it
A lively Latino club playing mostly salsa and samba. Closed Monday.

Rio Grande
Viale degli Olmi 1; tel: 055-352143
Huge late-night spot with a piano bar, disco and restaurant and themed music.

Space Electronic
Via Palazzuolo 37; tel: 055-293082; www.spaceelectronic.net
Lasers and videos are the hallmarks; this is the usual hang-out of foreign teenagers and would-be Latin lovers.

YAB
Via Sassetti 5r; tel: 055-215160; www.yab.it
Fashionable glassy disco-pub open Mondays in May, June and July.

SPORT

Participant Sports

There are numerous private sports and health clubs where you can take part in any popular sport. Below are a selection; for fuller listings visit the tourist office on arrival or purchase *Firenze Spettacolo*.

Gyms

Klab
Tel: 055-333621; www.klab.it
A chain of three new fitness

centres in Florence, which also run a number of classes.

Palestra Ricciardi
Borgo Pinti 75; tel: 055-2478444
A central gym where staff speak good English as well as some French and Spanish.

Tropos
Via Orcagna 20a; tel: 055-678381
A luxurious, and pricey, centre with gym and swimming pool.

Tennis

Tennis is popular in Italy. If you wish to play a game, try these clubs:

Circolo Carraia, Via Monti alle Croci, Florence; tel: 055-2346353

Zodiac, Via Grandi 2, Tavernuzze (near Florence); tel: 055-2022850

Swimming

Many luxury hotels outside the centre of Florence have swimming pools which may allow guests for a small fee. There are also public pools in towns – although these have erratic opening hours and can be by subscription only. The following swimming pools are in Florence:

Piscina Comunale Bellariva, Lungarno Aldo Moro 6; tel: 055-677521. Open-air during the summer.

Piscina Costoli, Viale Paoli, Campo di Marte; tel: 055-6236027. This is in the north of the city and has a clean outdoor pool in the summer.

Piscina Le Pavoniere, Via Cartena 2; tel: 055-362233. Set in the Cascine Park and only open in summer, this is one of the city's most appealing pools.

Horse Riding

For further information about horseback holidays contact the **Federazione Italiana Sport Equestri** (Viale Milton Giovanni 99, 50129 Florence; tel: 055-477999; www.fise.it).

For riding near Florence, try:
Scuola Equitazione Fiorentina,

Via Vicchio e Paterno 12, 50012 Bagno a Ripoli; tel: 055-632718; www.equitazionefiorentina.it

Maneggio Marinella, Via di Macia 21, Calenzano; tel: 055-8878066

For horse-riding centres in other parts of Tuscany, contact the **Centro Ippico Toscano**, tel: 055-315621.

Spectator Sports

The main spectator sport in Tuscany is football. Florentines are football fanatics and passionate supporters of the local team "La Fiorentina" (www.acffiorentina.it). They play regularly at the **Stadio Artemio Franchi** (tel: 055-5030190), and the season runs on Sundays from August to May with games in the afternoon or the evening.

Next to the stadium is the athletics arena, which also hosts a number of events during the year. The Firenze Marathon takes place annually – www.firenzemarathon.it

OUTDOOR ACTIVITIES

If you feel like getting out of the city, Tuscany is a perfect destination for holidays involving hiking, cycling or some other outdoor activity. In recent years, a number of specialist tour operators have started offering cycling and hiking tours of Tuscany. Some include a house-party element, attempting to combine people of similar backgrounds and tastes. Others mix the outdoor side with more leisurely pursuits, such as painting, cookery or history of art courses (suitable for those with less energetic partners). The tours range greatly in terms of the accommodation (from classic villas to simple farms). Nonetheless, the quality (and price) is usually well above that offered by a two-star hotel.

These holidays tend to be all-inclusive, except for optional

excursions. Some packages involve staying in different accommodation along the route; in this case, the company generally transports your luggage for you from hotel to hotel.

A fairly expensive but highly recommended UK company which arranges walks and other outdoor tours in Tuscany is **The Alternative Travel Group Limited**, 69–71 Banbury Road, Oxford OX2 6PJ; tel: 01865-315678; brochure line 01865-315665; www.atg-oxford.co.uk Its walking holidays are designed for anyone – not just serious walkers – and all transport and hotel accommodation is arranged.

Two other companies worth contacting are **Cycling for Softies** (2–4 Birch Polygon, Manchester M14 5HX; tel: 0161-2488282; www.cycling-for-softies.co.uk) and **Explore Worldwide** (1 Frederick Street, Aldershot, Hampshire GU11 1LQ, tel: 01252-760100 (brochures), 01252-760000 (bookings); www.exploreworldwide.com)

For a full list of reputable companies specialising in adventure, nature, walking and cycling tours, contact your national ENIT (Italian Tourist Board) office.

The **Italian Alpine Club** (CAI), the principal walking organisation in Italy, is also worth contacting. The branch in Florence can be contacted at Via del Mezzetta 2, 50135 Florence; tel: 055-6120467; www.cai.it

SHOPPING

Florence is probably the best city in Tuscany for shopping. The Florentines have been producing exquisite goods for centuries, from gilded furniture and gorgeous leather goods to silver jewellery and marbled paper. Despite tourism, consumerism and high labour costs, it still has a reputation as a city with high standards of craftsmanship in many spheres, and with a little care prices are fairly reasonable. There are hundreds of shops in Florence as well as markets and market stalls dotted around the centre. It is worth shopping around and bargaining, for which a little Italian will go a long way.

If you wish to visit craftsmen at work, consult the tourist office: the Santa Croce leather school, on Piazza Santa Croce, for example, is a popular place for visitors to watch skilled Florentine leather-workers.

What to Buy

Some suggested purchases are as follows:

Leather goods: jackets, handbags, wallets and belts are some of the items available in leather from the many shops and market stalls in the city. The quality is often excellent and the designs appealing.

Food: olive oil, coffee, herbs, fresh pasta, cheese, truffles, dried mushrooms *(porcini)*.

Alcohol: regional red wines (especially Chianti), Italian spirits, liqueurs and aperitifs such as Grappa or Averna.

Clothes and shoes: Florence is home to a number of the Italian designer labels, as well as cheaper shops where there is no noticeable drop in quality. Shoe shops abound, with gravity-defying heels and splendid designs.

Handicrafts: Lace and embroidered tablecloths; pottery and ceramics; gold and silverware; alabaster and marble objects; woodwork; straw and raffia goods; art books and reproductions; marbled paper; rustic household goods; prints; antiques; reproduction furniture; Tuscan impressionists and modern paintings.

Opening Times

Standard opening times for shops are from 8.30/9am to 1/1.30pm and 3.30/4 to 7.30/8pm Monday to Saturday. Some places are closed on Mon-day mornings or open only in the mornings on Saturday. Department stores and other shops in the centre of the city will stay open all day, and there is now limited Sunday opening. All shops normally stay open later in summer.

Food shops are usually closed on Wednesday afternoon in Florence, but this changes in the summer months, when early closing is usually on Saturday. Many of the bigger supermarkets now stay open through lunch and close at around 8.30pm.

Where to Shop

There are a number of small artisan shops as well as boutiques, chain stores and designer shops in Florence. For standard purchases, department stores and supermarkets are just as good and offer cheaper prices (included in listings below). Markets are also a feature of Italian life, where real bargains can be had. Apart from the permanent open-air markets in the city, many neighbourhoods have a weekly market where, if you are lucky, bargains can be found. Open-air markets are held usually once or twice a week in almost all tourist resorts.

Tobacconist's shops *(tabacchi)* are licensed to sell postage stamps, *schede* (telephone cards), salt and candles, besides cigarettes and tobacco. *Farmacie* (pharmacies) abound and take it in turns to open at night. They sell a range of things including baby food.

The following is a selection of recommended shops (English is spoken in many of them).

Antiques

There are two main areas for antiques shops: Via Maggio and the surrounding streets in the Oltrarno, and Borgo Ognissanti, west of the centre. Look out for old picture frames, antique jewellery, ceramics and statues, paintings and furniture; however, you are unlikely to find a bargain.

Books

After Dark

Via de' Ginori 47r; tel: 055-294203
English-language bookstore with a good supply of magazines.

Edison

Piazza della Repubblica 27; tel: 055-213110; www.libreriaedison.it
A large bookshop with an extensive range of language resources and guidebooks. Café on the first floor which hosts regular talks as well as internet points. Open daily until midnight.

Feltrinelli Internazionale

Via Cavour 12/20r; tel: 055-219524
The most comprehensive and respected bookshop in Florence, with a range of foreign-language books and guides.

Seeber-Melbookstore

Via Cerretani 16r; tel: 055-287339; www.melbookstore.it
This newly located bookshop has a range of books and music as well as a café.

The Paperback Exchange

Via Fiesolana 31r; tel: 055-2478154
North of the Santa Croce district, this is no ordinary bookshop. For a start, it stocks just about every book ever written on Florence still in print, and many that are no longer published. In addition, it operates a system whereby you get a credit based on a percentage of the original price of any book you trade in, which can be used to buy books from their vast stock of quality second-hand English and American paperbacks. The shop is run by enthusiasts who seem to know everything there is to know about Florence and books.

Ceramics

La Botteghina del Ceramista

Via Guelfa 5r; tel: 055-287367
Hand-painted ceramics – mostly from Deruta and Montelupo – in intricate designs and bright, jewel colours, including many by the renowned Franco Mari.

Sbigoli Terrecotte

Via Sant'Egidio 4r; tel: 055-2479713

Has a good choice of hand-painted ceramics, both traditional and contemporary designs.

Clothes

Florence is a high-spot for fashion, and the centre is full of top designer boutiques. The most elegant streets are Via de' Tornabuoni and Via della Vigna Nuova where Versace, Valentino Armani, YSL, Coveri and all the other big names in fashion have their outlets: the shop windows are an attraction in themselves. Via Calzaiuoli and Via Roma also contain expensive shops, whilst along Via del Corso and the streets leading from the Duomo to the railway station are some cheaper options. Below is a selection of the best of both.

Designer shops:
Giorgio Armani
Via della Vigna Nuova 51r;
tel: 055-212081
Emporio Armani
Piazza Strozzi 14–16r;
tel: 055-284315
For more affordable Armani, although quality is not always guaranteed.
Brioni
Via Roma 1; tel: 055-282771
Classic men's style; exquisitely made clothes. Brioni has dressed James Bond in his latest films.
Ferragamo
Palazzo Spini-Feroni, Via de' Tornabuoni 2; tel: 055-271121
This famous Florentine shoe-maker has now branched out into accessories and clothes.
Gucci
Via de' Tornabuoni 73r;
tel: 055-2645432
This international Florentine firm has developed a tighter, more sophisticated range in recent years; but the belts and hand-bags are still their trademark.
Raspini
Via Roma 25–29r,
tel: 055-213077
Prada
Via de' Tornabuoni 67r;
tel: 055-283439

One of the biggest names in fashion today; highly desirable, sophisticated designs.
Pucci
Via dei Tornabuoni 20–22/r;
tel: 055-2658082
Christian Lacroix heads up the team that produces these well-known and extraordinary prints.
Valentino
Via dei Tosinghi 52r;
tel: 055-293142
Versace
Via de' Tornabuoni 13r; tel: 055-2396167

Other:
Echo
Via dell'Oriuolo 37r;
tel: 055-2381149
An interesting selection of women's clothing arranged by colour.
Ethic
Borgo Albizi 37;
tel: 055-2344413
One of the few shops to offer clothing at reasonable prices, this shop has constantly changing stock.

Department Stores:
Coin
Via Calzaiuoli 56r;
tel: 055-280531
This department store has a good selection of women's and men's fashions as well as accessories and shoes.
Limoni
Via dei Panzani 31r;
tel: 055-2658929
Adjoined to Oviesse, the best shop in Florence for a range of cosmetics and make-up.
Oviesse
Via dei Panzani 31r;
tel: 055-2658929
A cheaper department store which is useful for forgotten items.
La Rinascente
Piazza della Repubblica 1;
tel: 055-218765
Cosmetics, household items, clothes, shoes and accessories are sold in this store, which has a rooftop café.

Fabrics

Antico Setificio
Via L. Bartolini 4;
tel: 055-213861
This wonderful shop specialises in fabrics produced along traditional lines, above all silk, which is still woven on 18th-century looms.
Casa dei Tessuti
Via de' Pecori, 20–24;
tel: 055-215961
Fine silks, linens and woollens.

Food and Wine

Boscovino
Borgo degli Albizi 85-87r; tel: 055-2001447; www.boscovivo.com
This is one of the best specialist Tuscan food and wine stores in Florence. Items can be shipped home.

Gifts and Paper

Marbled paper is very closely associated with Florence, and many of the designs echo ancient themes or Medici crests. If you are interested in buying some marbled paper, you should attempt to visit at least one of the following:
Giulio Giannini e Figlio
Piazza Pitti 37r; tel: 055-280814
This is Florence's longest-established marbled paper shop.
Il Papiro
Via Cavour 55r; tel: 055-215262.
Piazza del Duomo 27r; tel: 055-281628
Marbled-paper designs are on display in Il Papiro's Florentine branches.
Signum
Various branches around town including Borgo de' Greci and Lungarno Medici.
These shops sell postcards, pens, paper and jigsaws, all of high quality.
Il Torchio
Via de' Bardi 17; tel: 055-2342862
Cheaper than some of the other shops and with interesting designs. You also see the artisans at work here. They sell to Liberty, where prices are sky-high.

Gloves

Madova
Piazza San Felicità 4;
tel: 055-210204
Every kind of glove you could imagine, all of them beautifully made in the factory round the corner.

Jewellery

The Ponte Vecchio is the main place visitors first encounter Florentine jewellery. The setting is atmospheric, but most craftsmen work in very different conditions. There is still a flourishing jewellery trade in Florence (particularly in Oltrarno), although most gold jewellery is in fact made in Arezzo nowadays. Nevertheless, the following traditional goldsmiths and silversmiths remain:

Brandimarte
Via Bartolini 18r; tel: 055-239381
Handcrafted silver goods and jewellery in a large store. This is where Florentine *signore* go to buy wedding presents. Good prices.

Gatto Bianco
Borgo SS Apostoli 12r; tel: 055-282989
Contemporary designs in gold and silver.

Marzio Casprini
Via Rosso Fiorentino 2a; tel: 055-710008
Silversmith.

If you can afford to push the boat out, these two Florentine establishments are well worth adding to your itinerary:

Buccellati
Via de' Tornabuoni 71r; tel: 055-2396579
Torrini
Piazza del Duomo 10r; tel: 055-2302401

Leather

Leather goods are, of course, the best buy in the city. Quality ranges from the beautifully tooled creations of local artisans to shoddy goods aimed at undiscerning tourists. For top-of-the-range quality (and prices), you should start with the designer boutiques in the Via de' Tornabuoni or shops in streets around the Piazza della Repubblica. Try the following outlets:

Raspini
Via Roma 25r; tel: 055-213077
Sells superb leather bags and coats as well as high-quality fashions.

Il Bisonte
Via del Parione 11; tel: 055-211976
This internationally famous name started life in this very street. Chunky bags, luggage and other leather goods at high prices.

Furla
Via della Vigna Nuova 47r; tel: 055-281416
Bags and accessories in contemporary designs.

For more down-to-earth prices, head for the San Lorenzo market northwest of the Duomo, where numerous street stalls sell shoes, bags, belts and wallets. The straw market also sells bags and accessories, and the Santa Croce area is the place to go to find leather shops.

Markets

Cascine Market (Parco delle Cascine, Tues 8am–2pm)
Sells clothes, produce and household goods; popular with locals.
Sant'Ambrogio (Piazza S. Ambrogio, 8am–2pm)
Vegetables, foods, meats and flowers; again popular with the locals.
San Lorenzo Market (Mercato di San Lorenzo, Via dell'Ariento/Piazza San Lorenzo)
The covered market sells a range of foods, whilst the street market has clothes, shoes, leather goods and jewellery.
Straw Market (Mercato del Porcellino, Mercato Nuovo)
Now selling fewer straw goods and more tourist items, this small market is just behind Piazza della Repubblica.

Pharmacy

Officina Profumo Farmaceutica di Santa Maria Novella
Via della Scala 16; tel: 055-216276

Housed in a frescoed chapel, this fascinating shop was founded by monks in the 16th century. It sells herbal remedies, but more tempting is the range of beautifully packaged perfumes, shampoos, lotions and room scents.

Shoes

Calvani
Via degli Speziali 7r; tel: 055-2654043
A good range of shoes both in terms of type and price, with some unusual designs.
Cresti
Via Roma 14r; tel: 055-214150
You will find beautifully crafted shoes on sale here, and available at much lower prices than at Ferragamo.
Ferragamo
Via de' Tornabuoni 2; tel: 055-292123
Italy's most prestigious shoemaker, providing hand-tooled shoes and beautifully crafted ready-to-wear collections. Ferragamo boasts that once one has worn its shoes, nothing else feels good enough.
Francesco
Via di Santo Spirito 62r
This is the place to have unpretentious hand-made shoes tooled in classic designs by a traditional craftsman.

The roads leading from the Duomo to Santa Maria Novella station have a good range of slightly cheaper shoe shops.

Supermarkets

Food and wine can be purchased here at cheaper prices than the smaller shops in town. These are just some of the branches in Florence:
Esselunga (www.esselunga.it)
Via Masaccio
Via del Ginoro
Standa
Via Pietrapiana
Coop (www.coop.it)
Via Salvia Cristiani
Conad (www.conad.it)
Via L. Alamanni
Via dei Servi

A – Z

A HANDY SUMMARY OF PRACTICAL INFORMATION, ARRANGED ALPHABETICALLY

A ddresses

If the letter "r" appears after numbers in an address, it refers to *rosso* (red) and denotes a business address; Florentine addresses operate a dual numbering system, with "red" numbers usually denoting businesses and blue or black numbers usually denoting residential addresses.

B ehaviour

Italians are an expressive people: they are very friendly but will have no qualms about showing you their displeasure should you do something to offend them. Being polite and trying to speak a little Italian goes a long way. Both men and women greet each other with a kiss on each cheek.

Business Hours

Offices are usually open from 8am–1pm and from 2–4pm, though many now stay open all day. For details on shop opening hours, see *Shopping (above)*. On Italian national holidays, all shops, offices and schools are closed.

C hildren

At first sight, Tuscany does not appear an immediate choice for kids, but there are some museums and other sights in Florence which hold a certain amount of appeal. Teenagers may well be interested in a study holiday focusing on crafts, sports, cooking or languages. Most importantly, finding a place to eat with

the kids in tow is never a problem in Italy. Florence is full of ice-cream parlours and child-friendly restaurants.

In Florence

The newly expanded Egyptian collection at the Archaeological Museum *(see page 152)* is full of mummies. The Science Museum *(see page 107)* contains working experiments of Galileo. The Anthropological Museum *(see page 116)* is crammed with curiosities including Peruvian mummies, Indian shadow puppets and Eskimo anoraks made from whaleskins. For children with a gruesome fascination for the human body, La Specola (in the Museo di Zoologia, *see page 171)* exhibits realistic anatomical waxworks of body parts.

The Boboli Gardens and the Cascine are Florence's two main parks where kids can run around and let off steam, whilst one of the few children's playgrounds is to be found in Piazza dell'Azeglio.

Canadian Island (Via Gioberti 15; tel: 055-677567) is an English-speaking company which runs summer camps, courses and day centres for children in Tuscany. The Ludoteca Centrale (Via Fibbiai 2; tel: 055-2478386) is a fun children's centre with books, games and audio-visual equipment.

Outside Florence

Outside of Florence are a number of parks and the coast which offer possibilities for children. The resorts of Viareggio and Elba are well set-up for children, and most coastal cities have permanent funfairs. The Maremma is a good place for wildlife-spotting, whilst the Parco di Pinocchio at Collodi near Pisa (tel: 0572-429342) is an obvious choice for children. There is a compact but interesting zoo open daily at Pistoia: Pistoia Zoo, Via Pieve a Celle 160a; tel: 0573-911219; www.zoodipistoia.it

Climate

The climate in Florence can be extreme. Its position, lying in a bowl surrounded by hills, accounts for the high degree of humidity that is often a feature of the weather in mid-summer. The heat and humidity are generally at their most intense between mid-July and mid-August, when temperatures frequently climb into the 30s Celsius (high 90s Fahrenheit). Winters can be very cold and damp, but there are a good number of cold, crisp and sunny days, and visiting the city at this time of year, without the crowds, can be very pleasant.

The city seems to get more and more crowded each year, the peak periods being around Easter time and from June to the end of August. The only relatively tourist-free months are Novem-

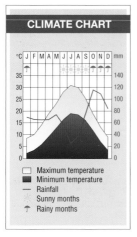

CLIMATE CHART

- ☐ Maximum temperature
- ■ Minimum temperature
- — Rainfall
- ☼ Sunny months
- ☂ Rainy months

ber to February. Overall, the best months to visit Florence are May, September and early October, when the temperatures are pleasantly warm but not too hot for sightseeing.

Clothing

Casual wear is acceptable in all but the grandest hotel dining rooms and restaurants. Clothing should be as light as possible for summer, but take a light jacket or sweater for the evenings, which can be surprisingly cool. If you go in spring or autumn, it's worth taking a light raincoat or umbrella. In winter (Nov–Mar), the temperature frequently drops to freezing or below, and warm clothing is essential for the outdoors. A pair of comfortable shoes is invaluable for sightseeing and walking the cobbled streets. Shorts and bare shoulders are frowned upon and frequently forbidden in churches.

Crime and Safety

Petty crime is a major problem in Florence, particularly pickpocketing and the snatching of handbags and jewellery in the street and on buses. Always carry valuables securely, either in a money belt or handbag which can be worn strapped across the body. One popular scam is for someone to approach you to distract your attention while someone else steals your purse or wallet.

Cars are also vulnerable, so avoid leaving personal belongings out of view, and always lock the doors and boot. Car radios are a common target, so take your radio with you if you have one of the detachable types; most Italians do – you often see local people going for their evening stroll with a radio tucked under their arm.

Make sure you report any thefts to the police, since you will need evidence of the crime in the form of a police report to claim insurance.

Customs and Duty-Free

It is no longer possible to buy duty-free or tax-free goods on journeys within the European Union. VAT and duty are included in the purchase price. Shops at ports and airport terminals will sell goods duty- and tax-paid to those travelling within the EU; they may choose not to pass on price increases. Airports can have separate duty-free shops for those travelling outside the EU or single shops selling duty-free goods alongside duty- and tax-paid goods.

Since the sale of duty-free goods in any EU country has been abolished there are no longer any limits on how much you can buy on journeys within the European Union, provided it's for your own personal use. However, there are certain suggested limits, and if you exceed them, Customs may seize your goods if you can't prove they are for your own use. The guidance levels are 800 cigarettes or 400 cigarillos or 200 cigars or 1 kg of smoking tobacco; 10 litres of spirits; 20 litres of fortified wine; 90 litres of wine; 110 litres of beer.

Duty-free is still available to those travelling outside the EU.

TRANSPORT

ACCOMMODATION

ACTIVITIES

A – Z

LANGUAGE

D isabled Travellers

Despite difficult cobbled streets and poor wheelchair access to tourist attractions and hotels, many people with disabilities visit Florence and Tuscany every year. However, unaccompanied visitors will usually experience some difficulty, so it is best to travel with a companion.

Conditions and disability awareness are improving slowly in Italy in general, although the situation is certainly not ideal, and access is not always easy. More museums now have lifts, ramps and adapted toilets, newer trains and buses are accessible (although wheelchair-users may need help when boarding), and recent laws require restaurants, bars and hotels to provide the relevant facilities. These laws, however, do not always cover access to those facilities. This sometimes results in the absurdity of a new wheelchair-accessible room being located on the fourth or fifth floor of a hotel with a lift that is too narrow to admit a wheelchair.

For details of which sights and museums are accessible and to what degree, contact the tourist office (see below). For drivers with disabilities, there are plenty of reserved parking places in Florence and these are free.

In the United Kingdom, you can obtain further information from **RADAR** (12 City Forum, 250 City Road, London EC1V 8AF; tel: 020-72503222; www.radar.org.uk). In the United States, contact **SATH** (5th Avenue, Suite 610, NY 10016; tel: 212-447-7284; www.sath.org).

E mbassies and Consulates

Australian Embassy: Via Antonio Bosio 5, 00161 Rome; tel: 06-852721
UK Embassy: Via XX Settembre 80a, 00187 Rome; tel: 06-42200001
UK Consulate: Lungarno Corsini 2, 50123 Florence; tel: 055-

ELECTRICITY

Italy uses 220v and two-pin plugs – adaptors can be purchased from airports or departments stores in the city.

284133
US Embassy: Via Vittorio Veneto 119a, 00187 Rome; tel: 06-46741
US Consulate: Lungarno A. Vespucci 38, 50123 Florence; tel: 055-266951

Emergencies

Police (Carabinieri): 112
Police (Polizia): 113
Fire Brigade (Vigili del Fuoco): 115
Medical Aid/Ambulance (Misericordia): 118
Police HQ (Questura, to report theft, including vehicles): Via Zara 2; tel: 055-49771
Tourist Aid Police: Via Pietrapirda 50; tel: 055-203911 Help with reporting theft, lost property or any other police problems; interpreters available.
Railway Police: 055-212296
Tourist Medical Service: (24-hour home visits, with English- or French-speaking doctors) Via Lorenzo il Magnifico 59; tel: 055-475411
Associazione Volontari Ospedalieri: Via Carducci 4; tel: 055-2344567. This group of volunteers will translate (free) for foreign patients.
Lost Property Office: Via Circondaria 19; tel: 055-3283942
Automobile Club d'Italia (Soccorso ACI): 803116
24-hour breakdown: 116
Car Pound (Veicoli Rimossi): tel: 055-308249.

Entry Regulations

Visas and Passports

Subjects from European Union countries require either a passport or a Visitor's Identification Card to enter Italy. A visa is not required.

Holders of passports from most other countries do not require visas for stays of less than three months, except for nationals of Eastern European countries, who need to obtain visas from the Italian Embassy in their own country.

Police Registration

A person may stay in Italy for three months as a tourist, but police registration is required within three days of entering Italy. If staying at a hotel, the management will attend to the formality. Although this regulation seems to be rarely observed, it is advisable that you carry a set of passport photos in case you need them for registration.

You are legally obliged to carry a form of identification (passport, driving licence, etc.) with you at all times. This rule is often flouted, but bear in mind that it would be unwise to call the police or attempt to report a problem (e.g. theft) unless you are carrying appropriate identification.

H ealth and Medical Care

Insurance

With an E111 from the Department of Health (available from main UK post offices), UK visitors are entitled to reciprocal medical treatment in Italy. There are similar arrangements for citizens of other EU countries. As few Italians have faith in their own state health service, it may be advisable to take out insurance for private treatment in case of accident. Holiday insurance policies and private patients' schemes give full cover during your stay abroad and are recommended for non-EU visitors.

In summer, the weather in Florence can be very hot; sunscreen, a shady hat and mosquito repellent are recommended. Tap water is safe provided there is no warning sign – acqua non potabile. Many visitors prefer to drink bottled mineral water, either fizzy (gassata) or still (naturale).

See Emergencies (above) for health-related telephone numbers.

Medical Services

Pharmacies: the staff in chemist's shops (farmacie) are usually very knowledgeable about common illnesses and sell far more medicines without prescription than their colleagues in other Western countries (even so, most drugs still require a prescription).

Every farmacia has a list of the local pharmacies which are open at night and on Sundays. Chemist's shops which are open 24 hours (farmacie aperte 24 ore su 24) in Florence are:
Farmacia Comunale, in Florence station; tel: 055-216761.
Farmacia Molteni, Via Calzaiuoli 7r; tel: 055-215472.
Farmacia all'Insegna del Moro, Piazza San Giovanni 20r; tel: 055-211343.

In addition, you can call 800 420 707 to find out which chemists are on the night rota.

There is an **accident and emergency department** in the city centre at Ospedale Santa Maria Nuova, Piazza Santa Maria Nuova 1; tel: 055-27581.

Other emergency numbers are listed above.

▐I▐ nternet and E-mail

Internet services are good in Florence, with wireless just having been brought to the city. Many hotels offer access, and there are a huge number of internet cafés which are open until late. Some charge by the period of use, whilst others require that a prepaid card be bought in advance. Below is one recommendation.

Internet Train

A number of points including: Via Porta Rossa 38r, Via de' Benci 36r, Railway station, Via dell' Oriuolo 40r; www.internettrain.it

This company offers internet access from its terminals or personal laptops as well as a number of other services including phonecards and mobile telephone rental.

A list of useful pages is listed below under Websites.

▐M▐ edia

Print

La Stampa, Il Corriere della Sera and La Repubblica are national papers with local sections, while the gossipy La Nazione is the region's paper favoured by most Florentines for its coverage of local news. Free commuter papers City and Leggo contain useful information. A wide variety of foreign press is available.

Firenze Spettacolo is the most informative monthly listings magazine on nightlife, clubs, bars, restaurants and the live arts in Florence. It is available from all news-stands.

Television and Radio

Television is deregulated in Italy. In addition to the state network, RAI (which offers three channels), there are many channels, of which the main ones are Canale 5, Rete 4, Italia 1 and La Sette. There are also a vast number of radio stations, including many regional ones. Satellite gives access to Sky and BBC channels in some locations.

Money

In common with the other Eurozone countries of the EU, Italy's monetary unit is the euro (€), which is divided into 100 cents. Bank notes are issued in denominations of 5, 10, 20, 50, 100, 200 and 500 euros. Coins are denominated in 1 and 2 euros, and 1, 2, 5, 10, 20 and 50 cents.

Travellers' Cheques

Dollar, sterling or euro travellers' cheques (preferably issued by a major bank or well-known company such as Thomas Cook or American Express) can be used to obtain cash in any commercial bank and in exchange for goods and services in shops and hotels. Expect to pay a small commission charge.

Credit Cards

Most major credit cards, including Visa, American Express and MasterCard, are accepted in hotels, restaurants and shops, for air and train tickets, and for cash in any bank and some cash dispensers. The **American Express** office in Florence is at Via Dante Alighieri 22r; tel: 055-50981.

Direct Money Transfers

Western Union has a number of agents for direct money transfers. A central one is Changepoint, Via dei Calzaiuoli 3r; tel: 055-290798.

Banks, Exchange Bureaux and ATMs

Normal banking hours are Mon–Fri 8.30am–noon and at varied times between 2.30–4.30pm. Changing money in a bank can be time-consuming, but the rates are generally better than in exchange offices. Exchange rates are displayed outside banks and exchange offices and are also printed in daily newspapers.

Exchange rates tend to be most favourable in the summer months, although rates obviously fluctuate according to world markets. There is one rate for buying euros and one for selling. €1 is roughly equivalent to £0.65 or $1.20.

Major banks have several branches in the city as well as ATMs dotted around. A high concentration of banks, including some foreign companies, is to the west of Piazza della Repubblica, around Via de' Tornabuoni.

Exchange offices (negozi di cambio) are to be found all over the city as well as at the train station.

TRANSPORT

ACCOMMODATION

ACTIVITIES

N I A

LANGUAGE

Tipping

Restaurants in Florence all levy a *coperto* of around €2 – a charge for linen, bread and service – and so tipping isn't expected unless you patronise very expensive hotels and restaurants. If you want to give a tip, leave the small change in a bar; leave 10 percent in a restaurant, and round up the taxi fare to a suitable figure (between 5 and 10 percent).

P ostal Services

The main **post office** in Florence is in Via Pellicceria 3 (near Piazza della Repubblica; www.poste.it) and it is open Monday–Saturday 8.15am–7pm. It offers a full range of postal and telegraph services. There is also a postal courier service which provides a quick and efficient way to send letters and parcels worldwide in 24/48 hours.

There are local post offices in each area of the city, and these are generally open from Monday–Friday 8.15am–1.30pm and until 12.30pm on Saturday.

PUBLIC HOLIDAYS

The dates of the national holidays are:
1 January: *Capodanno* (New Year's Day)
Easter: *Pasqua*
Easter Monday: *Pasquetta*
25 April: *Anniversario della Liberazione* (Liberation Day)
1 May: *Festa del Lavoro* (Labour Day)
24 June: *San Giovanni* (St John the Baptist – Florence's patron saint)
15 August: *Ferragosti* (Assumption of the Blessed Virgin Mary)
1 November: *Tutti Santi* (All Saints' Day)
8 December: *Immacolata Concezione* (Immaculate Conception)
25 December: *Natale* (Christmas Day)
26 December: *Santo Stefano* (Boxing Day)

Stamps are sold at post offices and tobacconist's shops *(tabacchi)*. There are yellow post-boxes (usually set into the wall) on most main streets, at post offices and at railway stations.

Poste Restante

Correspondence sent Poste Restante *(Fermo Posta)* should be addressed to Fermo Posta Centrale, Florence. They will arrive at the post office in Via Pellicceria and will be handed over from the *Fermo Posta* counter on the ground floor on production of proof of identification – usually a passport – and in exchange for a small fee.

R eligious Services

Florence is full of Catholic churches, and Mass is celebrated in Italian at varying times. The **Duomo** holds a Mass in English every Saturday at 5pm. Services are held in English at the **American Episcopal Church of St James**, Via B. Rucellai 9 (tel: 055-294417) and the **Anglican Church of St Mark**, Via Maggio 16 (tel: 055-294764). The **Synagogue** is at Via L.C. Farini 4 (tel: 055-245252). Florence's Islamic Association can be contacted on 055-711648.

Anyone who attempts to enter a church in shorts or with bare shoulders will be ejected.

S moking

A ban on smoking in enclosed public places was brought into force in January 2005 and, owing to the hefty penalties with which owners are threatened, it is the most obeyed law in Italy.

Strikes

Italy has active trade unions, and strikes are frequent, causing disruptions to transport and other services, although a limited service must be executed. Strikes are usually publicised in advance by posters or in newspapers.

T elecommunications

Italy has plenty of telephone kiosks, and almost every bar has a public phone. Not all of them can be used for long-distance calls, but you can make international calls from any kiosk that takes cards. The phone kiosks at railway stations take coins and cards, although the latter are becoming the norm. **Telephone cards** *(schede telefoniche)* – both Telecom Italia and others – can be purchased from tabacconists *(tabacchi* – look out for the black-and-white "T" sign), newspaper stands and other shops with the appropriate sticker in the window. A number of call centres have opened up in Florence and these are often more convenient and offer better rates.

To make calls within Italy, first use the three- or four-number city codes (including the initial zero), even if you are calling locally. When calling Italy from outside the country, you should retain the initial zero of the local city code. Directories are easy to understand and give comprehensive information – www.paginegialle.it is Italy's Yellow Pages online.

Telegrams may be sent from any telecom office, post office or railway station. Main offices and stations have fax facilities, as do many stationery shops *(cartolerie)*. Both internal and overseas telegrams may be dictated over the phone 24 hours a day (call 186).

Photocopying machines can be found at the main railway station and in many stationer's shops.

International Calls

To telephone Florence from overseas: dial the number for an international call in the country you are calling from (usually 00); dial Italy's country code (39), then the area code for Florence with the initial zero (055), and the number of the person you are contacting.

TIME ZONE

Italy works on GMT + 1 and switches to DST – daylight saving time, GMT + 2 – at the same time as the rest of Europe.

To telephone/fax overseas from Florence: dial the overseas connection number (00) followed by the country code (e.g. UK: 44, US: 1), then the area code, without the initial zero, and then the contact number.

Toilets

Public toilets are few and far between and not always clean. All bars have facilities, and so visitors are best off purchasing a coffee and making use of these. Otherwise, La Rinascente in Piazza della Repubblica has clean toilets on the top floor.

Tourist Offices

The headquarters of the tourist board, the **APT** (**Azienda per il Turismo**; www.firenzeturismo.it) is at Via Manzoni 16 (tel: 055-23320), but this is a long way from the city centre. The most central office of the APT is Via Cavour 1r; tel: 055-290832/290833. It is open 8.30am–6.30pm Mon–Sat and until 1.30pm Sun; the rest of the year it closes at 1.45pm and on Sundays. Other offices are at:
• Borgo Santa Croce 19r; tel: 055-2340444. Open Mon–Sat 9am–7pm and Sun 8.30am–2pm.
• Piazza Stazione; tel: 055-212245. Open Mon–Sat 9am–7pm and Sun 8.30am–2pm.

In Fiesole the office is at Via Portigiani 3–5; tel: 055-5978372.

U seful Addresses

United Kingdom
Accademia Italiana: 8–9 Grosvenor Place, London SW1X 7SH; tel: 020-7235 0303. Art

ABOVE: from Botticelli to Uccello.

shows, events, bookshop and restaurant.
Italian Embassy: 14 Three Kings Yard, London W1Y 2EH; tel: 020-7312 2200. General enquiries, commercial office and residence.
Italian Consulate: 38 Eaton Place, London SWIX 8AN; tel: 020-7235 9371.
Italian Cultural Institute: 39 Belgrave Square, London SWIX 8NT; tel: 020-7235 1461. Advice on culture, events, language and art courses in London and Italy.
Italian Trade Centre (ICE): 37 Sackville Street, London W1X 2DQ; tel: 020-7734 2412.
Italian Chamber of Commerce: 1 Princes Street, London W1B 2AY; tel: 020-7495 8191.
Italian State Tourist Office (ENIT): 1 Princess Street, London W1B 2AY; tel: 020-7408 1254.
Alitalia: 2a Cains Lane, Bedfont TW14 9RL; tel: 0870-544 8259; www.alitalia.co.uk.
Meridiana: 48 Grosvenor Gardens, London SW1W 0EB; tel: 020-7730 3454; www.meridiana.it.
Ryanair: tel: 0906-270 5656; www.ryanair.com.
easyJet: tel: 0905-821 0905; www.easyjet.com.

North America
Italian State Tourist Office: 1 Place Ville Marie, Montreal, Quebec H3B 2C3, Canada; tel: (514) 866-7667.
Italian State Tourist Office: 630 Fifth Avenue, Suite 1565, New York, NY 10111; tel: (212) 245-4822.
Italian State Tourist Office:

12400 Wilshire Bvd, Suite 550, Los Angeles, CA 90025; tel: (310) 820 1898; www.italiantourism.com
Italian State Tourist Office: 500 N. Michigan Avenue, Chicago, Suite 3030, Illinois, IL 60611; tel: (312) 644-0996

W ebsites

Websites are given throughout the book in the relevant sections. Some of the more important are:
General Information: www.enit.it
Information plus hotels and restaurants: www.firenzeturismo.it
Museums: www.firenzemusei.it and www.polomuseale.firenze.it
Events: www.firenzespettacolo.it and http://english.firenze.net

Women Travellers

The difficulties encountered by women travelling in Italy are overstated. However, women do, especially if they are young and blonde, have to put up with male attention. Ignoring whistles and questions is the best way to get rid of unwanted attention. The less you look like a tourist, the fewer problems you are likely to have.

WEIGHTS AND MEASURES

The metric system is used for weights and measures. Italians refer to 100 grams as *un etto*; 200g are therefore *due etti* and so on.

LANGUAGE

UNDERSTANDING ITALIAN

Language Tips

In Tuscany, the Italian language is supplemented by regional dialects. In large cities and tourist centres you'll find many people who speak English, French or German. In fact, due to the massive emigration over the past 100 years, do not be surprised if you are addressed in a New York, Melbourne or Bavarian accent: the speaker may have spent time working abroad.

It is worth buying a good phrase book or dictionary, but the following will help you get started. Since this glossary is aimed at non-linguists, we have opted for the simplest options rather than the most elegant Italian.

Pronunciation and Grammar Tips

Italian speakers claim that pronunciation is straightforward: you pronounce it as it is written. This is approximately true, but there are a couple of important rules for English-speakers to bear in mind: *c* before *e* or *i* is pronounced "ch", e.g. *ciao, mi dispiace, la coincidenza*. *Ch* before *i* or *e* is pronounced as "k", e.g. *la chiesa*. Likewise, *sci* or *sce* are pronounced as in "sheep" or "shed" respectively. *Gn* in Italian is rather like the sound in "onion", while *gl* is softened to resemble the sound in "bullion".

Nouns are either masculine (*il*, plural *i*) or feminine (*la*, plural *le*). Plurals of nouns are most often formed by changing an *o* to an *i*

and an *a* to an *e*, e.g. *il panino, i panini*; *la chiesa, le chiese*.

Words are stressed on the penultimate syllable unless an accent indicates otherwise.

Like many languages, Italian has formal and informal words for "You". In the singular, *Tu* is informal while *Lei* is more polite. Confusingly, in some parts of Italy or in some circumstances, you will also hear *Voi* used as a singular polite form. (In general, *Voi* is reserved for "You" plural.) For visitors, it is simplest and most respectful to use the formal form unless invited to do otherwise.

There is, of course, rather more to the language than that, but you can get a surprisingly long way towards making friends with a few phrases.

Basic Communication

Yes *Sì*
No *No*
Thank you *Grazie*
Yes please *Sì grazie*
Many thanks *Mille grazie/tante grazie/molte grazie*
You're welcome *Prego*
All right/OK/That's fine *Va bene*
Please *Per favore* or *per cortesia*
Excuse me (to get attention) *Scusi* (singular), *Scusate* (plural)

Excuse me (to get through a crowd) *Permesso*
Excuse me (to attract attention, for example of a waiter) *Senta!*
Excuse me (sorry) *Mi scusi*
Wait a minute! *Aspetta!*
Could you help me? (formal) *Potrebbe aiutarmi?*
Certainly *Ma, certo*
Can I help you? (formal) *Posso aiutarLa?*
Can you help me? *Può aiutarmi, per cortesia?*

I need... *Ho bisogno di...*
Can you show me...? *Può indicarmi...?*
I'm lost *Mi sono perso*
I'm sorry *Mi dispiace*
I don't know *Non lo so*
I don't understand *Non capisco*
Do you speak English/French/German? *Parla inglese/francese/tedesco?*
Could you speak more slowly, please? *Può parlare piu lentamente, per favore?*

Could you repeat that please?
Può ripetere, per piacere?
slowly/quietly *piano*
here/there *qui/là*
What? *Quale/come?*
When/why/where?
Quando/perchè/dove?
Where is the lavatory? *Dov'è il bagno?*

Days and Dates

morning/afternoon/evening *la mattina/il pomeriggio/la sera*
yesterday/today/tomorrow
ieri/oggi/domani
the day after tomorrow
dopodomani
now/early/late
adesso/presto/ritardo
a minute *un minuto*
an hour *un'ora*
half an hour *un mezz'ora*
a day *un giorno*
a week *una settimana*
Monday *lunedì*
Tuesday *martedì*
Wednesday *mercoledì*
Thursday *giovedì*
Friday *venerdì*
Saturday *sabato*
Sunday *domenica*
first *il primo/la prima*
second *il secondo/la seconda*
third *il terzo/la terza*

Numbers

1	*uno*
2	*due*
3	*tre*
4	*quattro*
5	*cinque*
6	*sei*
7	*sette*
8	*otto*
9	*nove*
10	*dieci*
11	*undici*
12	*dodici*
13	*tredici*
14	*quattordici*
15	*quindici*
16	*sedici*
17	*diciassette*
18	*diciotto*
19	*diciannove*
20	*venti*
21	*ventuno*
30	*trenta*
40	*quaranta*
50	*cinquanta*
60	*sessanta*
70	*settanta*
80	*ottanta*
90	*novanta*
100	*cento*
200	*duecento*
500	*cinquecento*
1,000	*mille*
2,000	*duemila*
5,000	*cinquemila*
50,000	*cinquantamila*
1 million	*un milione*

Greetings

Hello (Good day) *Buon giorno*
Good afternoon/evening *Buona sera*
Good night *Buona notte*
Goodbye *Arrivederci*
Hello/Hi/Goodbye (familiar) *Ciao*
Mr/Mrs/Miss *Signor/Signora/Signorina*
Pleased to meet you (formal) *Piacere di conoscerLa*
I am English/American *Sono inglese/americano*
Irish/Scottish/Welsh
irlandese/scozzese/gallese
Canadian/Australian
canadese/australiano
Do you speak English? *Parla inglese?*
I'm here on holiday *Sono qui in vacanze*
Is it your first trip to Florence? *E il suo primo viaggio a Firenze?*
Do you like it here? (formal) *Si trova bene qui?*
How are you? (formal/informal) *Come sta/come stai?*
See you later *A più tardi*
See you soon *A presto*
Take care *Sta bene*

Emergencies

Help! *Aiuto!*
Stop! *Fermate!*
I've had an accident *Ho avuto un incidente*
Watch out! *Attenzione!*
Call a doctor *Per favore, chiama un medico*
Call an ambulance *Chiama un'ambulanza*
Call the police *Chiama la Polizia/i Carabinieri*
Call the fire brigade *Chiama i pompieri*
Where is the telephone? *Dov'è il telefono?*
Where is the nearest hospital? *Dov'è l'ospedale più vicino?*
I would like to report a theft *Voglio denunciare un furto*
Thank you very much for your help *Grazie dell'aiuto*

In the Hotel

Do you have any vacant rooms? *Avete camere libere?*
I have a reservation *Ho fatto una prenotazione*
I'd like... *Vorrei...*
a room with twin beds *una camera a due letti*
a single/double room (with a double bed) *una camera singola/doppia (con letto matrimoniale)*
a room with a bath/shower *una camera con bagno/doccia*
for one night *per una notte*
for two nights *per due notti*
We have one with a double bed *Ne abbiamo una matrimoniale*
Could you show me another room please? *Potrebbe mostrarmi un'altra camera?*
How much is it? *Quanto costa?*
on the first floor *al primo piano*
Is breakfast included? *E compresa la prima colazione?*
Is everything included? *E tutto compreso?*
half/full board *mezza pensione/pensione completa*
It's expensive *E caro*
Do you have a room with a balcony/view of the sea? *C'è una camera con balcone/con una vista del mare?*
a room overlooking the park/the street/the back *una camera con vista sul parco/che da sulla strada/sul retro*
Is it a quiet room? *E una stanza tranquilla?*
The room is too hot/cold/noisy/small *La camera è troppo calda/fredda/rumorosa/piccola*
Can I see the room? *Posso vedere la camera?*
What time does the hotel close? *A che ora chiude l'albergo?*

TRANSPORT
ACCOMMODATION
ACTIVITIES
A – Z
LANGUAGE

I'll take it *La prendo*
big/small *grande/piccola*
What time is breakfast? *A che ora è la prima colazione?*
Please give me a call at... *Mi può chiamare alle...*
Come in! *Avanti!*
Can I have the bill, please? *Posso avere il conto, per favore?*
Can you call me a taxi please? *Può chiamarmi un tassì, per favore?*
dining room *la sala da pranzo*
key *la chiave*
lift *l'ascensore*
towel *l'asciugamano*
toilet paper *la carta igienica*
pull/push *tirare/spingere*

Eating Out

Bar Snacks and Drinks
I'd like... *Vorrei...*
coffee *un caffè* (espresso: small, strong and black)
  un cappuccino (with hot, frothy milk)
  un caffelatte (like *café au lait* in France)
  un caffè lungo (weak, served in a tall glass)
  un corretto (laced with alcohol, probably brandy or grappa)
tea *un tè*
lemon tea *un tè al limone*
herbal tea *una tisana*
hot chocolate *una cioccolata calda*
orange/lemon juice (bottled) *un succo d'arancia/di limone*
fresh orange/lemon juice *una spremuta di arancia/di limone*
orangeade *un'aranciata*
water (mineral) *acqua (minerale)*
fizzy/still mineral water *acqua minerale gasata/naturale*
a glass of mineral water *un bicchiere di minerale*
with/without ice *con/senza ghiaccio*
red/white wine *vino rosso/bianco*
beer (draught) *una birra (alla spina)*
a bitter (Vermouth, etc.) *un amaro*
milk *latte*
a (half) litre *un (mezzo) litro*
bottle *una bottiglia*

ice cream *un gelato*
pastry *una pasta*
sandwich *un tramezzino*
roll *un panino*
Anything else? *Desidera qualcos'altro?*
Cheers *Salute*
Let me pay *Offro io*
That's very kind of you *Grazie, molto gentile*

Bar Notices
Prezzo a tavola/in terrazza Price at a table/terrace (often double what you pay standing at the bar)
Si paga alla cassa Pay at the cash desk
Si prende lo scontrino alla cassa Pay at the cash desk, then take the receipt (*lo scontrino*) to the bar to be served – a common procedure
Signori/Uomini Gentlemen (lavatories)
Signore/Donne Ladies (lavatories)

In a Restaurant
I'd like to book a table *Vorrei riservare una tavola*
Have you got a table for...? *Avete una tavola per ...?*
I have a reservation *Ho fatto una prenotazione*
lunch/supper *il pranzo/la cena*
We do not want a full meal *Non desideriamo un pasto completo*
Could we have another table? *Potremmo spostarci?*
I'm a vegetarian *Sono vegetariano/a*
Is there a vegetarian dish? *C'è un piatto vegetariano?*
May we have the menu? *Ci dia la carta?*
wine list *la lista dei vini*
What would you like? *Che cosa prende?*
What would you recommend? *Che cosa ci raccomanda?*
home-made *fatto in casa*
What would you like as a main course/dessert? *Che cosa prende di secondo/di dolce?*
What would you like to drink? *Che cosa desidera da bere?*
a carafe of red/white wine *una caraffa di vino rosso/bianco*

fixed-price menu *il menu a prezzo fisso*
the dish of the day *il piatto del giorno*
VAT (sales tax) *IVA*
cover charge *il coperto/pane e coperto*
That's enough; no more, thanks *Basta (così)*
The bill, please *Il conto, per favore*
Is service included? *Il servizio è incluso?*
Where is the lavatory? *Dov'è il bagno?*
Keep the change *Va bene così*
I've enjoyed the meal *Mi è piaciuto molto*

Menu Decoder

Antipasti (hors d'oeuvres)
antipasto misto mixed hors d'oeuvres (including cold cuts, possibly cheeses and roasted vegetables – ask, however)
buffet freddo cold buffet (often excellent)
caponata mixed aubergine, olives and tomatoes
insalata caprese tomato and mozzarella salad
insalata di mare seafood salad
insalata mista/verde mixed/green salad
melanzane alla parmigiana fried or baked aubergine (with parmesan cheese and tomato)
mortadella/salame salami
pancetta bacon
peperonata grilled peppers (drenched in olive oil)

Primi (first courses)
il brodetto fish soup
il brodo consommé
i crespolini savoury pancakes
gli gnocchi dumplings
la minestra soup
il minestrone thick vegetable soup
pasta e fagioli pasta and bean soup
il prosciutto (cotto/crudo) ham (cooked/cured)
i suppli rice croquettes
i tartufi truffles
la zuppa soup

Secondi (main courses)

La Carne (Meat)
arrosto roast meat
al ferro grilled without oil
al forno baked
alla griglia grilled
stufato braised, stewed
ben cotto well-done (steak, etc.)
al puntino medium (steak, etc.)
al sangue rare (steak, etc.)
l'agnello lamb
il bresaolo dried salted beef
la bistecca steak
il capriolo/cervo venison
il carpaccio lean beef fillet
il cinghiale wild boar
il controfiletto sirloin steak
le cotolette cutlets
il fagiano pheasant
il fegato liver
il fileto fillet
il maiale pork
il manzo beef
l'ossobuco shin of veal
il pollo chicken
le polpette meatballs
il polpettone meat loaf
la porchetta roast suckling pig
la salsiccia sausage
il saltimbocca (alla romana) veal escalopes with ham
le scaloppine escalopes
lo stufato stew
il sugo sauce
la trippa tripe
il vitello veal

Frutti di Mare (Seafood)
Beware the word *surgelati*, meaning frozen.
affumicato smoked
alle brace charcoal-grilled
alla griglia grilled
fritto fried
ripieno stuffed
al vapore steamed
le acciughe anchovies
l'anguilla eel
l'aragosto lobster
i bianchetti whitebait
il branzino sea bass
i calamaretti baby squid
i calamari squid
la carpa carp
i crostacei shellfish
le cozze mussels
il fritto misto mixed fried fish

i gamberetti shrimps
i gamberi prawns
il granchio crab
il merluzzo cod
le molecche soft-shelled crabs
le ostriche oysters
il pesce fish
il pescespada swordfish
il polipo octopus
il risotto di mare seafood risotto
le sarde sardines
la sogliola sole
le seppie cuttlefish
il tonno tuna
la triglia red mullet
la trota trout
le vongole clams

I Legumi/La Verdura (Vegetables)
a scelta of your choice
i contorni accompaniments
ripieno stuffed
gli asparagi asparagus
la bietola similar to spinach
i carciofini artichoke hearts
il carciofo artichoke
le carote carrots
il cavolo cabbage
la cicoria chicory
la cipolla onion
i funghi mushrooms
i fagioli beans
i fagiolini French (green) beans
le fave broad beans
il finocchio fennel
l'indivia endive/chicory
l'insalata mista mixed salad
l'insalata verde green salad
la melanzana aubergine
le patate potatoes
le patatine fritte chips
i peperoni peppers
i piselli peas
i pomodori tomatoes
le primizie spring vegetables
il radicchio red, slightly bitter lettuce
i ravanelli radishes
la rucola rocket
gli spinaci spinach
la verdura green vegetables
la zucca pumpkin/squash
gli zucchini courgettes

I Dolci (Desserts)
al carrello from the trolley
un semifreddo semi-frozen

dessert (many types)
la bavarese mousse
la cassata Sicilian ice cream with candied peel
le fritelle fritters
un gelato (di lampone/limone) (raspberry/lemon) ice cream
una granita water ice
una macedonia di frutta fruit salad
il tartufo (nero) (chocolate) ice-cream dessert
il tiramisù cold, creamy rum-and-coffee dessert
la torta cake/tart
lo zabaglione sweet dessert of eggs and Marsala wine
lo zuccotto ice-cream liqueur
la zuppa inglese trifle

La Frutta (Fruit)
l'albicocca apricot
l'arancia orange
le ciliege cherries
il cocomero watermelon
i fichi figs
le fragole strawberries
i frutti di bosco berries
i lamponi raspberries
la mela apple
il melone melon
la pera pear
la pesca peach
il pompelmo grapefruit
le uve grapes

Basic foods
l'aceto vinegar
l'aglio garlic
il burro butter
la focaccia oven-baked snack
il formaggio cheese
la frittata omelette
la grana/il parmegiano parmesan cheese
i grissini bread sticks
la marmellata jam
l'olio oil
il pane bread
il pane integrale wholemeal bread
il pepe pepper
il riso rice
il sale salt
la senape mustard
le uova eggs
lo yogurt yoghurt
lo zucchero sugar

TRANSPORT

ACCOMMODATION

ACTIVITIES

A – Z

LANGUAGE

FURTHER READING

General

Italy, Tuscany and Florence have inspired a huge number of books of all genres – below is just a small selection. For general information about Italy, you should consult the Italian State Tourist Office's *Italy Traveller's Handbook*, which is updated yearly. Italian Touring Club regional guides and maps are available from **Stanfords**, 12–14 Long Acre, Covent Garden, London WC2E 9LP; tel: 020-7836 1321; www.stanfords.co.uk.

Art and Architecture

Much has been written on the art and architecture of Florence. A good reading list would include: Giorgio Vasari, *Lives of the Most Excellent Painters, Sculptors And Architects* (1568 and later editions); Benvenuto Cellini, *Autobiography* (1562 and later editions); C. Avery, *Florentine Renaissance Sculpture* (J. Murray, 1970); M. Baxandall, *Painting and Experience in Fifteenth-Century Florence* (Oxford, 1972); J. Beck, *Italian Renaissance Painting* (Konemann, 1999); A. Blunt, *Artistic Theory in Italy 1450–1600* (Oxford, 1940, and later editions); J. Burckhardt, *The Civilisation of the Renaissance in Italy* (Phaidon, 1944, and later editions); S. Greedberg, *Painting in Italy 1500–1600* (Yale, 1993); J. White, *Art and Architecture in Italy 1250–1400* (Yale, 1993); and, R. Wittkower, *Art and Architecture in Italy 1600–1750* (Yale, 1982).
The Architecture of the Italian Renaissance. Peter Murray (Schocken, 1997) Originally published in 1967, this volume remains the classic guide to art and architecture of the Renaissance period. Written by a professor of Birkbeck College, London.
Autobiography. Benvenuto Cellini (Penguin Classics, 1999) The troubled life of the Florentine artist is charted in his work, which gives an insight into life in the Renaissance period.
Brunelleschi's Dome: The Story of a Great Cathedral in Florence. Ross King (Pimlico, 2005) This book charts one of the greatest architectural feats to have ever been accomplished – the dome of Santa Maria del Fiore cathedral – and its creator.
Florence: The City & Its Architecture. Richard Goy (Phaidon, 2002) Organised thematically as opposed to chronologically, this is a modern account of the history, culture, politics and art of Florence. Includes drawings and photographs.
The Florentine Renaissance. Vincent Cronin (Pimlico, 1993) A comprehensive guide to the years of the Renaissance and its intellectual output.
Italian Architecture from Michelangelo to Borromini. Antony Hopkins (Thames & Hudson, 2002) Tracking the artistic period from the High Renaissance through Mannerism to Baroque, this helps explain the backgraound to much of Florence's artistic patrimony.
The Italian Painters of the Renaissance. Bernard Berenson (Phaidon, 1968) Hard to find, the essays in this book provide a good guide to a number of important figures in Italian art, including Caravaggio and Giotto.
Lives of the Artists: Volumes 1 and 2. Giorgio Vasari (Oxford World Classics, 1998) An account of the lives of many important figures in Florentine art by the figure renowned for the corridor linking the Palazzo Vecchio to Palazzo Pitti via the Uffizi.
Villas of Tuscany. Carlo Cresti & Massimo Listri (IB Tauris and Co., 2003) Writing and photographs about Tuscan houses including the Medici villas around Florence designed by masters such as Buontalenti.

Culture and History

The City of Florence: Historical Vistas and Personal Sightings. R.W.B. Lewis (Henry Holt and Co., 1996) A personal view on Florence and its legacy, which makes the perfect travel companion.
The Civilisation of Renaissance Italy. Jacob Burckhardt (Penguin,

BELOW: waiting for the bus.

1990) Published in 1860, this was a defining work in the study of the Italian Renaissance. It remains an illuminating account of the myriad of developments of the era.

Florence: The Biography of a City. Christopher Hibbert (Penguin, 1994) This book weaves together the history and culture of Florence, with photographs and illustrations to make the narrative come to life.

Italians. David Willey (BBC Publications, 1984) Although now slightly out of date, this provides a colourful portrait of the Italian people.

The Italians. Luigi Barzini (Penguin, 1991) Originally published in the sixties, this is still worthwhile reading for the frankness of Barzini's portrait of his fellow countrymen.

The Oxford Illustrated History of Italy. George Holmes (Oxford, 2001) An extensive, though concise, insight into Italy's colourful past for those who want a deeper understanding of the country as a whole.

The Rise and Fall of the House of Medici. Christopher Hibbert (Penguin, 1979) By an author who has written extensively on Florence, this book provides a witty insight into the dynasty who ruled Florence and are responsible for gathering much of the art to be found there today.

Tuscany and Its Wines. Hugh Johnson and Andy Katz (Chronicle Books, 2005) Providing a guide to the best wines in the region with stunning pictures by photographer Andy Katz.

Literature

A Room with a View. E.M. Forster (Penguin Classics, 2000) Classic novel and social study of the English holidaying in Florence.

The Da Vinci Code. Dan Brown (Corgi, 2004) This best-selling fictional thriller is based in Western history and includes interesting titbits relevant to Italy and Florence.

D.H. Lawrence and Italy. D.H Lawrence (Penguin, 1997) Three books based on Lawrence's jour-

nals during his travels in Italy, the text is an interesting travel companion.

Italian Hours. Henry James. (Penguin Classics, 1995) Essays on nineteenth-century travel in Italy by another classic author.

Love and War in the Apennines. Eric Newby (Hodder & Stoughton 1971) A story of the escape of a British prisoner of war in Italy during World War II.

Pictures from Italy. Charles Dickens (Penguin Classics, 1998) A travelogue of Dickens's tour of Italy which he took during a break from writing.

The Prince. Niccolò Machiavelli (Oxford World Classics, 2005) A new translation by Peter Bondanella of Machiavelli's classic treatise on power in the Renaissance.

The Stones of Florence. Mary McCarthy (Penguin, 2000) A travel companion which is an accessible introduction to art history and Florence.

A Traveller's Companion to Florence. Harold Acton and Edward Chaney Eds (Interlink, 2002) A guide to Florence based on letters, memoirs and other materials from renowned Florentine personalities.

Florence Explored. Rupert Scott. (New Amsterdam Books, 1990) A great little book which is presented through a series of walks around the city.

War in the Val d'Orcia. Iris Origo (HarperCollins, 2002) A true story of civilian life in Tuscany during the World War II.

Films

The following English-language films are set in or around Florence and show the area in its full glory:

A Room with a View (1985, directed by James Ivory) An acclaimed adaptation of the novel by E.M. Forster starring Maggie Smith, Helena Bonham-Carter and Simon Callow.

Tea with Mussolini (1999, directed by Franco Zefferelli) Starring Judi Dench and Maggie

Smith, the film charts the life of a boy left in the care of a million-airess and three eccentric British women in Florence during the Fascist occupation of Italy.

Under the Tuscan Sun (2003, directed by Audrey Wells) The story of a woman in search of a new life in Tuscany.

Italian cinema has also produced some classic films (*Cinema Paradiso*, *La Dolce Vita*, *La Vita è Bella*), actors and actresses (Sophia Loren, Monica Bellucci) and directors (Franco Zefferelli, Federico Fellini). The most famous films can be found subtitled.

FEEDBACK

We do our best to ensure the information in our books is as accurate and up to date as possible. The books are updated on a regular basis, using local contacts, who painstakingly add, amend and correct as required. However, some mistakes and omissions are inevitable and we are ultimately reliant on our readers to put us in the picture. We would welcome your feedback on any details related to your experiences using the book "on the road". Maybe we recommended a hotel that you liked (or another that you didn't), as well as interesting new attractions, or facts and figures you have found out about the country itself. The more details you can give us (particularly with regard to addresses, e-mails and telephone numbers), the better. We will acknowledge all contributions, and we'll offer an Insight Guide to the best letters received.

Please write to us at:
Insight Guides
PO Box 7910
London SE1 1WE
United Kingdom
Or send e-mail to:
insight@apaguide.co.uk

TRANSPORT ACCOMMODATION ACTIVITIES A – Z LANGUAGE

ART & PHOTO CREDITS

FLORENCE STREET ATLAS

The key map shows the area of Florence covered by the atlas section. An index of street names and places of interest shown on the maps can be found on the following pages. For each entry there is a page number and grid reference.

Map Legend

═══	Autostrada with Junction	✦✦	Airport	═══	Autostrada
═ ═ ═	Autostrada (under construction)	✝✝	Church (ruins)	═══	Dual Carriageway
═══	Dual Carriageway	✝	Monastery	═══	Main Roads
═══	Main Road	🏰🏯	Castle (ruins)		
───	Secondary Road	∴	Archaeological Site	═══	Minor Roads
───	Minor road	∩	Cave		
───	Track	★	Place of Interest	───	Footpath
─ ─ ─	International Boundary	⌂	Mansion/Stately Home	┅┅	Railway
─ ─ ─	State Boundary	※	Viewpoint		Pedestrian Area
─ ● ─	National Park/Reserve	⌇	Beach		Important Building
─ ─ ─	Ferry Route				Park

🚌	Bus Station
❶	Tourist Information
✉	Post Office
✚	Cathedral/Church
☪	Mosque
✡	Synagogue
⚊	Statue/Monument
▯	Tower
🗼	Lighthouse

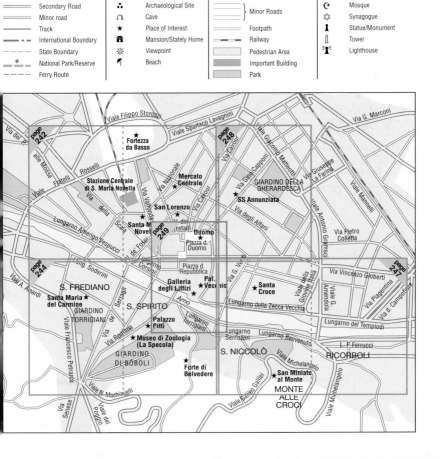

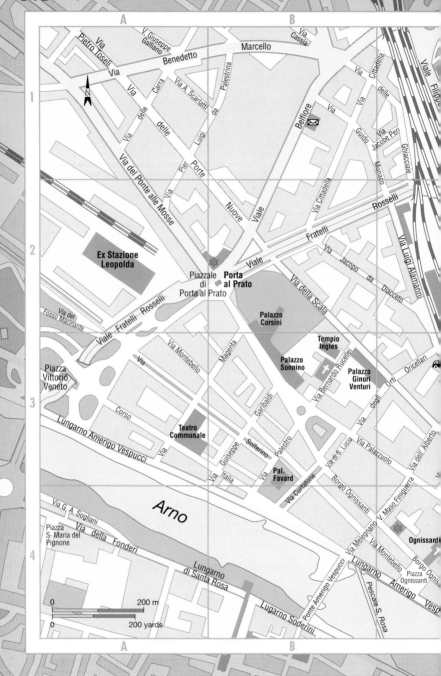

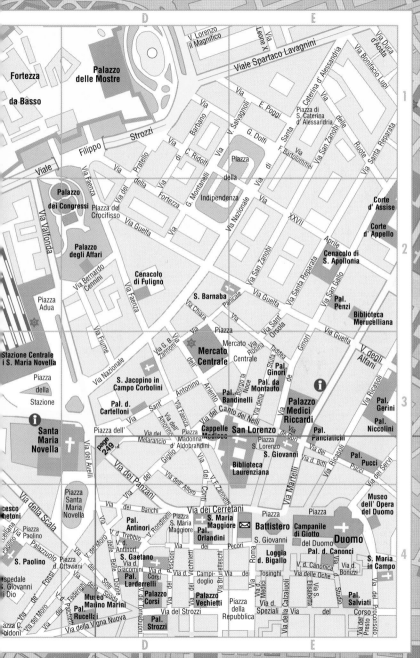

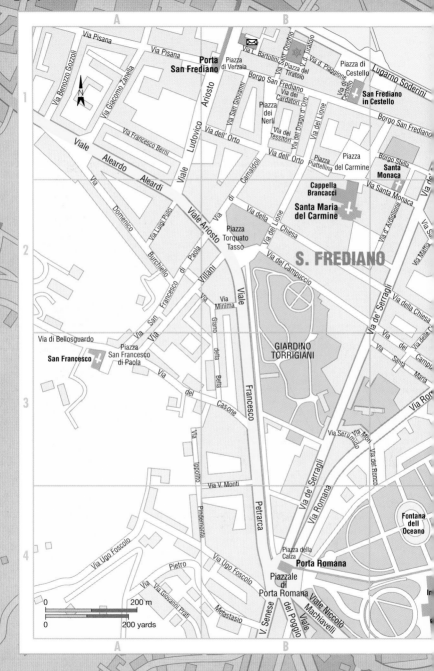

Via Pisana

Via Pisana

Porta San Frediano

Piazza di Verzaia

Via L. Bartolini

Sant' Onofrio

Piazza del Tiratoio

Via d. Piaggione

Via di Cestello

Piazza di Cestello

Via di Cestello

San Frediano in Cestello

Borgo San Frediano

Lugarno Soderini

Borgo San Frediano

Via dei Cardatori

Via del Drago d'Oro

Via del Leone

Piazza dei Nerli

Via dei Tessitori

Via dell' Orto

Via dell' Orto

Borgo Stella

Piazza Piattellina

Piazza del Carmine

Santa Monaca

Via Santa Monaca

Camaldoli

Cappella Brancacci

Santa Maria del Carmine

Via della Chiesa

S. FREDIANO

Via del Campuccio

Via de' Serragli

Via della Chiesa

Via d' Ardiglione

Via Santa

Via del Leone

Piazza Torquato Tasso

Via Minima

Viale

Giano

della

Bella

GIARDINO TORRIGIANI

Via del Campuccio

Via di Bellosguardo

San Francesco

Piazza San Francesco di Paola

Via San Francesco di Paola

Via del Casone

Via Ippolito Pindemonte

Via Francesco Petrarca

Via Serumido

Via Moin

Via del Ronco

Via V. Monti

Via Romana

Via de' Serragli

Via Romana

Fontana dell' Oceano

Via Ugo Foscolo

Via Ugo Foscolo

Pietro

Via Giovanni Prati

Metastasio

V. Sesese

del Poggio

Piazza della Calza

Porta Romana

Piazzale di Porta Romana

Viale Niccolò Machiavelli

| 0 | | 200 m |
| 0 | | 200 yards |

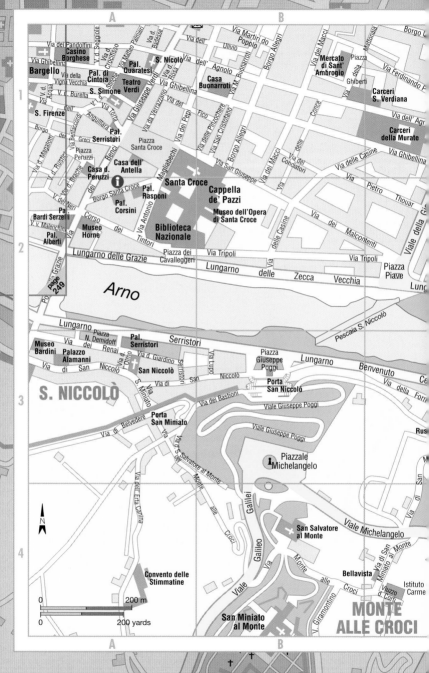

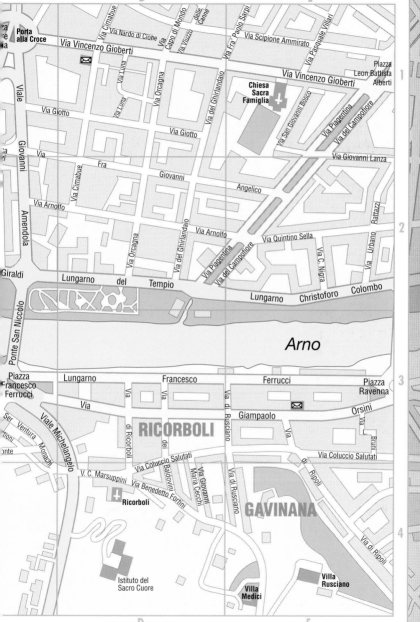

Porta
alla Croce

Via Cimabue

Via Nardo di Cione

Via Capo di Mondo

Via delle Canne

Via Fra Paolo Sarpi

Via Scipione Ammirato

Via Pasquale Villari

Via Vincenzo Gioberti

Via Vincenzo Gioberti

Piazza
Leon Battista
Alberti

Via Luna

Via Orcagna

Via Ghirlandaio

Chiesa
Sacra
Famiglia

Via San Giovanni Bosco

Via Piagentina

Via del Campofiore

Via Giotto

Via Giotto

Via
Giovanni
Fra

Via Cimabue

Giovanni

Angelico

Via Giovanni Lanza

Viale Giovanni Amendola

Via Arnolfo

Via Arnolfo

Via Quintino Sella

Via C. Nigra

Via Urbano

Ricciazzi

Via Orcagna

Via del Ghirlandaio

Via Piagentina

Via del Campofiore

Giraldi

Lungarno   del   Tempio

Lungarno   Christoforo   Colombo

Ponte San Niccolò

Arno

Piazza
Francesco
Ferrucci

Lungarno   Francesco   Ferrucci

Piazza
Ravenna

Via

Via

Via

Via di Rusciano

Orsini

Via

Viale Michelangelo

Ser Ventura Monachi

Giampaolo

Via di Ripoli

Bruni

Ponte

Via di Ricorboli

RICORBOLI

del Ricorboli

Via Coluccio Salutati

V. C. Marsuppini

Via Benedetto Fortini

Via Coluccio Salutati

Via Giovanni Maria Cecchi

Via Giovanni Baldovini

Via di Rusciano

GAVINANA

Via di Ripoli

Ricorboli

Istituto del
Sacro Cuore

Villa
Medici

Villa
Rusciano

0   200 m
0   200 yards

A

Via Duca d' Aosta
V. Zara
Via di Campolreggi
Via San Salvestrina
Via San Gallo
Via Sant' Anna
Via Venezia

Questura

Pal. Pandofini

Chiesa Inglese

Corte d' Assise
Casino Mediceo
Corte d' Appello

San Marco

Museo di San Marco

Piazza San Marco

Università

Galleria dell' Accademia

Academia di Belle Arti
Opificio delle Pietre Dure
Palazzo Grifoni

Via degli Alfani

Pal. Gerini

Pal. Niccolini

Via dei Servi
Via Sei Castellaccio

page 249

S. Maria d. Angeli
Piazza Brunelleschi

Ospedale

S. Michele Visdomini

Via Maurizio Bufalini

S. Maria Nuova

Piazza S. M. Nuova

Pal. Guadagni

Museo Firenze Com'Era
Museo Fiorentina di Preistoria

S. Maria in Campo

Via dell' Oriolo

Teatro Stabile

Museo di Antropologia e Etnologia

Pal. Altoviti

Pal. Albizi

Borgo   degli   Albizi

Pal. Pazzi

Pal. Alessandri

S. Pier Maggiore

B

Via Alfonso Lamarmora
Viale
Via Pier Capponi
Via Francesco Valori

Via Gustavo Cherubini

Via Giacomo Matteotti

Via Salvatore
Via Modena
Via Luigi

Piazza I. del Lungo

Via Venezia

Via Pier Antonio Micheli

Museo Botanico

GIARDINO DEI SEMPLICI

Museo di Mineralogia e Litologia

Via Gino Capponi

Pal. Capponi

Via Giuseppe Giusti

GIARDINO DELLA GHERARDESCA

Santissima Annunziata

Via Cesare Battisti

Piazza d. Santissima Annunziata

Museo Archeologico

Spedale degli Innocenti

Via Laura
Via della Colonna

Via della Pergola

Borgo Pinti

Via Nuova dei Caccini

Teatro della Pergola

S. Maria Maddalena dei Pazzi

Via degli Alfani

Via della Pergola

Borgo Pinti

Fiesolana

Via de' Pepi

Via Luigi Carlo Farini

Sinagoga (Tempio Israelitico)

Via dei Pilastri

Piazza Salvemini

S. Pier Maggiore

Piazza dei Ciompi

Via Mezzo

Piazza S. Ambrogio

Pietrapiana

Sant' Ambrogio

Via Pietrapiana
Via la Croce

C

Via G. Pico della Mirandola
Via Fra Domenico Buonvicini
Via Girolamo Benecieni

Piazza Savonarola

Via Marsilio Ficino

Via dei Della Robbia

Piazza A. Cont

CIMITERO DELLA MISERIC

Via degli Artisti

Piazzale Donatello

CIMITERO DEGLI INGLESI

Via Vittorio Alfieri

Palazzo Paneiatichi Ximenes

Via Giuseppe Giusti

Piazza Massimo d' Azeglio

Via della Colonna

Via G. Battista Nic

Via Giosue Carducci

Via della Mattonaia

Borgo   la   Croce

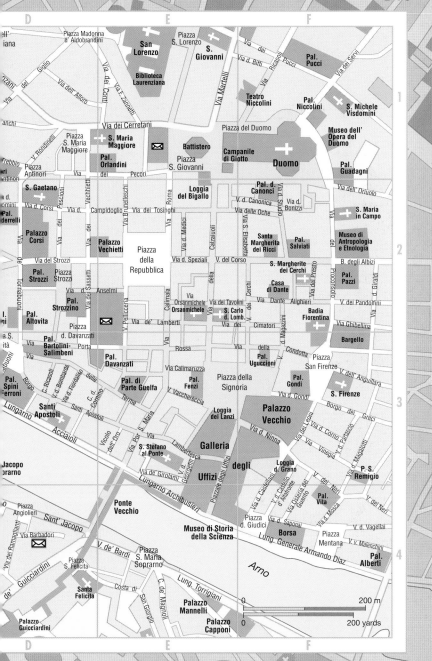

STREET INDEX

GENERAL INDEX